JOURNAL FOR THE STUDY OF THE NEW TESTAMENT
SUPPLEMENT SERIES

273

Paul, Monotheism and the People of God

The Significance of Abraham Traditions
for Early Judaism and Christianity

Nancy Calvert-Koyzis

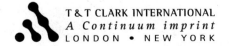

T&T CLARK INTERNATIONAL
A Continuum imprint
LONDON • NEW YORK

Copyright © 2004 T&T Clark International
A Continuum imprint

Published by T&T Clark International
The Tower Building, 11 York Road, London SE1 7NX
15 East 26th Street, Suite 1703, New York, NY 10010

www.tandtclark.com

British Library Cataloguing-in-Publication Data
A catalogue record for this book is available from the British Library

Library of Congress Cataloging-in-Publication Data
A catalogue record for this book is available from the Library of Congress

Typeset by CA Typesetting, www.sheffieldtypesetting.com
Printed on acid-free paper in Great Britain by CPI Bath

ISBN 0-567-08378-0

For David and Theresa

CONTENTS

PREFACE

This book is a revision of my doctoral dissertation, written under the supervision of Drs Philip R. Davies and Andrew T. Lincoln and submitted to the University of Sheffield in 1993. I am grateful to both of my supervisors for their exemplary scholarship and critical supervision.

During my doctoral studies, I was financially supported in part by Tyndale House, Cambridge and the British Committee of Vice Chancellors and Principals. Since that time, I found assistance in the form of a course reduction at Wheaton College in 1996 and at Tyndale Seminary in 2002 when I had a leave of absence. I am grateful to those committees and institutions for their generous support.

I was fortunate to have colleagues who were willing to comment upon developing chapters at both Redeemer University College and McMaster University. I am particularly grateful to Eileen Schuller, Steve Westerholm, Alan Mendelson and Al Wolters for their careful and critical reading of earlier versions of the chapters of which this book is composed.

I am also grateful to Sheila Pepper in administrative services at Mills Library, McMaster University, for providing me with a research office in which I was able to update earlier drafts of this book.

However the idea for the investigation of the figure of Abraham in early Judaism and the Pauline texts came from my New Testament courses with a devoted professor, Dr T. David Gordon, at Gordon-Conwell Theological Seminary. I will always be grateful for the way he and his wife, Diane, opened their home to seminary students and encouraged me to pursue doctoral studies.

My ultimate thanks, however, go to my husband David and my daughter Theresa for their emotional support and patience while I completed this book.

ABBREVIATIONS

Periodicals, Reference Works, and Serials

AB	Anchor Bible Commentary
AGJU	Arbeiten zur Geschichte des antiken Judentums und des Urchristentums
ALGHJ	Arbeiten zur Literatur und Geschichte des hellinistischen Judentums
AnBib	Analecta Biblica
ANRW	Hildegaard Temporini and Wolfgang Haase (eds.), *Aufstieg und Niedergang der römischen Welt: Geschichte und Kultur Roms in Speigel der neueren Forschung* (Berlin: W. de Gruyter, 1972–)
BA	*Biblical Archaeologist*
BASOR	*Bulletin of the American Schools of Oriental Research*
BBB	Bonner biblische Beiträge
BDAG	W. Bauer, F.W. Danker, W.F. Arndt, F.W. Gingrich, *A Greek-English Lexicon of the New Testament and Other Early Christian Literature* (Chicago: University of Chicago Press, 3rd. edn, 2000).
BDF	F. Blass, A. Debrunner and R. Funk, *A Greek Grammar of the New Testament and Other Early Christian Literature* (Chicago: University of Chicago Press, 1961).
Bib	*Biblica*
BibOr	Biblica et orientalia
BJRL	*Bulletin of the John Rylands University Library of Manchester*
BJS	Brown Judaic Studies
BNTC	Black's New Testament Commentaries
BR	*Bible Review*
BTB	*Biblical Theology Bulletin*
CBQ	*Catholic Biblical Quarterly*
CBQMS	*Catholic Biblical Quarterly*, Monograph Series
CRINT	Compendia rerum iudaicarum ad Novum Testamentum
CSCO	Corpus scriptorum christianorum orientalium
CSEL	Corpus scriptorum ecclesiasticorum latinorum
EKKNT	Evangelische-Katholischer Kommentar zum Neuen Testament
EvQ	*Evangelical Quarterly*
ExpTim	*Expository Times*
FOTL	The Forms of the Old Testament Literature
HDR	Harvard Dissertations in Religion
HSM	Harvard Semitic Monographs
HTR	*Harvard Theological Review*
HUCA	*Hebrew Union College Annual*
ICC	International Critical Commentary
Int.	*Interpretation*
JBL	*Journal of Biblical Literature*
JETS	*Journal of the Evangelical Theological Society*
JSHRZ	Jüdische Schriften aus hellenistisch-römischer Zeit

JSJ	*Journal for the Study of Judaism in the Persian, Hellenistic and Roman Period*
JSNT	*Journal for the Study of the New Testament*
JSNTSup	*Journal for the Study of the New Testament*, Supplement Series
JSOTSup	*Journal for the Study of the Old Testament,* Supplement Series
JQR	*Jewish Quarterly Review*
JSP	*Journal for the Study of the Pseudephigrapha*
JSPSup	*Journal for the Study of the Pseudepigrapha* Supplement Series
LCL	Loeb Classical Library
NICNT	New International Commentary on the New Testament
NIGTC	The New International Greek Testament Commentary
NovT	*Novum Testamentum*
NovTSup	*Novum Testamentum*, Supplements
NRSV	New Revised Standard Version
NTS	*New Testament Studies*
OTP	James Charlesworth (ed.), *The Old Testament Pseudepigrapha* (2 vols.; Garden City, NY: Doubleday, 1983).
RB	*Revue biblique*
RevExp	*Review and Expositor*
SBLBMI	The Society of Biblical Literature Bible and Its Modern Interpreters
SBLDS	Society of Biblical Literature Dissertation Series
SBLSCS	Society of Biblical Literature Septuagint and Cognate Studies
SBLSP	*Society of Biblical Literature Seminar Papers*
SBLTT	Society of Biblical Literature Texts and Translations
SBT	Studies in Biblical Theology
SCS	Septuagint and Cognate Studies
SJLA	Studies in Judaism in Late Antiquity
SJOT	*Scandinavian Journal of the Old Testament*
SJT	*Scottish Journal of Theology*
SNTSMS	Society for New Testament Studies Monograph Series
SPB	Studia postbiblica
SSEJC	Studies in Early Judaism and Christianity
SUNT	Studien zur Umwelt des Neuen Testaments
TAPA	*Transactions of the American Philological Association*
TDNT	*Theological Dictionary of the New Testament*
TNTC	Tyndale New Testament Commentaries
TZ	*Theologische Zeitschrift*
USQR	*Union Seminary Quarterly Review*
WBC	Word Biblical Commentary
WTJ	*Westminster Theological Journal*
WUNT	Wissenschaftliche Untersuchungen zum Neuen Testament
ZNW	*Zeitschrift für die neutestamentliche Wissenschaft*

Apocrypha and Pseudepigrapha

2 Bar.	*2 Baruch (Syriac Apocalypse)*
Jub.	*Jubilees*
4 Macc.	4 Maccabees
Apoc. Abr.	*Apocalypse of Abraham*
LAB	*Liber Antiquitatum Biblicarum (Biblical Antiquities)*
Sir.	Sirach
1 Macc.	1 Maccabees

Wis.	Wisdom of Solomon
Jdt.	Judith

Josephus

Ant.	*Jewish Antiquities* or *Antiquitates judaicae*
Apion	*Against Apion* or *Contra Apionem*
Life	*Life of Josephus* or *Vita Josephi*
War	*Jewish War* or *Bellum judaicum*

Philo

Abr.	*De Abrahamo*
Cher.	*De cherubim*
Congr.	*De congressu eruditionis gratia*
Deus Imm.	*Quod Deus sit immutabilis*
Ebr.	*De ebrietate*
Flacc.	*Contra Flaccum*
Fug.	*De fuga et inventione*
Gig.	*De gigantibus*
Leg. All.	*Legum allegoriae*
Leg. Gai.	*Legatio ad Gaium*
Migr. Abr.	*De migratione Abrahami*
Mut. Nom.	*De mutatione nominum*
Poster. C.	*De posteritate Caini*
Praem. Poen.	*De praemiis et poenis*
Prov.	*De providentia*
Quaest. in Exod.	*Quaestiones et solutiones in Exodum*
Quaest. in Gen.	*Quaestiones et solutiones in Genesin*
Rev. Div. Her.	*Quis rerum divinarum heres sit*
Somn.	*De somniis*
Spec. Leg.	*De specialibus legibus*
Virt.	*De virtutibus*
Vit. Cont.	*De vita contemplativa*

Greek and Latin Sources

Ant. Rom.	Dionysius of Halicarnassus, *Antiquitates romanae*
Cass Dio *Hist.*	Cassius Dio, *Historia romana*
Diog. L.	Diogenes Laertius
Ep.	Seneca, *Epistulae morales*
Flac.	Cicero, *Pro Flacco*
Geogr.	Strabo, *Geographica*
Hist.	Tacitus, *Historiae*
Juv. Sat.	Juvenal, *Satirae*
Metaph.	Aristotle, *Metaphysica*
Phaedr.	Plato, *Phaedrus*
Sat.	Horace, *Satirae*
Tib.	Suetonius, *Tiberius*

Early Christian Authors

Civ.	Augustine, *De civitate Dei*
Praep. Ev.	Eusebius, *Praeparatio Evangelica*
Strom.	Clement of Alexandria, *Stromata*

Chapter 1

Introduction:
Abraham, Monotheism and Method

1. *The Centrality of Abraham*

Even in the twenty-first century, the centrality of Abraham in religious thought and tradition cannot be denied. He is known as the forebear of the three monotheistic religions: Islam, Judaism and Christianity. Descent from Abraham in either physical or spiritual terms is often seen as central to what identifies each of these different groups as God's people in contrast to those who are not privileged with this lineage. This delineation provides a sense of identity and belonging for those who are members of each community – those who are 'inside'.

During the second temple era, spiritual or physical descent from Abraham also provided a sense of identity. The authors of early Jewish texts portrayed Abraham as a kind of cipher through whom the Jew could discern what it meant to be an ideal person of God. These depictions of Abraham usually also served to illustrate the authors' beliefs concerning what the people of God should believe and how they should behave in the different environments in which they found themselves.[1]

Of course Paul reworked traditions about Abraham in order to forge a new identity for the people of God in Christ. In both Galatians and Romans, Paul revised popular traditions about Abraham in order to define the new people of God by virtue of spiritual descent. Just like other Jewish authors, Paul used his portrayal of Abraham to make his points about the faith and behaviour of God's people as they responded to those around them.

2. *Previous Literature*

Previous literature on the portrayal of Abraham in early Jewish literature and the letters of Paul is extensive, but it deserves to be summarized so that this volume may be put into context. Scholars who previously addressed the topic approached the texts in a variety of ways. Many used rabbinic sources without considering the possibility that the dates of rabbinic texts are highly questionable and may not prove as useful for a study of Pauline literature as texts which can be dated more

---

1. O. Schmitz, 'Abraham im Spätjudentum und im Urchristentum', *Aus Schrift und Geschichte* (Stuttgart: Calwer Vereinsbuchhandlung, 1922), pp. 99–123; Sandmel, Abraham in Normative and Hellenistic Jewish Traditions' (PhD dissertation, Yale University Press, 1949), p. 326.

securely.[2] Scholars such as O. Schmitz, S. Sandmel, C.K. Barrett, C. Dietzfelbinger and M. Martin-Achard relied upon rabbinic texts in addition to other early Jewish documents to understand Paul's use of Abraham.[3]

A few authors tended to used New Testament categories as they approached Jewish texts instead of studying Jewish texts in their own right. For example, C. Dietzfelbinger approached the Jewish texts using categories gleaned from Paul: 'ἐπαγγελία, 'πίστις', and 'σπέρμα 'Αβρααμ'.[4] In his dissertation, 'Paul and the Abraham Tradition: A Challenge for the Church Today', Ik Soo Park followed the basic outline of Dietzfelbinger, imposing Pauline categories on Early Jewish texts.[5] Halvor Moxnes published *Theology in Conflict: Studies in Paul's Understanding of God in Romans* in 1980.[6] In part two of the book, he provides a study of Abraham in the Old Testament, the Apocrypha, Qumran, the *Genesis Apocryphon,* the works of Philo and rabbinic literature all under the heading of 'God and his Promise to Abraham' based upon the promise theme found in Romans 4.[7] While the study is profitable, once again a New Testament scholar begins by asking questions of early Jewish literature based upon New Testament categories rather than allowing the Jewish literature to speak for itself.

Scholars such as W.L. Knox and S. Sandmel long ago recognized the significance of the tradition of Abraham's discovery of the one God.[8] While New Testament scholars acknowledged this tradition linking Abraham and monotheism, they did not fully develop what the tradition might mean for Paul's argument or for the debates among those in Christian communities in Galatia and Rome. For example, although O. Schmitz noted the characterization in Jewish literature of Abraham as a zealous monotheist, when he came to the Pauline texts he focused on Paul's interpretation of Gen. 15.6.[9] F. Wieser noted the tradition in his appendix and pointed out that in Rom. 4 the faith Paul requires is like Abraham's faith in God because it is belief in God who had subsequently raised Christ from the dead, but he does not develop the theme of monotheism further.[10] P. Démann

---

2.   For discussions of the pitfalls of using rabbinic texts to interpret New Testament texts, see P.S. Alexander, 'Rabbinic Judaism and the New Testament', *ZNW* 74 (1983), pp. 237–46 (238); E.P. Sanders, 'Defending the Indefensible', *JBL* 110 (1991), pp. 463–77; Daniel Boyarin, *A Radical Jew: Paul and the Politics of Identity* (Berkeley: University of California Press, 1994), p. 2.

3.   Otto Schmitz, 'Abraham'; Sandmel, 'Abraham'; C.K. Barrett, *From First Adam to Last* (New York: Charles Scribner's Sons, 1962); Christian Dietzfelbinger, *Paulus und das Alte Testament: Die Hermeneutik des Paulus, untersucht an seiner Deutung der Gestalt Abrahams,* (München: Chr. Kaiser Verlag, 1961); R. Martin-Achard, *Actualité d' Abraham,* Bibliothèque théologique (Neuchâtel: Delachaux et Niestlé, 1969).

4.   Dietzfelbinger, *Hermeneutik,* p. 7.

5.   Ik Soo Park, 'Paul and the Abraham Tradition: A Challenge for the Church Today' (Unpublished PhD dissertation, Drew University, 1985), e.g., p. 12.

6.   Halvor Moxnes, *Theology in Conflict: Studies in Paul's Understanding of God in Romans,* (Leiden: E.J. Brill, 1980).

7.   See H. Moxnes, *Conflict,* pp. 117–206.

8.   W.L. Knox, 'Abraham and the Quest for God', *HTR* 28 (1935), pp. 55–60; Samuel Sandmel, 'Abraham's Knowledge of the Existence of God', *HTR* 44 (1951), pp. 137–39.

9.   Schmitz, 'Spätjudentum', pp. 119–21.

10.   Friedrich E. Wieser, *Die Abrahamvorstellungen im Neuen Testament* (Europäische Hochschulschriften, 23/307; Bern: Peter Lang, 1987), pp. 161–65 (65).

went so far as to say that no traditions similar to the monotheistic tradition about Abraham found in rabbinic, Alexandrian and Islamic literature are found in the New Testament.[11] When C.K. Barrett studied the role of Abraham in Jewish literature, including rabbinic texts, he noted that to Paul's Jewish contemporaries Abraham was the first convert, proselyte and father of Israelites.[12] Barrett began to develop the connection between Abraham, monotheism and Paul when he noted Abraham's faith closely resembled Christian faith because it was directed towards God, but like the others, he does not develop the theme further. G. Walter Hansen notes the tradition of Abraham's conversion from idolatry to monotheism in an appendix but writes primarily from the standpoint of the function of Abraham in terms of epistolary and rhetorical criticism and not from the standpoint of the possible significance of this tradition for Paul or the communities to which he writes.[13]

Jeffrey Siker has shown how early Christians eventually used Abraham as a device for excluding the Jews in *Disinheriting the Jews: Abraham in Early Christian Controversy*.[14] While Siker does explore the function of Abraham in early Christian literature, he does not fully develop the theme of Abraham and monotheism in the letters of Paul or its significance in early Judaism.

In his book *The Figure of Abraham in the Epistles of St. Paul: In the Footsteps of Abraham*, R.A. Harrisville III surveys an extensive array of Jewish literature in which Abraham is mentioned, from the Pseuedepigrapha to Philo to the Dead Sea Scrolls and rabbinic literature. After this extensive survey, Harrisville arrives at the rather surprising conclusion that, in his use of Abraham, Paul was aligned only with Scripture, and was not aligned with Jewish interpretations of his day or earlier. Harrisville states, 'Paul the Apostle was a maverick in disregarding the common views about Abraham'.[15]

In this volume, I intend to show that the tradition of Abraham's rejection of idolatry and embracing of monotheistic faith is significant for an understanding of Paul's arguments in his letters to the Galatians and the Romans and the debates in the communities to which he writes. By 'monotheism', I mean the doctrine or belief that there is only one God.[16]

---

11. P. Démann, 'La Signification d'Abraham dans la Perspective du Nouveau Testament', *Cahiers Sioniens* 5 (1952), pp. 31–43 (66).

12. Barrett, *Adam*, pp. 22–45.

13. *Abraham in Galatians: Epistolary and Rhetorical Contexts* (JSNTSup, 29; Sheffield: Sheffield Academic Press, 1989), pp. 185–86, 190.

14. *Disinheriting the Jews: Abraham in Early Christian Controversy* (Louisville, KY: Westminster/John Knox Press, 1991); see also 'From Gentile Inclusion to Jewish Exclusion: Abraham in Early Christian Controversy with Jews', *BTB* 19.1 (1989), pp. 30–36.

15. *The Figure of Abraham in the Epistles of St. Paul: In the Footsteps of Abraham* (San Francisco: Mellen Research University Press, 1992), p. 182; see also Sze-kar Wan who also finds Harrisville's conclusion surprising in 'Abraham and the Promise of the Spirit: Galatians and the Hellenistic-Jewish Mysticism of Philo', *SBL Seminar Papers 1994* (SBLSP, 34; Atlanta: Scholars Press, 1995), pp. 6-22 .(6 n. 1).

16. See also Larry Hurtado's work where he supports the monotheistic self-understanding of

So that we might be reasonably certain the Abraham traditions we examine are found in Jewish literature from roughly 168 BCE to 100 CE, rabbinic texts have not been included in this analysis. I will also endeavour to study Jewish texts in their own right without importing categories from the New Testament. Using this approach, it is my hope that we might first understand the texts from the standpoint of Jewish concerns rather than from the standpoint of Pauline categories.

3. *Abraham and Early Jewish and Christian Identity*

In the first section of this book, we will explore examples of the portrayal of Abraham in Jewish literature roughly contemporary with Paul. In essence, Abraham functioned as a key to how the Jewish people perceived their identity. The portrayals of Abraham also often reveal how the Jews of the time were to relate to members of nations other than their own.

Documents found both in Palestine and the Diaspora will be discussed based upon my earlier study in which each document was considered in its entirety in order that the fullest understanding of the depiction of Abraham might be gained.[17] These texts were originally chosen because they provided the most extensive portrayals of Abraham.

For the purposes of this volume we will focus upon the most frequently occurring traditions about Abraham: that he rejected idolatry for faith in the one God and that he was obedient to God especially through observance of the law. Questions to be asked of early Jewish texts include: What identifies people who belong to the people of God? What characterizes those who do not belong? We will discuss Abraham traditions in reference to the literary genres, dates and probable historical situations within which they occurred. Most often Abraham traditions are found in the corpus of literary works known as 'rewritten Bible' such as the *Book of Jubilees*, (c. 168 BCE) the *Biblical Antiquities*, (66–74 CE), the works of Philo (early first century CE) and Josephus (93–94 CE), all of which we will investigate. We will also discuss one apocalyptic work, the *Apocalypse of Abraham* (c. 70 CE).[18] Shorter allusions to Abraham found in other Jewish documents will be noted where appropriate. By 'traditions' I do not mean a direct quotation or paraphrase of the original text but 'an imaginative development stemming from reflection upon the figure of Abraham'.[19]

Graeco-Roman Judaism, *One God, One Lord* (London: SCM Press, 1988); 'First-Century Jewish Monotheism', *JSNT* 71 (1998), pp. 3–26.

17. Nancy L. Calvert, 'Abraham Traditions in Middle Jewish Literature: Implications for the Interpretation of Galatians and Romans' (Unpublished PhD dissertation, University of Sheffield, 1993).

18. While I discussed the *Genesis Apocryphon* and the *Testament of Abraham* in my dissertation, and they do not disprove my thesis, they do not contain strong attestation to the traditions about Abraham that I wish to investigate in this volume.

19. Daniel J. Harrington, 'Abraham Traditions in the Testament of Abraham and in the "Rewritten Bible" of the Intertestamental Period', *Studies on the Testament of Abraham* (SBLSCS, 6; Missoula, MT: Scholars Press, 1976), pp. 165–71 (165).

Fundamental to this study is the presupposition that during the time Paul was writing, fledgling Christianity still identified with Judaism to a very large extent. Abraham is central to both religions and his portrayal reveals fundamental elements of both early Jewish and Christian identity. My intent in section two is to further understand Paul's use of Abraham traditions to identify God's people by comparing it with a similar use of the patriarch in early Jewish literature. The questions we will consider as we approach Paul's letters to the Galatians and the Romans are: how does Paul's definition of the identity of the people of God through his use of Abraham differ from the definition expressed through the use of Abraham traditions in Jewish literature? As a result, who is included within and who is excluded from the people of God by virtue of this new identity? And, since the Abraham traditions were so tied up with monotheism which is central to Paul's gospel (which we shall see), how does Paul use his redefinition of monotheism and thereby Abraham to create this new definition of the people of God in Christ?

Of course, in order to answer these major questions, we will need to investigate whether or not Paul was influenced by early Jewish traditions of Abraham and whether he uses them in ways similar to or different from authors of early Jewish documents. We will also pursue whether the opponents in Galatia and the weak in Romans used traditions of Abraham for their own ends. In this way, we will get a sense of how his view of what it meant to be a child of Abraham differed from the views of those Christians in Galatia and Rome. By investigating Paul's understanding of what it meant to be a child of Abraham in contrast to Jewish authors and those in Galatia and Rome, we shall further understand the significance of Abraham for early Judaism and Christianity.

Chapter 2

ABRAHAM AS THE PROCLAIMER OF THE ONE GOD AND COVENANT STIPULATIONS IN THE *BOOK OF JUBILEES*

1. *Introduction*

During the era with which we are concerned, from the mid-second century BCE to the first century CE, Jewish authors often altered the biblical texts in order to attain their apologetic and parenetic goals. In their hands, the biblical patriarchs gained a prominence and a reputation embellished beyond all recognition.[1]

A few authors depicted Abraham as the originator of culture or as the author of astrology, which was regarded by some as the highest of all sciences. For example, Pseudo-Eupolemus (2nd century BCE) combines the accounts in Genesis with the origin of Babylonian and Hellenistic culture.[2] He believed that Abraham was born in Babylonia and surpassed all men in nobility and wisdom, and that Abraham discovered astrology and the Chaldaic arts. Another Jewish writer, Artapanus (c. 300–100 BCE), portrayed Enoch, his Hellenistic equivalent Atlas and Abraham as the inventors and communicators of astrological secret knowledge.[3] As we shall see, Abraham was also an important figure to the author of *Jubilees*.

2. *The* Book of Jubilees

Although *Jubilees* contains some characteristics of apocalyptic literature, most would agree that it is an example of the literary genre called rewritten Bible, which, according to Daniel Harrington, refers to those products of 'Palestinian Judaism at the turn of the era that take as their literary framework the flow of the biblical text itself and apparently have as their major purpose the clarification and actualization of the biblical story'.[4] The author of *Jubilees* began by using the biblical text but added extra-biblical traditions to the scriptural framework that will prove to be significant as we investigate the portrayal of Abraham in the book.

---

1.   D.S. Russell, *The Old Testament Pseudepigrapha: Patriarchs and Prophets in Early Judaism* (London: SCM Press, 1987), p. 1.

2.   Eusebius, *Praep. Ev.* 9.17.

3.   Eusebius, *Praep. Ev.* 9.18.

4.   Daniel Harrington, 'Palestinian Adaptations of Biblical Narratives and Prophecies', in Robert A. Kraft and George W.E. Nickelsburg (eds.), *Early Judaism and Its Modern Interpreters* (SBLBMI, 2; Atlanta, GA: Scholars Press, 1986), pp. 239–58 (239).

As is the case with most authors of works on *Jubilees*, I assume that the book was written as a literary unity.[5] Although the exact dating of the composition of the text differs among scholars, it is usually placed near the middle of the second century BCE, either just before the Hasmonaean era during the rule of Antiochus Epiphanes IV or not too long after the Hasmonaean era began, under the reign of the descendants of Mattathias.[6] As is well known, under Antiochus Epiphanes IV the tensions between proponents of different views of Judaism reached their climax. *Jubilees* itself reflects an ideological tension between those Jews who stood for strict maintenance of the law and separation from Gentiles and those who freely associated with Gentiles and assimilated aspects of Hellenistic culture.

For the author of *Jubilees* the particulars of the covenant had been in existence since creation; the distinctive practices of Judaism that had separated them from other nations had not begun with Moses but had been practised since the beginning. As VanderKam suggests, 'the true religion was detailed and separatist and had always been so. Sabbath-keeping and Israel's election out of the nations dated from the time of creation'.[7]

In *Jubilees*, covenantal stipulations that were introduced at the time of Moses in the Bible are revealed to and practised by the patriarchs. For example, Abraham is said to have celebrated the feast of tabernacles long before the institution of the festival (Lev. 23.34; Deut. 16.13–15; *Jub.* 16.21). Because those who lived before the time of Moses actually practised stipulations of what became known as the Mosaic Law, the law is made more credible. The law was not only given to Moses but was instituted at creation and exists in the form of heavenly tablets. For example, the laws for keeping the Sabbath were declared after the seventh day was made (*Jub.* 2.25); the laws of purification are different for men and women because Adam was created in the first week while Eve was not shown to Adam until the second week (*Jub.* 3.8). The Mosaic Law in essence is part of the created order.

Different from the covenants found in the Hebrew Bible, *Jubilees* presents the agreements with Noah, Abra(ha)m, and Moses as being renewals of the same covenant.[8] According to *Jubilees*, the covenant that God established with Noah

---

5. For example, see James VanderKam, *The Book of Jubilees* (Guides to Apocrypha and Pseudepigrapha; Sheffield: Sheffield Academic Press, 2001), pp. 17–18.

6. For a pre-Hasmonaean date, see G.W.E. Nickelsburg, 'The Bible Rewritten and Expanded', in Michael E. Stone (ed.), *Jewish Writings of the Second Temple Period* (CRINT, 2.2; Assen: Van Gorcum, 1984), pp. 89–156 (101–103); for a Hasmonaean-era date, see O.S. Wintermute, '*Jubilees*: A New Translation and Introduction', *OTP*, vol. 2, p. 44; John C. Endres, *Biblical Interpretation in the Book of Jubilees* (CBQMS, 18; Washington, DC: The Catholic Biblical Association of America, 1987), p. 13; James VanderKam, 'The *Book of Jubilees*', in M. De Jonge (ed.), *Outside the Old Testament* (Cambridge Commentaries on Writings of the Jewish and Christian World, 200 B.C. to A.D. 200, 4; Cambridge: Cambridge University Press, 1985), pp. 111–44 (116).

7. James VanderKam, 'Genesis 1 in *Jubilees* 2', in *From Revelation to Canon: Studies in the Hebrew Bible and Second Temple Literature* (Leiden: E.J. Brill, 2000), pp. 500–521 (521); see *Jub.* 2.19.

8. James VanderKam, *An Introduction to Early Judaism* (Grand Rapids, MI: Eerdmans, 2001), p. 98.

(*Jub.* 6) was renewed yearly during the feast of weeks (cf. Deut. 16.9–12; Lev. 23.15–21). The covenant established with Abraham that was a renewal of the feast celebrated by Noah is the next documented celebration of the feast of weeks (*Jub.* 14.20; cf. 15.1–20). The feast of weeks is central to *Jubilees*; its celebration allowed the community to observe the anniversary of the first covenant concluded between God and Noah after the deluge. The celebration of the feast of weeks at the final encounter between Abraham and Jacob emphasized the continuity of the covenant through Jacob (22.1, 10–24).[9] It may be significant that Abraham, not Isaac as in the biblical account, is the one to give his last words to Jacob and thus continue the covenant. In fact, the author attributes to Abraham the same words used by Isaac in Gen. 27.29 (*Jub.* 22. 11b).

After the feast, in his last words, Abraham blesses Jacob (*Jub.* 22.10–30) and expresses his desire that Jacob and his descendants conduct themselves right- eously in order that they may be a 'holy people' (*Jub.* 22.12). This portion of the blessing is not found in Genesis; it is one example of the author shifting attention from the promissory aspect of the disclosure to Abraham to the demand for cove- nant fidelity. This emphasis on the covenant that the author of *Jubilees* combines with the Abraham traditions is more characteristic of the Mosaic tradition.[10] For the author of *Jubilees*, fidelity to the stipulations of the covenant, no matter when those stipulations were communicated, was essential in maintaining a relation- ship with God. Thus because of the shift of emphasis from a promissory covenant to a Mosaic covenant of fidelity, the forebears are no longer so much examples of divine favour as they are examples for imitation by the Jewish community.[11]

Another important theme in *Jubilees* is separation from Gentiles, particularly in relation to obedience to covenant stipulations. God is faithful to his covenant with his nation, Israel (*Jub.* 1.17–18). Those who belong to Israel are to follow the stipulations of the covenant. Central among these stipulations is abstaining from idol worship (1.9; 11.4; 11.16; 12.2; 20.7; 22.22; 36.5), but other stipula- tions include keeping the Sabbath (2.18), covering nakedness (3.31), refraining from eating meat with blood in it (6.10; 21.18), observing the feast of weeks and the feast of tabernacles (6.17; 6.29), tithing (13.24), circumcising their sons (15.25–34), abstaining from sexual immorality (16.4–6; 20.3–6; 25.7; 50.5), not intermarrying with members of other nations (30.7) and not committing incest (33.10). Generally, members of the covenant are to avoid the uncleanness of the Gentiles particularly by avoiding idolatry, but also by avoiding other transgres- sions.[12] In order to be obedient to the covenant one needs to be separate from the Gentiles.

Circumcision is depicted as a covenant stipulation for those who are the elect in ch. 15. In fact, anyone who does not have the sign of circumcision, which was instituted at creation (*Jub.* 15.27), does not belong to the Lord (15.26a; see also

---

9. Endres, *Interpretation*, p. 40.
10. Endres, *Interpretation*, p. 49.
11. VanderKam, *Introduction*, p. 98.
12. E.P. Sanders, *Paul and Palestinian Judaism* (repr., Philadelphia: Fortress Press, 1983), p. 365.

Gen. 17.14) and is destined for annihilation (*Jub.* 15.26b). This discussion of the severity of the punishment for those who do not have the sign of circumcision would certainly speak loudly to those Jews who had succumbed to the assimilationist pressures of the day and had their marks of circumcision removed artificially. After the discussion of circumcision, the separation of Israel from the Gentiles is presented in a deterministic light:

> He sanctified them and gathered (them) from all mankind. For there are many nations and many peoples and all belong to him. He made spirits rule over all in order to lead them astray from following him. But over Israel he made no angel or spirit rule because he alone is their ruler. He will guard them and require them for himself from his angels, his spirits, and everyone, and all his powers so that he may guard them and bless them and so that they may be his and he theirs from now and forever.[13]

In his book *Identität durch Abgrenzung*, Eberhard Schwarz studied passages in *Jubilees* which command Israel's separation from the nations (*Jub.* chs. 7, 20–22, 25, 30 and 36). He maintains that *Jubilees* arose at a time when the separation of Israel from their environment was of special relevance and intense urgency and that the procedure of separation was disputed within the Jewish community.[14] He notes how the speeches of Abraham constitute a major component of these chapters, which will be discussed below.

Given that one major theme of *Jubilees* is separation from Gentile influence, it would make sense that the document was written during the years of severe ideological tension between nationalistic and assimilationist Judaism, either just before or during Hasmonaean rule. If this is the case, *Jubilees* is the response of a Jew who considers himself to be faithful to the stipulations of the covenant with God in the midst of many compatriots who by bowing to Hellenism are unfaithful in his eyes.

According to VanderKam, '*Jubilees* is an all-out defence of what makes the people of Israel distinctive from the nations and a forceful assertion that they were never one with them.'[15] Thus, *Jubilees* is a call to nationalistic fervour that is ultimately based upon monotheistic faith and covenantal stipulations.

3. *The Interpretation of Abraham in the* Book of Jubilees

In order to understand the character and function of Abraham in *Jubilees*, it is important to stress that through his adaptations of the Genesis narrative, the author is attempting to derive binding norms of behaviour which will guide the

---

13. Translations taken from James VanderKam's translation of the Ethiopic text as found in *The Book of Jubilees* (2 vols.; CSCO, 510–511; Scriptores Aethiopici, 87–88; Leuven: Peeters, 1989).

14. Eberhard Schwarz, *Identität durch Abgrenzung: Abgrenzungsprozesse in Israel im 2.vorchristlichen Jahrhundert und ihre traditionsgeschichtlichen Voraussetzungen. Zugleich ein Beitrag zur Erforschung des Jubiläenbuches* (Europäische Hochschulschriften, 23.162; Frankfurt/Bern: Peter Lang, 1982), pp. 18, 99.

15. James VanderKam, *The Book of Jubilees* (Guides to Apocrypha and Pseudepigrapha; Sheffield: Sheffield Academic Press, 2001), p. 140.

readers in their faithful observance of covenantal stipulations.[16] Our investigation will proceed along the lines of discerning how Abraham's behaviour and character are described, how Abraham functions within the text, and what this implies regarding norms of character and behaviour for the reader.

a. *Abraham's Separation from Idolatry for Belief in the One God*
The story of Abraham in *Jubilees* is reported from his birth in 11.15 through his death in 23.10. In the account of his birth, the author adds significant details to the account of the ancestors of Terah, the father of Abraham. Terah's ancestors, the children of Noah are making molten images and worshipping them as idols (11.4). Terah was the son of Nahor who had been practising divination and astrology since his early years. The stories of idols in Ur probably developed from Josh. 24.2 where Joshua says of their forefathers: 'Long ago your ancestors – Terah and his sons Abraham and Nahor – lived beyond the Euphrates and served other gods'.[17]

When Abram is born of Edna and Terah (11.15) the author immediately extols the character of Abram:

> the child began to realize the errors of the earth – that everyone was going astray after the statues and after impurity... When he was two weeks of years [=14 years], he separated from his father in order not to worship idols with him. He began to pray to the creator of all so that he would save him from the errors of mankind and that it might not fall to his share to go astray after impurity and wickedness (*Jub.* 11.16–17).

Within the account of Abraham, the author of *Jubilees* develops the theme of separation noted above. The separation of Abraham from his idolatrous father is symbolic of the separation of the people of God from the Gentiles who worship idols. According to *Jubilees,* Abraham is now the only one of the descendants of Noah – the entire population of the earth, or the Gentiles – who worships the true God. Most of the proscriptions of idolatry found in *Jubilees* are found in the story of Abraham. It is noteworthy that Abraham turns to the Creator in order that he might not make the same mistake as those around him of straying after idols and the consequent impurity and wickedness (11.17).

Abraham's first speech as recorded in *Jubilees* echoes the tradition that Abraham left behind idolatry for belief in the one God. In the speech Abraham pleads with his father to stop worshipping idols:

> What help and advantage do we get from these idols before which you worship and prostrate yourself? For there is no spirit in them because they are dumb. They are an error of the mind. Do not worship them. Worship the God of heaven who makes the rain and dew fall on the earth and makes everything on the earth. He created everything by his word; and all life (comes) from his presence. Why do you worship those things which

16. James L. Kugel and Rowan A. Greer, *Early Biblical Interpretation* (Library of Early Christianity, 3; Philadelphia: Westminster Press, 1986), p. 60; see also James VanderKam, 'Biblical Interpretation in *1 Enoch* and *Jubilees*', in *From Revelation to Canon: Studies in the Hebrew Bible and Second Temple Literature* (Leiden: E.J. Brill, 2000), p. 297.
17. Unless otherwise noted, all biblical translations are taken from the NRSV.

have no spirit in them? For they are made by hands and you carry them on your shoulders. You receive no help from them, but instead they are a great shame for those who make them and an error of the mind for those who worship them. Do not worship them (*Jub.* 12.2b–5).

This speech contains three sections. The first concerns the worthlessness of idols (12.2b–3): they have no spirit because they are dumb, and they are misleading of the mind. This section ends with 'do not worship them'. In the second section (12.4), Abraham adjures his father to worship the God of heaven. This God is the Creator who, contrary to the mute idol, makes everything by his word. Thirdly (12.5) Abraham points out that in contrast to the God who created the world, idols are created by human beings and serve to hinder and shame them rather than to help them. The entire speech ends with the statement, 'Do not worship them.'

Endres maintains that 'speeches often provide an interpretive clue to the events which they accompany'.[18] As is well known, Thucydides often used his speeches in a similar way. For Thucydides, the speechmakers became 'mouthpieces of the historian, their speeches being designed to penetrate to underlying causes and motives, reveal general truths, and bring out the viewpoints and characters of the major participants in events'.[19]

Our author, like Thucydides, is using speeches to bring out what is of significance in each situation in which the speech is found. He is also using the speeches to make the Torah relevant to his contemporaries through the guidelines found in the speeches. Through his mouthpiece Abraham, the author of *Jubilees* is telling his reader the reasons for the worthlessness of idolatry and encouraging the reader to worship the one, true Creator God of Abraham.

Abraham's father does not listen to his words but succumbs to the pressure of those around him who will kill him and his family should he refrain from worshipping idols. Abraham himself is in danger of death (12.7) and his brothers are angry with him (12.8). Abraham subsequently burns the house of idols (12.12–14); his brother, Haran, rushes in to save the idols and dies in the fire. Thus in contrast to members of his family who assimilate to the pressure to conform to idolatrous practices, even going so far as to die to protect idols, Abraham is committed to the one God, facing possible death for his actions and his convictions.

In his article, 'Die Abraham-Gestalt im Jubiläenbuch: Versuch einer Interpretation', Mogens Müller sees Abraham in *Jubilees* as the prototype for the Jewish group behind the work that stands against Gentile assimilation.[20] Abraham's recognition of God as portrayed in *Jubilees* occurs during the era of the idolatry of the sons of Noah. Abraham, however, has looked to the one God, the knowledge of whom has again reached human beings. For the author, contem-

18. Endres, *Interpretation*, p. 198.
19. Michael Grant (ed.), *Greek and Latin Authors* (New York: The H.W. Wilson Co., 1980), p. 441; cf. *Thucydides* 1.22.1.
20. Mogens Müller, 'Die Abraham-Gestalt im Jubiläenbuch: Versuch einer Interpretation', *SJOT* 19 (1996), pp. 238–57.

porary Israel had strayed just like the sons of Noah. However, in the time of the author of *Jubilees*, a faction had developed in which the true worship of God was revived.[21] Abraham then becomes the prototype and spokesman for this nationalistic faction who models a new beginning by his recognition of the one, true God.

Later Abram sits up 'to observe the stars' in order to ascertain the rainfall patterns of the coming year (*Jub.* 12.16). This would not be unusual for one of Mesopotamian origins since astrology was a type of divination for which Mesopotamia was especially famed.[22] Yet he soon realises his mistaken dependence upon the movement of the stars. Because astrology and meteorology were inextricably linked in the ancient world, the author believes that by following this course of action, Abraham was participating in astrology. As Vermes explains, 'A critical attitude towards astrology first appears in the *Book of Jubilees*. Its author...who...held the...opinion concerning the ungodly origin of the science of the stars, hesitates even to consider Abraham as an astrologer'.[23] After rejecting astrology, Abraham prays,

> My God, my God, God most High,
> You alone are my God.
> You have created everything;
> Everything that was and has been is the product of your hands.
> You and your lordship I have chosen.
> Save me from the power of the evil spirits who rule the thoughts
> of people's minds.
> May they not mislead me from following you, my God.
> Do establish me and my posterity forever.
> May we not go astray from now until eternity (*Jub.* 12.19–20).

Besides recognizing God as the Creator, Abraham discerns in this prayer that it is evil spirits who rule people's minds and cause them to practice idolatry. He asks for God's guidance in maintaining devotion to him alone not only for himself, but also for his descendants forever.

Significantly, after Abraham's rejection of astrology, the author of *Jubilees* inserts a section based upon Gen.12.1–3, which is God's call to Abraham and his promise that Abraham's would bear numerous progeny and bring blessing to all the nations. As VanderKam states, '*Jubilees* maintains...that Abram had recognized and confessed the true God before the scene described in Gen. 12.1–3 (*Jub.* 12.16–20); so the revelation came to one who already believed in God and had brought that belief to expression.'[24] God responds to Abraham's recognition of the one God and separation from his father's idolatrous family through election and blessing.

21. Müller, 'Abraham-Gestalt', p. 253.
22. A. Leo Oppenheim, *Ancient Mesopotamia: Portrait of a Dead Civilization* (Chicago: University of Chicago Press, 1964), p. 224.
23. *Scripture and Tradition in Judaism* (Leiden: E.J. Brill, 1961), p. 81.
24. VanderKam, *Jubilees* (2001), p. 110.

b. *Abraham's Adherence to the Mosaic Law and Faithful Obedience to God*
The author of *Jubilees* is also concerned to show how it is that Abraham is obedient to the Mosaic Law before the law was actually given. For example, Abraham celebrates the feast of the firstfruits when he offers sacrifices of animals, cereal and libations (*Jub.* 15.1–2). Our author also takes Gen. 21.8, which mentions the feast Abraham celebrated upon the birth of Isaac, and uses it as an occasion to depict Abraham as observing the feast of tabernacles (16.20–31).

These reported observations of festal celebrations are an example of using an ancient biblical character to strengthen the author's contemporary tradition. If in the diverse religious milieu of the second century the Jewish people were looking for foundations and authority for their traditions, this kind of depiction provided it. Abraham not only observed the feast, but did so 'in accord with the testimony of the heavenly tablets' (16.28). The 'heavenly tablets' are important to the author as regulators of religious festivals. Because Abraham celebrated the feast for seven days in the seventh month (16.29), Israel should observe it in a similar fashion. Abraham, who acted in accordance with the previously established sacred days, is an example for the readers of *Jubilees* to follow.

Our author also waxes eloquent concerning the laws of circumcision in *Jub.* 15.25–32 (see also above). He states that a son who is not circumcised on the eighth day according to what is written on the heavenly tablets 'does not belong to the people of the pact which the Lord made with Abraham but to the people (meant for) destruction…he has violated the covenant of the Lord our God' (15.26). The author of *Jubilees* puts the covenant of circumcision within the context of the 'eternal ordinance' (15.25) of circumcision on the eighth day. As such, the account functions in the story of Abraham to encourage his readers to continue to circumcise their children: not to be circumcised is akin to being among those who are meant for destruction, namely, the nations. The prophetic passage ('They will not circumcise their sons' 15.33–34) functions to warn those adults who were never circumcised as children or those who have not had their children circumcised or have practised epispasm that by not having the sign of circumcision they have made themselves like the nations. They are condemned by this eternal error (15.34).

Thus in *Jubilees* Abraham is portrayed as one who rejects idolatry for faith in the one God and practises covenantal stipulations. This in turn provides a model for *Jubilees'* readers of the necessity of monotheistic faith and obedience to covenantal stipulations for remaining within God's people. Thus, through the example of Abraham the author of *Jubilees* legitimates the people of God and provides the necessary boundaries for their continued existence.

c. *Abraham's Proclamation of Separation from Gentiles, Idolatry and Sin*
Much of the remaining material in *Jubilees* (20.1–23.10) in which Abraham appears is made up of speeches. In the first speech, Abraham speaks to his descendants: Ishmael and his twelve children, Isaac and his two children, and Keturah's six children and their sons. His second speech is his testament to Isaac,

and the third and most important speech is given to his grandson and primary covenant transmitter, Jacob.

In these speeches, Abraham instructs his immediate descendants, Isaac and Jacob, how to be obedient to their God. Through this depiction of Abraham and his descendants, the author of *Jubilees* is portraying for his readers the very same thing – these are the commandments by which they can put the desires of God above their own.

Abraham's first speech is concerned with following the way of the Lord in contrast to going after idols and their uncleanness (20.1–10). In the prelude (20.1–5) he commands them to practise righteousness and love towards all people, to circumcise their sons, not to deviate either to the right or left from all the ways which the Lord commanded them, to keep themselves from all sexual impurity and uncleanness and to set aside such activity among themselves. Abraham drives his point home by telling his listeners about the judgements of Sodom based on sexual impurity and the giants who were judged and destroyed because of their evil.

An extensive section of poetry follows (20.6–10) that is broken up into five sections. It is plausible that the second section (20.7) contains the summary of the speech both because it contains Abraham's only command in the first person found in the speech and it is the only section that is not extensively dependent upon the Old Testament or *1 Enoch*. Abraham states, 'I testify to you, my sons: love the God of heaven, and hold fast to all his commandments. Do not follow their idols and their uncleanness' (20.7).

The worthlessness of worshipping idols is described in v. 8 and is much like Abraham's earlier speech to his father that also addressed the vanity of idol worship. In both speeches, Abraham contends that idol worship is worthless because idols have no spirit and they are created by human beings whereas the true God created everything (12.4) and sends rain (12.4; 20.9).

The speech may best be described in the following outline:

1.   The result of corruption (especially of a sexual nature) is cursing and judgement (20.6).
2.   It is necessary to love God and follow his commands and not to go after idols and their defilement (20.7).
3.   Making and worshipping idols is worthless (20.8).
4.   Worshipping the Most High God and doing what is righteous leads to great blessing (20.9).
5.   The result of worshipping and obeying God is becoming a blessing upon the earth (20.10).

As was seen earlier in the text, Abraham is concerned with following God and his commands while avoiding idols and their sure defilement. Since the Gentiles were those outside of the covenant community who were regarded as idol worshippers, in effect Abraham is commanding avoidance of Gentile ways and Gentile idol worship. If one follows the observation made earlier that the author's use of speeches may be similar to that of the precedent set by Thucydides, then the author is capitalizing upon this theme of separation from Gentiles as an especially important one for the reader to draw from the Abraham narrative.

Abraham's second speech is his testament to Isaac. In Jewish literature, testaments are among the last words of an important character, which may emphasize not only what the author considered pertinent in the previous narrative concerning that character, but also what the author is trying to express to his readers at the present time.[25]

In order to ascertain the central message of Abraham's testament it will be analysed according to the components of the covenant formulary found in the work of Klaus Baltzer. Baltzer maintains that the testament closely follows the covenant formulary in its components. Of the three final speeches in *Jubilees*, Abraham's testament to Isaac is the only one that fits the form delineated precisely. Using Baltzer's components, the speech appears as follows:

Preamble: Who is concerned (Isaac; 21.1)
The age of the patriarch (175 years; 21.2)
1a. Antecedent History: (21.2–3)
'Throughout my entire lifetime I have continually remembered the Lord and tried to do his will wholeheartedly and to walk a straight course in all his ways. I have personally hated idols in order to keep myself for doing the will of the one who created me.'
1b. Statement of Faith: (21.4)
'For he is the living God. He is more holy, faithful, and just than anyone and [he] exercises judgment against all who transgress his commands and despise his covenant.'
2a. Statement of Substance (21.5)
'Now you, my son, keep his commands, ordinances and verdicts. Do not pursue unclean things, statues or molten images'.
2b. Corpus of Individual Stipulations (21.6–20)
Items included here are the prohibition of eating the blood of animals or birds, the proper way to offer burnt offerings and purity laws. Following these laws results in the protection of God and safety from the evil one and every kind of death.
3. Conclusion (21.21–26)
'I see...that all the actions of mankind (consist of) sin and wickedness and all their deeds of impurity, worthlessness, and contamination. With them there is nothing that is right. Be careful not to walk in their ways or to tread in their paths so that you may not commit a mortal sin before the most high God... Depart from all their actions and from all their impurity. Keep the obligations of the most high God... He will bless you'.[26]

The most noticeable section here for the purposes of this chapter is 2a (21.5), the statement of substance. What is significant is the similarity between this statement and the summary statement found above in *Jub.* 20.7. In both statements Abraham adjures the hearers to keep the commands of God, and not to go after Gentile idols and pollution. Again, Abraham appears as a prototype of one who rejects idolatry for faith in and obedience to the one God, who follows the commands of God and separates from Gentiles and their defiling ways.

25. Endres, *Interpretation*, p. 198; Walter Harrelson, 'The Significance of "Last Words" for Intertestamental Ethics', in James L. Crenshaw and John T. Willis (eds.), *Essays in Old Testament Ethics* (New York: KTAV, 1974), pp. 205–23.
26. Adapted from Klaus Baltzer, *The Covenant Formulary* (Philadelphia: Fortress Press, 1971), pp. 137–41. Note that while I have used the form that Baltzer recommends, I am using VanderKam's translation.

Before the final speech (22.10–24), Abraham is described as celebrating the festival of weeks. As was mentioned above, this feast is central to the *Book of Jubilees*; it celebrated the anniversary of the first covenant between God and Noah after the deluge (6.17). The celebration of the feast of weeks at the final encounter between Abraham and Jacob emphasized the continuity of the covenant through Jacob.[27]

In his final speech, Abraham first blesses Jacob (22.11–15). Because this speech takes place at the time of Abraham's death and contains his final advice for the primary continuator of the covenant, its themes are of utmost importance. The main point of the speech appears in vv. 16–19:

> Now you…Jacob…keep the commandments of your father Abraham.
> Separate from the nations,
> and do not eat with them.
> Do not act as they do,
> and do not become their companion,
> for their actions are something that is impure,
> and all their ways are defiled and something abominable and detestable.
> They offer their sacrifices to the dead,
> and they worship demons.
> They eat in tombs,
> and everything they do is empty and worthless.
> They have no mind to think,
> and their eyes do not see what they do
> and how they err in saying to (a piece of) wood:
> «you are my god»;
> or to a stone:
> «you are my Lord;
> you are my deliverer».
> (They have) no mind (*Jub.* 22.16–18).

The speech continues with a description of the coming judgement for Canaanites and those who worship idols as well as a final blessing upon Jacob (22.20–30). Abraham's epitaph follows shortly thereafter: 'For Abraham was perfect with the Lord in everything that he did – being properly pleasing throughout his lifetime.'

Once again, the speech revolves around the themes of forsaking idolatry, of keeping the commandments and separating oneself from the Gentiles. Endres contends, 'the command to separate from the Gentiles provides a focal point of the covenant renewal for this author; as he viewed the life of his Jewish community, its primary obligation was to remain free of Gentile influences'.[28]

4. *Conclusion: The Function and Significance of Abraham in* Jubilees

Within the *Book of Jubilees*, Abraham has several functions. With Noah and Jacob, he is a central transmitter of the covenant. Like others such as Noah

---

27. Endres, *Interpretation*, p. 40.
28. Endres, *Interpretation*, p. 45.

(*Jub.* 6.17–29) he is obedient to the Law of Moses before it is given because it has been ordained in the heavenly tablets. In addition, like others such as Moses (*Jub.* 30.7–17), he symbolizes the necessity of separation from Gentiles.

In *Jubilees*, Abraham's unique contribution is that he is the first to reject idolatry and embrace monotheism. He is the first among the sons of Noah to search for and find the true God and Creator. He recognizes the folly of idolatry. He announces separation from Gentiles because of their idolatry and because of the sin that is a consequence of this idolatry.

What does the character and function of Abraham described in the text of *Jubilees* mean in reference to implied norms of behaviour for the Jew especially in light of the historical and cultural circumstances of *Jubilees* described earlier? First, Abraham is the first person from among the sons of Noah to believe in the one true God. We are told that Mastema is responsible for the delusion of the sons of Noah (11.4–5), otherwise known as the Gentiles. It is Abraham alone who separates from his father (11.16) and begins to pray to and seek the true God and his ways (11.17). After Abraham exhorts his father not to worship the idols that are mute and created by human beings in contrast to the true God who creates by his word (12.2–5), his father replies tellingly, 'I know…my son…if I speak to them in righteousness, they will kill me because their souls cleave to them' (12.6–7). It seems reasonable that Terah, who knows the truth yet fears for his life if he does not worship idols, represents at least one faction of the Jewish people. Terah represents the Jews who at present worship idols or even Jews who worshipped them under Antiochus Epiphanes' command that they worship idols or die (cf. 1 Macc. 1.47).

In the speech attributed to Abraham in *Jub.* 12, the author commands his readers to forsake the folly of idol worship. Abraham sees beyond astrology and recognizes the Creator God (12. 17–20). Abraham represents the ideal Jew who worships the true God and destroys idols, although it may cost him his life.

According to the author of *Jubilees*, Abraham obeys the law. He celebrates feasts (cf. 15.20–31) and he circumcises his son and his household (15.23–34). The author adds a warning of the annihilation of those Jews who were not circumcised on the eighth day (15.26). Faithlessness regarding circumcision is even predicted (15.33–34), presumably a *vaticinium ex eventu*.

Jewish avoidance of circumcision occurred under the reign of Antiochus Epiphanes IV when he proclaimed that any Jew who circumcised a son was to die (1 Macc. 1.48–50). Jews who bore the marks of circumcision could very well be subjected to mild to severe persecution. Abraham provides the example of one who circumcises his son and his household according to the ordinance in the heavenly tablets.

The celebration of feasts also became associated with persecution. According to another decree by Antiochus Epiphanes, the Jewish people were to profane Sabbaths and festivals or die (1 Macc. 1.45). As in the case of circumcision, the author of *Jubilees* attributes eternal validity to the keeping of the Sabbath and festivals because they were ordained in the heavenly tablets. Abraham was depicted as observing both the feast of tabernacles and the feast of weeks. If the readers of *Jubilees* were to emulate Abraham, obviously they were to observe their holy days – perhaps even in the face of persecution.

Those who do not follow the commands of the Lord, even if they are Jews, can expect the wrath of God to fall upon them. Lot and his daughters, having committed incest, are judged just like Sodom (16.5–9). This is the kind of sin about which the author warns his readers using Abraham as his mouthpiece. Much of the sin consists of sexual impurity (cf. 20.6), although the eating of sacrifices incorrectly offered is also sin (21.6–20). For the most part, sin is attributed to Gentiles (22.16–19) who worship and offer sacrifices to idols (22.17–18). The true Jew is to separate (22.16) from Gentiles lest with association come assimilation and sin. The Jewish readers are then strictly warned; those who associate with Gentile idolaters run the risk of taking on the sins of the Gentiles and consequently the wrath and judgement of God.

Thus, like Abraham, the readers of *Jubilees* are to forsake idolatry and sin by remaining true to their God and his commandments, even though the cost of this loyalty may be death. The author of *Jubilees* considers this to be an extremely important message for his readers who are caught between the polemical ideologies of the nationalistic and assimilationist Jewish factions.

The author's purpose is to provide an uncompromising warning of the consequences of his readers' behaviour should they forsake their religion. Even though they may die for the observance of the very aspects of Judaism that made them unique – circumcision, holy days and monotheism – the exhortation of *Jubilees* still stands. If their forefather Abraham was willing to die instead of worship his father's idols, why should these Jews not avoid association with Gentiles? The worship of the one God and the separation from idolatrous Gentiles characterized Abraham as God's own and should still characterize the readers of *Jubilees*. The only outcome of association with Gentiles could be idol-worship and departure from following the commands of God.

Thus, in *Jubilees*, those who are within the boundaries of God's people are those who reject idolatry and obey the stipulations of the covenant. Those who are outside of the boundary, of course, are the Gentiles who are idolaters and sinners and the Jews who assimilate with their ways. Monotheism excludes anyone who would venture into this sphere of assimilation, and Abraham represents the legitimation of this monotheistic boundary and the prototype for those who would heed *Jubilees'* warning.

Chapter 3

ABRAHAM THE PROSELYTE AND PHILOSOPHER
IN THE WORKS OF PHILO

1. *Philo and the Jewish Community in Alexandria*

Philo, an Alexandrian Jew (c. 20 BCE–40 CE) belonged to one of the wealthiest and most prominent families in Alexandria.[1] During his boyhood, he studied topics such as grammar, geometry, rhetoric and music.[2] However, to Philo, these subjects were only in preparation for what he and many other writers of antiquity considered to be the most worthy of subjects: philosophy.[3] From his writings, it is evident that he was familiar with Stoic, Pythagorean, and Platonic traditions, Greek literature, and Hellenistic mystic philosophy.[4]

Philo's writings may have been used later in a synagogue-school where Philo taught his interpretive methods of scripture to a select group of initiates. Philo's works reveal a strongly Hellenized Judaism. Mendelson has gone so far as to say that although Hellenism permeated the Mediterranean world, the 'fusion of Judaism and Hellenism actually reached its acme not in Palestine, but in Alexandria'.[5]

By Philo's lifetime, the Jewish people had lived in Egypt for hundreds of years. Artapanus, who is thought to have lived in Alexandria in the third to second centuries BCE, provided an apologetic for the ancient history of the Jewish people in Egypt in order to prove that they were not recent immigrants.[6] E.M. Smallwood contends that the community of Jews in Alexandria at the time of the appointment of Agrippa I (37–44 CE) was probably 'the largest and most important single Diaspora community in the world at that time.'[7] The Jewish people formed a cross

---

1. Peder Borgen, 'Philo of Alexandria', Michael E. Stone (ed.), in *Jewish Writings of the Second Temple Period* (CRINT, 2.2; Assen: Van Gorcum, 1984; Philadelphia: Fortress Press, 1984), pp. 233–82 (252–54).

2. *Congr.* 74–78; *Rer. Div. Her.* 105. Cf. Alan Mendelson, *Secular Education in Philo of Alexandria* (Cincinnati: Hebrew Union College Press, 1982), pp. 1–45.

3. Mendelson, *Education*, p. xxiii.

4. E. Bréhier, *Les idées philosophiques et religieuses de Philon d'Alexandrie* (Paris: Librairie Alphonse Picard & Fils, 1908); E.R. Goodenough, *By Light, Light: The Mystic Gospel of Hellenistic Judaism* (New Haven: Yale University Press, 1935).

5. Mendelson, *Education*, p. xvii.

6. Eusebius, *Praep. Ev.* 9.18.1.

7. E.M. Smallwood, *The Jews Under Roman Rule* (SJLA, 20; Leiden: E.J. Brill, 1976), p. 220.

section of the Egyptian population, comprising all grades of wealth and social position.[8]

Whether or not the Jews possessed citizenship in Ptolemaic or even Roman Alexandria has been a matter of debate.[9] They were concentrated in at least two of the five geographical divisions of Alexandria.[10] Their official form of government, known as a *politeuma*, was a recognized, semi-autonomous civic body, which 'had its own constitution and administered its internal affairs as an ethnic unit through officials distinct from and independent of those of the host city'.[11] Separate administration and the concentration in areas of the city simultaneously ensured that the Jews retained their cohesion as a racial entity.[12]

Although relations between the Jews and the Ptolemies had been harmonious, anti-Jewish tensions grew with the annexation of Egypt by the Romans in 30 BCE. The Jews in Alexandria benefited from the Roman annexation 'by coming automatically under the protection which it was by then Roman policy to afford to all Jews in the empire in the practice of their religion and the preservation of their national identity'.[13]

Tension grew when the Romans based the rate of the poll tax upon personal status. Those who were citizens of the Greek cities were exempt from the tax, while the Hellenes of the provincial towns paid a lower rate. The native Egyptians paid the tax in full. 'For the Jews the matter of their personal status was therefore of considerable importance, and they seem to have been resolved to hold out for equal status with the Greeks and for being considered citizens of Alexandria'.[14]

According to Peder Borgen, 'Greek education and the gymnasium were burning issues to the Jews in Alexandria, since they served as the condition for full civil rights. The *encyclia* therefore played an important part both in matters of taxes and in the question of gaining access to political offices.'[15] Philo supported the policy that Jews should participate actively in the social life of Alexandria. It is probably the case that Philo's allegory of Gen. 16.1–16, in which Abraham proceeds from Hagar and Ishmael to Sarah and Isaac, represents progression from encyclical education (Hagar and Ishmael), which the Jews shared with pagans, to genuine, Jewish philosophy (Sarah).[16]

8.   Smallwood, *Rule*, pp. 222–23.

9.   P.M. Fraser, *Ptolemaic Alexandria* (Oxford: Clarendon Press, 1972), p. 54; Smallwood, *Rule*, pp. 227–35; Aryeh Kasher, *The Jews in Hellenistic and Roman Egypt: The Struggle for Equal Rights* (Tübingen: J.C.B. Mohr [Paul Siebeck], 1985), pp. 75–105.

10.   *Flacc.* 55.

11.   Smallwood, *Rule*, p. 225.

12.   Smallwood, *Rule*, p. 225.

13.   Smallwood, *Rule*, p. 231.

14.   M. Stern, 'The Jewish Diaspora', in S. Safrai, *et al.* (eds.), *Jewish People in the First Century* (CRINT, 1.1.; Assen: Van Gorcum, 1974), pp. 117–83 (125).

15.   Peder Borgen, 'Philo: Survey of Research since World War II', *ANRW* 21.1 (Berlin: W. de Gruyter, 1984), pp. 98–154 (116).

16.   *Mut. Nom.* 253–263; *Congr.* 35.

Tension further increased with the accession of Gaius Caligula in March, 37 CE. Although Avilius Flaccus, the Roman governor of Egypt, had governed excellently until this point, his position was precarious under the new emperor and his post was eventually terminated.[17] Consequently, Flaccus held the office for the present, but his recall was inevitable. At this point, the Greek nationalist party posed as Flaccus' friends and took advantage of the situation. They promised to intercede on behalf of Flaccus at the imperial court, provided he supported them in their conflict with the Jews.

Initial violence against the Jews occurred in the form of a counter-demonstration to a visit from Agrippa I who made an ostentatious parade through the streets of Alexandria. Flaccus made no attempt to prevent the Greeks from chanting gibes and mocking the Jewish ruler.[18] The Greek mob burned or demolished many synagogues in parts of Alexandria where comparatively few Jews lived and in the Jewish districts they made the synagogues unfit for use by placing portraits of Gaius in them.[19]

The situation was only to get worse, as attested by Philo's statements in *Flaccus* 53–54:

> He [Flaccus] proceeded to another scheme…the destruction of our citizenship, so that when our ancestral customs and our participation in political rights, the sole mooring on which our life was secured, had been cut away, we might undergo the worst misfortunes with no cable to cling to for safety. For a few days afterwards he issued a proclamation in which he denounced us as foreigners and aliens and gave us no right of pleading our case but condemned us unjudged.

According to Aryeh Kasher, the problem with Flaccus' actions was not so much that it curtailed the hopes of the Jews for full citizenship, but that it dissolved the rights accorded to those in the *politeuma*. The political organizational structure of Alexandria was a collection of *politeumata*. What concerns Philo about the decree that they are now 'foreigners and aliens' is the loss of their protection in reference to their ancestral laws, to their property and to themselves. 'Consequently, the Jews were no longer recognized as an organized group with political privileges, and being "foreigners and aliens" they were handed over to the *polis* (as individuals) for good or for evil.'[20] Thus, the request on the part of the Alexandrian Greeks that the Jewish people be surrendered to them was granted.

The Greeks put Flaccus' ruling into effect of their own accord. After Greeks chased Jews into one part of the city, Flaccus ordered them to remain there or they cruelly tortured or massacred them before they could take refuge.[21] The 'refuge' eventually became a virtual ghetto. People died not only from the famine and sickness that resulted from such actions but also from being burned alive in

17. *Flacc.* 8.
18. *Flacc.* 25–35.
19. *Leg. Gai.* 132–139.
20. Kasher, *Rights*, p. 244.
21. *Flacc.* 55–72; see also *Leg. Gai.* 120–131.

the middle of the city.[22] Finally, on Gaius' birthday, numbers of Jews were taken
to the theatre and were scourged, some of them to death, or they were tortured.[23]

Two embassies went to Rome. The Greeks went to exculpate themselves and
to keep the Jews in their unprivileged position. The five Jews who went under the
leadership of Philo sought redress for their injuries and the restoration of their
rights and the reinstatement of the *politeuma*. The Jews drew up a statement to
submit to the emperor that was based upon matters raised by the riots. When
Gaius returned to Rome from his military campaigns, he was virtually no help to
them at all but, as Philo reports, he seemed to be most concerned about why they
could not consider him to be a god.[24]

After Gaius' death, Claudius became emperor. It was he who, after listening to
both delegations, reaffirmed the traditional Augustan policy of allowing the Jews
to observe their laws freely but warned them not to try to win more privileges
than they formerly had. The synagogues in Alexandria were safeguarded and the
politeuma was reinstated.

2. *Philo's Literary Works*

The works of Philo that will be used in this chapter may be broken up into three
categories. First, the form of literature based on the interpretation of the Pentateuch that lacks an opening series of verses and the content of which flows from
the title of the particular essay will be designated as the 'exposition of the law'.
Secondly, the form of literature that begins with a series of biblical verses, the
content of which is shaped by these verses, will be called the 'allegory of the
law'. The third group contains works that can simply be called 'questions and
answers' because they follow the form of the asking of a brief question about the
meaning of a biblical passage or verse and the answer in response.[25]

The texts that will be used in this study of Abraham in Philo which fall under
the category of the exposition of the law are *De Abrahamo*, *De virtutibus* and *De
praemiis et poenis*. Texts which fall under the category of the allegory of the law
used in this chapter are *De migratione Abrahami*, *Legum allegoriae*, *De
ebrietate*, *Quis rerum divinarum heres sit*, *De cherubim*, *De fuga et inventione*,
De gigantibus, *De mutatione nominum* and *De somniis I and II*. Citations from
the third category are taken from *Quaestiones et solutiones in Genesin* and
Quaestiones et solutiones in Exodum.

For whom were Philo's works intended? Philo was probably writing for both
Jewish and Gentile readers. In his works in the category the exposition of the law
(hereafter called 'exposition'), Philo was probably writing at a simpler, more
literal level for a Gentile readership. In his works in the category the allegory of
the law (hereafter called 'Allegory'), Philo was probably writing for those who

---

22. *Leg. Gai.* 130; *Flacc.* 68.
23. *Flacc.* 73–85, 95–96.
24. *Leg. Gai.* 350–372.
25. These categories, which are still used by scholars of Philo today, are based upon those of Samuel Sandmel in *Philo of Alexandria: An Introduction* (New York, Oxford: Oxford University Press,
1979), pp. 30, 41–51.

were already acquainted with Judaism, presumably Jews.[26] In the midst of tensions between the Jews of Alexandria and those around them as described above, it is reasonable to assume that one of Philo's underlying motives may have been to provide an apologetic for Judaism and its distinctive beliefs and practices to the Hellenistic Gentile reader.

Another reason for Philo's work was to prevent Jews who were sympathetic with Hellenism and on the verge of apostasy from totally forsaking Judaism. From Philo's accounts, it appears that there were not only Jews in Alexandria who were opposed to the kind of philosophical allegorizing of the law that Philo practised, but also those who were so allegorical in their treatment of the law that they rejected the literal sense of the law.[27] In his work *De providentia* Philo is depicted as debating the belief in divine providence with his nephew, Tiberius Julius Alexander, whom H.A. Wolfson categorizes as belonging to the class of apostates known as 'uprooted Jewish intellectuals'.[28] This type of presentation would reasonably find readership among those Jews who had similar concerns. V. Nikiprowetzky has stated,

> Il est certain que c'est toute l'oeuvre exégétique de Philon, et non pas seulement une partie de cette oeuvre, que est marquée du caractère apologétique…toute l'oeuvre exégétique de Philon est née du désir de comprendre l'Ecriture d'une manière légitime. Cette explication philosophique et scientifique de la Bible rend Philon capable de méditer, ou de contempler, en quelque sorte, la parole de Dieu…Une telle exégèse doit réconcilier *par voie de conséquence,* les Juifs perplexes avec la Loi de leurs pères; aux païens elle doit montrer tous les motifs qu'ils ont de respecter la législation de Moïse ou même de l'adopter.[29]

In his apologetic mission, Philo most likely used popular Jewish exegetical traditions, probably from the synagogue communities in Alexandria. Mack contends that fundamentally there has been 'a failure to…explore the possibility that the [Philonic] corpus may contain a great deal of material from the traditions of Jewish interpretation which can not be attributed directly to Philo at all'.[30] Hamerton-Kelly has suggested that source analysis is pertinent to the

26. Samuel Sandmel, *Philo's Place in Judaism: A Study of Conceptions of Abraham in Jewish Literature* (New York: KTAV, 1971), p. 107; see also Birnbaum, *The Place of Judaism in Philo's Thought: Israel, Jews, and Proselytes* (Studia Philonica Monographs 2, no. 290; Atlanta, GA: Scholars Press, 1996), pp. 221–22.

27. *Migr. Abr.* 92.

28. *Philo: Foundations of Religious Philosophy in Judaism, Christianity, and Islam* (2 vols.; repr., Cambridge, MA: Harvard University Press, rev. edn, 1948), vol. I, p. 82.

29. 'It is certain that all the exegetical work of Philo, and not solely a fraction of this work, is marked by an apologetic character…all the exegetical work of Philo is born of the desire to understand Scripture in a legitimate manner. This philosophical and scientific explication of the Bible makes Philo capable of meditating on or of contemplating the word of God in some way… Such an exegesis must, *by way of consequence*, reconcile those Jews who are perplexed with the Law of the fathers; to Gentiles it must show them the grounds that they have to respect the legislation of Moses, or even to adopt it.' V. Nikiprowetzky, *Le commentaire de l'écriture chez Philon d'Alexandrie* (ALGHJ, 11; Leiden: E.J. Brill, 1977), pp. 182–83.

30. B. Mack, 'Philo Judaeus and Exegetical Traditions in Alexandria', *ANRW* 2.21.1 (Berlin: W. de Gruyter, 1984), pp. 227–71 (231).

study of Philo's works. By source analysis, he does not mean merely a written source but something less definable. 'One must be prepared to entertain as a source – or more precisely, a tradition – something less defined than a verbatim reproduction of a written document – for instance, notes expanded by Philo on the basis of oral tradition'.[31] Philo's use of Jewish tradition will be kept in mind as a study of the traditions of Abraham in Philo is pursued.

3. *The Interpretation of Abraham in the Works of Philo*

Because the concern of our study at this point is not to discuss all of the traditions of Abraham found in Philo, this section is divided according to the traditions of Abraham as rejecting idolatry for monotheism and obedience to the Mosaic Law. We will begin with the works that fall into the category of the exposition, particularly *De Abrahamo,* because these works provide the primary traditions about Abraham in the most comprehensible fashion. We will then proceed to discuss selections from both the allegory category and *Quaestiones et solutiones in Genesin*, which substantially supplement traditions from the first category.

a. *Abraham the First Monotheist in the Exposition of the Law*
In *De Abrahamo,* Philo describes Abraham's migration from Chaldaea in both the literal and the allegorical senses (*Abr.* 62–88). Literally, Abraham is a man of wisdom.[32] Wisdom was a revered characteristic in Philo's world; Abraham is described as having contemplative wisdom. Abraham emigrates for the noblest of reasons – he has neither, for example, been banished nor is he interested in making money via commerce. Abraham's emigration is 'one of soul rather than body' (*Abr.* 66). Allegorically, Abraham is in search of the true God (*Abr.* 68– 69).[33] Philo uses allegory much like the Stoics who converted Homeric personalities into symbols representing 'aspects of human characteristics or dispositions [which] could enable one to continue a sense of personal connection with the ancient past…by making it contemporary and universal in the sense that these human characteristics still abided among men'.[34]

One example of such allegory from *The Odyssey* is the maxim, which may be attributed to Gorgias of Leontini, 'Those who neglect philosophy and spend their time on ordinary studies are like the Suitors who desired Penelope but slept with her maids.'[35] Hellenistic allegory used by Philo was characterized by being unhistorical. He took no account at all of the historical situation, and very little of the original meaning of the material allegorized. Allegory served as the device by

---

31. Robert G. Hamerton-Kelly, 'Sources and Traditions in Philo Judaeus: Prolegomena to an Analysis of His Writings', *Studia Philonica* 1 (1972), pp. 3–26 (16).

32. *Abr.* 68; cf. *Rer. Div. Her.* 18; *Poster. C.* 7.

33. Cf. *Abr.* 85–87.

34. Samuel Sandmel, 'Philo: The Man, His Writings, His Significance', *ANRW* 2.21.1 (Berlin: W. de Gruyter, 1984), pp. 3–46 (13).

35. Kathleen Freeman, *Ancilla to the Pre-Socratic Philosophers* (Oxford: Basil Blackwell, 1948), p. 139.

which Philo interpreted Scripture as a repository of Platonism and Stoicism. Philo's belief that Greek philosophy could be found in the Jewish Scriptures attested to the greater antiquity of Judaism in comparison with the Greek world and provided an apologetic for Judaism.[36]

i. *Abraham Migrates from Chaldaea and Astrological Knowledge.* According to Philo's rendition, Abraham's migration from Chaldaea to Haran was, allegorically, from the worship of the Creation to the worship of the Creator.

> The migrations as set forth…are made…according to the laws of allegory by a virtue-loving soul in its search for the true God. For the Chaldeans were especially active in the elaboration of astrology and ascribed everything to the movements of the stars. They supposed that the course of the phenomena of the world is guided by influences contained in numbers and numerical proportions. Thus they glorified the visible existence, leaving out of consideration the intelligible and invisible. But while exploring numerical order as applied to the revolution of the sun, moon, and other planets and fixed stars, and the changes of the yearly seasons and the interdependence of phenomena in heaven and on earth, they concluded that the world itself was God, thus profanely likening the created to the Creator. In this creed Abraham had been reared, and for a long time remained a Chaldean. Then opening the soul's eye as though after profound sleep…he followed the ray and discerned what he had not beheld before, a charioteer and pilot presiding over the world and directing in safety his own work' (*Abr.* 68–70).[37]

To Philo and much of the Roman world, being called a Chaldaean connoted someone who foretold the future based upon astrology. While in the citation above Philo literally states that Abraham was involved in astronomy, in Philo's culture astronomy would mean the same thing as astrology.

A similar depiction of Abraham is found in *De virtutibus*:

> The most ancient member of the Jewish nation was a Chaldaean by birth, the son of an astrologer, one of those who study the lore of that science, and think that the stars and the whole heaven and universe are gods, the authors, they say, of the events which befall each man for good or for ill, and hold that there is no originating cause outside the things we perceive by our senses. What could be more grievous or more capable of proving the total absence of nobility in the soul than this, that its knowledge of the many, the secondary, the created only leads it to ignore the one, the Primal, the Uncreated and Maker of all (*Virt.* 212–213).[38]

Again, Abraham is described as coming from a family and nation that practises astrology. Philo contrasts the base belief accorded to astrologers that secondary causes that are perceived with one's senses are responsible for human events with the belief in the one God who is the maker of all things, including those things that one perceives with the senses.

While my purpose here is not to discuss fully Philo's complicated relationship to Stoicism and Pythagoreanism, the brief consideration of relevant Stoic and

---

36. Sandmel, 'Significance', p. 14.

37. All translations from *Philo in Ten Volumes (and Two Supplementary Volumes)* (trans. F.H. Colson, G.H. Whitaker and Ralph Marcus; LCL, London: Heinemann, 1968).

38. Cf. *Abr.* 77–80.

Pythagorean principles that follow should illumine aspects of Philo's texts. Specifically, Philo appears to be grappling with an aspect of Stoic belief in which everything in nature contained a portion of the divine. As A.A. Long states, 'The existence of God, or what comes to the same thing in Stoicism, the divinity of Nature, is a thesis which the Stoics devoted great energy to proving'.[39] Consequently, everything on earth has a part of the divine Nature in it. Long even goes so far as to say 'Fundamentally, Stoic theology is pantheist'.[40]

A central position of Stoicism was that the divine bears the same relation to the universe as a man's soul to his body. Just as it was questioned whether the soul was situated in the head or in the heart, in the case of the universe it was questioned whether its 'principate' was in the sun or the sky.[41] The universe was thought to be God, but divinity was further ascribed to God's manifestations, particularly the heavenly bodies, sun, moon and stars.

To the Stoics, the mind was what the human being had in common with the divine and it was the divine that ultimately created the world. In contrast to Plato who believed in five causes, and Aristotle who believed in four causes of creation, to the Stoics only one cause existed who was the maker of the universe.[42] Seneca speaks of the cause not only as being single, but as 'creative reason, the deity…"the maker"'.[43]

By concentrating on numerical proportions (*Abr.* 68–69), Philo is also grappling with principles set forth by the Pythagoreans who believed that the universe was controlled by numbers and the proportions between numbers. Aristotle spoke of the Pythagoreans as those who believe 'that numbers are the ultimate things in the whole physical universe, they assumed the elements of numbers to be the elements of everything, and the whole universe to be a proportion or number.'[44] While Philo does not speak literally of harmony (literal musical intervals), which the Pythagoreans believed to be the outcome of the movement of the planets, the proportions between the planets is reflected in his choice of words. Because not everything could be counted, the idea of proportion between numbers was a central Pythagorean principle.

It seems most reasonable to assume that Philo is responding to some of the presuppositions of Stoicism and Pythagoreanism: that matter contained an element of the divine, that the planets were themselves gods, and that everything was controlled by arithmetic and numerical principles.

Philo describes Abraham as leaving the presuppositions of astrology behind (Chaldaea) in order to seek the true God. He is described as beginning to see and discern 'a charioteer and pilot presiding over the world and directing in safety his own work…' (*Abr.* 70). According to David Runia's interpretation of the Logos

---

    39. *Hellenistic Philosophy: Stoics, Epicureans, Sceptics* (Berkeley/Los Angeles: University of California Press, 2nd edn, 1986), p. 149.
    40. Long, *Philosophy*, p. 150; cf. p. 152.
    41. *Praep. Ev.* 15.15, 7; *Diog. L.* vii.138.
    42. *Ep.* 65.7.
    43. *Ep.* 65.11–14.
    44. *Metaph.* 1.5.2.

in Philo, 'the Logos permeates and holds together the entire cosmos. Heaven is…the highest and chief residence of the divine Logos in the cosmos. Philo likes to illustrate this with the image of the chariot, familiar to him from both the Platonic *Phaedrus* myth and Judaic tradition'.[45] In the *Phaedrus* myth Zeus, 'the great leader in heaven…[drives] a "winged chariot"' from which he arranges everything.[46] Paraphrasing Plato, in *Quaestiones et solutiones in Genesin,* Philo states, '"Heaven is a flying chariot" because of its very swift revolution which surpasses in speed even the birds in their course'.[47] In this chariot, the Logos is the reinsman and God its charioteer. According to Runia, 'The charioteer passes on to the reinsman the directions necessary for the correct guidance of the universe'.[48] According to Philo, Abraham is a good philosopher who, leaving behind his former misconceptions, begins to understand that the divine and first Cause exists beyond the phenomena and numerical proportions of the universe.

ii. *Abraham Migrates to Haran or the Knowledge of God Based upon Self-knowledge.* Abraham's migration to Haran occurs when, in order to establish the sight (discernment), which had been revealed to him, the holy word (logos) encourages Abraham to find the 'great' by self-observation (*Abr.* 71). In *De Abrahamo*, Haran is symbolic for the senses that are of no use unless the invisible mind is there to govern them. From this observation, Abraham comes to apprehend what it is he wanted to know: that just as he has an invisible mind to rule his own senses, so an invisible king governs the world. Philo continues by saying, 'anyone who reflects on these things…will know for certain that the world is not the primal God but a work of the primal God and Father of all' (*Abr.* 74–75).

Philo's description of Abraham's reasoning to the existence of God from analysing himself sounds much like the stoic description of Reason which rules the world and which is parallel to the mind that rules the body. Philo's argument using the figure of Abraham proves 'as is contended by the Stoics, that as there is a mind within man so there must be a mind within the world'.[49] This Stoic principle is articulated by Diogenes Laertius:

> The world…is ordered by reason and providence…inasmuch as reason pervades every part of it, just as does the soul in us… For through some parts it passes as a 'hold' or containing force, as is the case with our bones and sinews; while through others it passes as intelligence, as in the ruling part of the soul. Thus, then, the whole world is a living being, endowed with soul and reason…[50]

Even Abraham's change of name is based upon his turning from his former beliefs in astrology to his recognition of the one who governs the world (*Abr.* 81–84). His former name, Abram, signified one 'called astrologer and meteorologist

---

45. *Philo of Alexandria and the Timaeus of Plato* (Leiden: E.J. Brill, 1986), p. 214.
46. *Phaedr.* 246e.
47. *Quaest. in Gen.* 3.3.
48. *Timaeus,* p. 215. Cf. *Somn.* 1.157; *Fug.* 101.
49. Goodenough, *Light,* p. 138.
50. *Diog. L.* vii.138–139.

who takes care of the Chaldaean tenets as a father would of his children'; his new name, Abraham, signifies the 'elect father of sound' who is called elect based upon his merits. [51] Philo then describes the basis of the merits, 'Now to the meteorologist nothing at all seems greater than the universe, and he credits it with the causation of what comes into being. But the wise man with more discerning eyes sees something more perfect perceived by mind, something which rules and governs, the master and pilot of all else' (*Abr.* 84).

At the conclusion of this section on the migration of Abraham, Philo says that he has shown how Abraham was drawn away from his former life, and his mind 'did not remain…in the realm of sense, nor suppose that the visible world was the Almighty and Primal God, but using its reason, sped upwards and turned its gaze upon the intelligible order which is superior to the visible and upon Him who is maker and ruler of both alike' (*Abr.* 88).

As above, in tandem with one aspect of Stoic cosmology, Abraham's mind saw the intelligible order, which was the Maker and Ruler of the world. Unlike some Stoic philosophy in which the visible creation was believed to contain the divine, Abraham saw beyond the visible to the Primal, Creator God.

iii. *Abraham the Proselyte.* Abraham is spoken of as the first to believe in God in Gen. 15.6. In *De virtutibus,* Philo implicitly refers to this passage when he describes Abraham by saying, 'he is the first person spoken of as believing in God, since he first grasped a firm and unswerving conception of the truth that there is one Cause above all and that it provides for the world and all that there is therein' (*Virt.* 216).[52] Philo later clarifies how it is that Abraham might be viewed in his day as:

> the standard of nobility for all proselytes, who, abandoning the ignobility of strange laws and monstrous customs which assigned divine honours to stocks and stones and soulless things in general, have come to settle in a better land, in a commonwealth full of true life and vitality, with truth as its director and president' (*Virt.* 219; cf. *Ebr.* 106–110).

Abraham is not only the first one to believe in God, but because of his leaving behind astrology which Philo equates with idolatry, he is the prototype of the Gentile proselyte who leaves behind his idols of wood and stone for the worship of the one, true God.

Birnbaum points out that Philo 'frequently uses similar terms to describe Abraham's migration from Chaldea and the proselyte's "migration". As someone who leaves behind his family and background of false beliefs to discover the one true God, Abraham serves as a prototype of the proselyte.'[53] Philo does not provide information as to what legal requirements proselytes to Judaism in Alexandria were expected to fulfil, but indicates that '[t]he hallmark of the proselyte …is that he or she abandons belief in and worship of many gods, leaving behind

---

51. Cf. *Cher.* 4, 7; *Gig.* 62, 64; *Mut. Nom.* 66–67.
52. Cf. *Praem Poen.* 27; *Abr.* 262; see also Birnbaum, 'What Does Philo Mean by "Seeing God"? Some Methodological Considerations', *SBL Seminar Papers, 1994* (*SBLSP*, 34; Atlanta, GA: Scholars Press, 1995), pp. 535–52 (551).
53. Birnbaum, *Place*, p. 202, cf. p. 205.

a community of family and friends, to adopt belief in and worship of the one true God, becoming part of a new social community,' the only community that believes in and worships the one God.[54]

b. *Abraham the Monotheist in the Allegory of the Law*
i. *Abraham's Stages of Migration.* Most of the depictions of Abraham in this category are found in *De Migratione Abrahami*. His migration consists of a variety of stages, many of which Philo allegorizes from Gen. 12.1–3. The first stage towards full salvation is removal from three localities: land (body), kindred (sense perception) and his father's house (speech). Abraham is adjured to 'make thyself a stranger to them in judgment and purpose; let none of them cling to thee; rise superior to them all' (*Migr. Abr.* 7).

After expounding allegorically upon a number of subjects including Abraham and the law (see below), Philo resumes his allegory with Gen. 12.4, saying:

> Abraham migrated from Chaldea and dwelt in Haran, and…after his father's death there, he removes from that country also… What remark does this call for? The Chaldeans have the reputation of having, in a degree quite beyond that of other peoples, elaborated astronomy and the casting of nativities. They have set up a harmony between… heavenly things and earthly… These men imagined that this visible universe was the only thing in existence, either being itself God or containing God in itself as the soul of the whole. And they made Fate and Necessity divine, thus filling human life with much impiety, by teaching that apart from phenomena there is no originating cause… but that the circuits of sun and moon and of the other heavenly bodies determine for every being in existence both good things and their opposites (*Migr. Abr.* 177–179).

Philo proceeds with the interpretation of finding God allegorically (*Migr. Abr.* 184–185). Although the text is based upon the account of Abraham, he does not refer to Abraham but exhorts his reader to migrate, just as Abraham was depicted as migrating in *De Abrahamo*. In order to leave Chaldaea allegorically, the reader is to relinquish astrology, realizing that the universe is not the primal God but the handiwork of the primal God, and that the movements of the constellations are not the causes of fortune (*Migr. Abr.* 194).

Next, the reader is to examine the inner self.[55] Just as this examination should lead to the discovery of the reason which is master of all that is good and bad within itself, so should it lead to the discovery that there is a mind in the universe that controls it. This self-examination should lead to the discernment of the Universal Father through a mystical detachment from the physical self of senses (Haran) (*Migr. Abr.* 195).[56]

In his description of migration from Chaldaea to Haran to God, Philo makes his migration of Abraham found above in *De Abrahamo* directly applicable to the reader. The analogy between his depiction of the migration of Abraham and the reader is direct; he describes aspects of human characteristics that have a personal connection with the ancient past. He makes the migration of Abraham

54. Birnbaum, *Place*, pp. 224, 228.
55. Cf. *Som.* 1.52–60.
56. Cf. *Rer. Div. Her.* 69–70.

contemporary and universal in the sense that these human characteristics still existed among people.

However, what specifically is he telling his readers to do? It seems most reasonable from the earlier discussion based upon *De Abrahamo* to assume that he is addressing some of the beliefs of the Stoics and others, viz., that the created universe itself was a god or gods, and that apart from what exists there is not an originating Cause.

In the above citation from the *Migratione Abrahami*, Philo also speaks of the soul and of fate. Both of these were important concepts in Stoicism. The idea of the soul of the world represents the view of the Stoics 'whose God…is variously described by them either as the…"mind of the world", or "the soul of the world"'.[57] The idea of fate was equally important to the Stoics. It is in fact related to the concepts of the Chaldaeans. As E.V. Arnold explains, for some Stoics:[58]

> The heavenly bodies move incessantly in their orbits; there is no force either within or without them that can turn them aside a hair's breadth, or make their pace quicker or slower. No prayers of men, no prerogatives of gods can make them change… What will be, will be; what will not be, cannot be…all things take place according to fate; and fate is…the system by which the universe is conducted.

Philo is acting against a kind of determinism manifested in the signs of the stars and planets. Nothing is outside of this system of the phenomena of the world. Philo's problem with deifying fate is that this system then becomes God, rather than the First Cause that is outside of the system. Philo is defending the concept of Jewish monotheism: 'The attack on the "Chaldaeans" is for Philo an important element in his defence of Jewish monotheism against the threats to it contained in philosophies contemporary not with Abraham but with himself.'[59]

In his discussion of Gen. 15.6 in *Quis rerum divinarum heres sit*, Philo interprets 'Abraham believed God' as meaning that Abraham distrusted what was created, and trusted in God alone (*Rer. Div. Her.* 93). Philo continues by saying that Abraham's faith is greater than the faith of others because his faith 'is a task for a great and celestial understanding which has ceased to be ensnared by aught of the things that surround us' (*Rer. Div. Her.* 93). In his subsequent interpretation of Gen. 15.6b, Philo states, 'And…"his faith was counted to him for justice", for nothing is so just or righteous as to put in God alone a trust which is pure and unalloyed' (*Rer. Div. Her.* 94). Philo reasons that since Abraham had such a celestial understanding, his faith itself is considered to be an act of justice, and nothing more (*Rer. Div. Her.* 95).

Runia maintains that to Philo, different types of human beings exist after their souls come to dwell in their bodies. Some are men of earth, who are ensnared by their bodily desires; some are men of heaven, who are hardly hindered by their

---

57. Wolfson, *Philo*, vol. I, pp. 176–77.

58. *Roman Stoicism* (repr., New York: The Humanities Press, 1958), pp. 199–200.

59. Ronald Williamson, *Jews in the Hellenistic World: Philo* (Cambridge Commentaries on Writings of the Jewish and Christian World, 200 BC to AD 200, I.2; Cambridge: Cambridge University Press, 1989), p. 30.

bodies at all; and some are men of God, who are enrolled in the noetic world. Abraham began as one who was a Chaldaean, a man of heaven, but progressed to become a man of God. Because of this, he is privileged by being given the knowledge of God.[60]

Yet, elsewhere Philo suggests that although Abraham reaches the level of the logos, he has not yet reached the essence of God. This is stated, for example, in Philo's interpretation of the apparent discrepancy in Gen. 22.3b–4 where Abraham is said to have both reached the place for the sacrifice of Isaac and to be looking at it from afar:

> But when he has his place in the divine Word he does not actually reach Him Who is in very essence God, but sees Him from afar…all he sees is the bare fact that God is far away from all Creation, and that the apprehension of Him is removed to a very great distance from all human power of thought…what is signified is something like this: 'he came to the place and looked up and saw with his eyes' the place itself to which he had come, that it was a long way off from God for Whom no name nor utterance nor conception of any sort is adequate (*Somn.* I.66–67; cf. *Poster. C.* 18–20).

Through his interpretation of Gen. 22.3b–4 Philo shows that 'though what is said appears to involve a contradiction, there is no contradiction if the statement in question is interpreted allegorically'.[61] Although Abraham has found that God exists through the evidence of his handiwork, and had intended to go further in his understanding of God, he stops because he sees, once the eyes of his understanding have been opened, that he has been in chase of an elusive quarry that is difficult to capture and leaves its pursuers far behind. Although Philo believes in the superiority of reason, he is also aware that reason has limitations in the search for the knowledge of God. According to Williamson, 'All that even the wisest mind can know of God is in fact that he exists'.[62]

ii. *Israel: Those who 'See' God.* Another important theme connected with Abraham in the works of Philo is that he 'sees' that God exists. In the examples above, the word for seeing (ὁράω) is used in the sense of comprehending. While it is true in the above examples that Abraham sees or comprehends that he knows God exists but he does not know the essence of God (*Abr.* 70, 78), Philo's portrayal of Abraham 'seeing' God has further significance.

Built upon the example of their forebears who have 'seen' God, Israel is often called the 'nation of vision'.[63] Abraham, who discerned or saw the Maker of the world by contemplating nature (*Rer. Div. Her.* 96–99) is the 'founder of the nation and the race since from him as root sprang the young plant called Israel, which observes and contemplates all the things of nature' (*Rer. Div. Her.* 279) and which 'has eyes to see Him that IS'(*Migr. Abr.* 54). Philo also states in *Quaest. in Gen.* 4.4 that Abraham saw God in His oneness. According to Runia, 'In spite of

---

60. Runia, *Timaeus*, pp. 124–25; see also Mendelson, *Education*, pp. 47–65. The idea that Abraham's faith here is somehow meritorious is doubtful. See *Leg. All.* 3.228; *Migr. Abr.* 44.
61. Williamson, *Philo*, p. 189.
62. Williamson, *Philo*, p. 190.
63. *Mut. Nom.* 258; *Deus. Imm.* 144; *Abr.* 57.

the harsh attitude which Philo often displays towards sense-perception in general, there are numerous passages where he singles out the sense of sight for praise'.[64] It is also true that in Philo an intimate connection between seeing and contemplation exists.[65] Wisdom and philosophy have their origin in the sense of sight because by considering the cosmos, one considers who its creator is and what living according to nature requires.

Scholars have argued whether Israel who 'sees God' represents the concrete nation of Israel or whether it is developed as a spiritualized concept only. Strangely enough, Goodenough maintained both views.[66] Wolfson and Borgen contended that the nation that 'sees God' is a description of Judaism.[67] More recently, Birnbaum has convincingly argued that when Philo speaks of the 'Israel that sees God' in the allegory of the law, he is speaking primarily to anyone, both Jews and non-Jews, who have the ability to see God. On the other hand, when Philo speaks of 'Jews' in the exposition of the law, he is speaking primarily to those who believe in and worship God by observing specific laws and customs.[68]

Earlier the suggestions of Hamerton-Kelly concerning the discernment of traditions were noted.[69] One of his suggestions was that etymologies were evidence of a source that Philo used. From *Quaestiones et solutiones in Genesin* 3.49 and elsewhere, it appears that Philo's understanding of Israel as the nation that sees God is based upon an etymology: 'that nation to which was given the command to circumcise (children) on the eighth (day) is called "Israel" in Chaldean, and in Armenian (this means) "seeing God"'.[70] Scholars have speculated that the etymology of Israel who 'sees God' is based upon the Hebrew for that phrase which, in turn, sounds like 'Israel'.[71]

It is reasonable to assume Philo has gleaned this etymology from exegesis practised in the synagogues in Alexandria. And, since Abraham is spoken of as being the founder of the nation that 'contemplates all the things of nature' (*Rer. Div. Her.* 279, see also above) by virtue of which they see God, it is also plausible that the tradition may be contingent upon extra-biblical traditions about Abraham as well.[72]

In the portrayal of Abraham discerning the existence of God in *De Abrahamo*, he discerns that the aspects of creation around him, particularly the heavenly

---

64. Runia, *Timaeus*, p. 270.

65. Runia, *Timaeus*, pp. 273–74.

66. Goodenough, *Light*, p. 136; *The Politics of Philo Judaeus: Practice and Theory* (New Haven, NJ: Yale University Press, 1938), p. 12.

67. Wolfson, *Philo*, vol. II, pp. 51–52; Borgen, *Bread from Heaven: An Exegetical Study of the Concept of Manna in the Gospel of John and the Writings of Philo* (NovTSup, 10; Leiden: E.J. Brill, 1965), pp. 117–18.

68. Birnbaum, *Place*, pp. 223–24.

69. See above and Hamerton-Kelly, 'Sources', p.16.

70. *Abr.* 57; *Rer. Div. Her.* 78; Thackeray notes, 'Here, as elsewhere, the Arm. translator substitutes "Armenian" for "Greek"' (*Quaest. et sol. Gen.* 3.49, p. 249, n. *b*).

71. *Quaest. et sol. Gen.* 3.49, p. 249, n. *c*.

72. See also Nancy L. Calvert, 'Philo's Use of Jewish Traditions about Abraham', *SBL Seminar Papers, 1993* (SBLSP, 33; Scholars Press, 1994), pp. 463–76.

phenomena, are not God but are the evidence for God (*Abr.* 68–71; cf. *Migr. Abr.* 176–179, 194). Abraham is said next to look within and see that just as his mind rules his body and the emotions therein, so God rules the universe (*Abr.* 72–76; 185–186). However, in a passage found in *De somniis* (*Somn.* 1.52–60), Philo writes that Abraham and his family left astrology and speculation about the heavenly phenomena behind without mentioning that this was the occasion when Abraham first discerned the existence of God. On the contrary, in *De somniis*, Abraham first discerns God by looking into himself. It is as if Philo feels that it is necessary to include the tradition about Abraham and the stars even though it does not lead to Abraham's recognition of God. If we use Hamerton-Kelly's suggestion about discerning the traditions of Abraham via incongruity within Philo's works, then this incongruity in *De somniis* may be telling. [73] Philo continues to portray Abraham in a way that it related to astrology even when it does not exactly fit his argument about how Abraham discovered the existence of God.

c. *Abraham the Monotheist in the Works of Philo*

In the chapter on Josephus it will be shown how Abraham was the first to discern from his observation of the natural phenomena that one God existed. In Philo, Abraham also comes to his belief by discerning it is not the physical universe that is divine, but that God is its governor. For example, in *De Abrahamo*, above, Philo was cited as saying that Abraham did not believe that what he could sense was divine, but believed in the Deity that lay behind it. A similar concept of Abraham finding God through observing the natural phenomena was seen in *Jubilees*.

Philo uses the same traditions of Abraham as many of the Jewish authors represented in this book. He portrays Abraham as the first to believe in the one God, as the first to leave idolatry behind, and as able to discern God from nature. His portrayals of Abraham most naturally reflect those things that were distinctive about the Jewish nation. If, as has been noted above, Abraham is the founder of the nation that contemplates God, he is the founder of that nation which is distinctively Jewish – the nation that 'sees God'.

As W.L. Knox said, 'In Judaism, the great "convert" is Abraham'.[74] In Josephus, as in Philo, it will be shown that Abraham left astrology behind. However, Philo is clearer in the belief that Abraham's leaving astrology behind was equivalent to his forsaking a form of idolatry. Similarly in the chapter on *Jubilees,* it was shown how Abraham separated himself from his family who practised idolatry in order to follow the one God.

Philo interprets the Pentateuch using the philosophy he believes is allegorically inherent in the text. Abraham is a philosopher who reasons that one invisible, intelligible Cause, Ruler and Creator exists above all, and that what is visible certainly is not God but leads to belief in the existence of God. The traditions about Abraham the first monotheist and rejecter of idolatry certainly are not

---

73. Hamerton-Kelly, 'Sources', p. 16.
74. 'Abraham and the Quest for God', *HTR* 28 (1935), pp. 55–60 (55).

found in the Genesis text, although Abraham is said to have been an idolater in Josh. 24.2–3. These are the traditions that Philo has in common with the other Jewish authors mentioned above. Because these traditions already existed in *Jubilees,* and are later found in the *Biblical Antiquities* and the works of Josephus, it is reasonable to assume that they existed in Jewish communities other than those in Alexandria. In this case, they are examples of the traditions that Hamerton-Kelly refers to as those Jewish traditions that cannot be attributed originally to Philo.[75] If Philo's work is the product of exegetical traditions and methods from the activities in the synagogue in first-century Alexandria, it is also reasonable to assume that these traditions about Abraham were not only known to Philo, but were prevalent in the synagogues of Alexandria.

This being the case, as the foundational monotheist, Abraham symbolically performs an important function for Philo and for his readers. As Birnbaum points out in her discussion of Philo's relationship to particularism and universalism, Philo was not a particularist in that he did not believe that only Jews could see God. Abraham, for example, was said to be a Gentile when he saw God (see above) and, as Birnbaum suggests, Philo speaks of 'non-Jews such as the Persian Magi and other unidentified Gentile sages in a way that suggests that they too may be capable of seeing God'.[76]

However, at the same time, Birnbaum argues that Philo was only a potential universalist because while he aspired to encompass all people either within 'Israel' or the Jewish community, he believed that 'a prerequisite for anyone who belongs to either entity [Israel or the Jews] is belief in the existence of the one true God'.[77] In order to be a member of Israel, one must 'see' God and believe that He exists. Moreover, in order 'to worship God – as the Jews do – one again must believe that He exists'.[78] Proselytes, for example, must leave behind their idolatrous beliefs and worship the one true God. She continues:

> Although Philo may envision "Israel" and the Jews, then, as potentially open to all people, in his view, neither entity can encompass all people as they are. To be sure, he speaks quite disparagingly of polytheists, idolaters, and atheists – that is, people who believe in many gods, created gods, or no god. For Philo to embrace such individuals as part of "Israel" or the Jews, these individuals would first have to relinquish their wrong beliefs and adopt the monotheistic premise.[79]

Alan Mendelson has also seen monotheism as central to Philo. For Mendelson, Philo believed in five articles of faith that provided 'the lowest common denominator of religious belief, which Philo would have regarded as essential for the preservation of Jewish identity'.[80] These five articles of faith summarized in Philo's *De opificio mundi* 172 include the declaration that God is and is from eternity, that He that really is one, that He has made the world, that He has made

---

75. Hamerton-Kelly, 'Sources', p. 15.
76. *Place*, p. 225.
77. Birnbaum, *Place*, p. 226.
78. Birnbaum, *Place*, p. 226.
79. Birnbaum, *Place*, p. 226; cf. *Spec. Leg.* 1.327–44.
80. *Philo's Jewish Identity* (BJS, 161; Atlanta: Scholars Press, 1988), pp. 29–30.

it one world, unique as Himself is unique, and that He exercises forethought for His creation.[81] However, after Mendelson considers each of these articles, he states that within these five articles there is a convergence of ideas. 'In fact, if Philo had been so inclined, he might have stated that the alpha and the omega of orthodoxy was a belief in monotheism. The rest for him is commentary'.[82]

Scholars such as Maren R. Niehoff have argued that since Philo may have used 'terms which can be identified as monotheistic', he cannot be said to have embraced orthodox monotheism since an orthodox monotheism did not yet exist.[83] While Niehoff may be correct that Philo did not argue for monotheism in a way that we might consider now to be orthodox, it is true that faith in the one God of the Jews was important to Philo and this faith was in important factor that identified them in contrast to other nations.

What is noteworthy for our purposes is that Abraham is the one who first believes in God through discerning that he exists, and in this case represents those who can call themselves members of Israel. However, for Philo, being a Jew requires not only faith in God, but it requires that one worship him through observing specific laws and customs. How Abraham embodies the worship of God is found in Philo's attestation that he was obedient to the law.

d. *Abraham and the Law in the Exposition of the Law*
For Philo, a fundamental problem regarding Abraham was the relationship between Abraham, his descendant, Moses and the Law. Sandmel poses the question this way: 'If Moses' Law was the divine law, how could Abraham (and the other patriarchs) have flourished without it?'[84] Philo gives part of his answer in *De Abrahamo* when he states,

> Since it is necessary to carry out our examination of the law in regular sequence, let us postpone consideration of particular laws, which are, so to speak copies, and examine first those which are more general and may be called the originals of those copies. These are such men as lived good and blameless lives, whose virtues stand permanently recorded in the most holy scriptures, not merely to sound their praises but for the instruction of the reader and as an inducement to him to aspire to the same; for in these men we have laws endowed with life and reason, and Moses extolled them for two reasons. First he wished to show that the enacted ordinances are not inconsistent with nature; and secondly that those who wish to live in accordance with the laws as they stand have no difficult task, seeing that the first generations before any at all of the particular statutes was set in writing followed the unwritten law with perfect ease, so that one might properly say that the enacted laws are nothing else than memorials of the life of the ancients preserving to a later generation their actual words and deeds... [T]hey gladly accepted conformity with nature, holding that nature itself was...the most venerable of statutes, and thus their whole life was one of happy obedience to law *(Abr. 3–6)*.

81. Mendelson, *Identity*, pp. 29–30.
82. Mendelson, *Identity*, p. 49.
83. Maren R. Niehoff, *Philo on Jewish Identity and Culture* (Texts and Studies in Ancient Judaism, 86; Tübingen: Mohr Sieback, 2001), p. 79; cf. pp. 78–81, 83.
84. *Place*, p. 107.

The law of nature was a popular philosophical concept at the time of Philo. To Philo, the law of nature and the Law of Moses were identical. The law of nature that the cosmos obeys must be transposed to the level of humanity. This is achieved by the Law of Moses, which has God as the ultimate author.[85] To Philo the Law of Moses was the only truly natural law. Wolfson points out that 'the concept of natural law in Greek philosophy was to show that, according to Plato, Polemo, Aristotle, and the Stoics, enacted laws, if they are enacted by wise legislators on the basis of reason, are in a certain sense also laws in accordance with nature'.[86] However, despite all this, these enacted laws, even when based on reason, are the work of people and not the work of nature. As such, 'the "natural law"…sought by the Greek philosophers, could not possess the universality and eternity possessed by the Law of Moses, revealed by God, the sole Creator of nature'.[87] To Philo, only law that was revealed by God, the Creator of nature, can really be in accordance with natural law. This law, being the work of God, 'is like nature itself, and like nature it is universal and eternal and immutable'.[88] As Sandmel points out, in contrast to the rabbis who 'take as their norm the Mosaic (and Oral) Law, and…bring Abraham up to the norm by portraying him as an observer…Philo…takes Abraham (and the Patriarchs) as the norm, and shows in what way the Law of Moses fits in with the norm'.[89]

In the section from *De Abrahamo* quoted above, Philo is writing in order that his readers might follow the examples of their Jewish ancestors. He proceeds to name the ancestors whom he has in mind: Enos, Enoch, Noah, Abraham, Isaac, and Jacob. According to Philo, obedience to the Jewish law is not too difficult because even though those who lived before the Mosaic Law did not have a written law to follow, they followed the law of nature. In contrast, the readers do have a written law that they can follow.

Abraham belongs to the second and greater trinity (the first trinity being Enos, Enoch, and Noah). Abraham, Isaac and Jacob are described as being 'God-lovers and God-beloved' *(Abr.* 50). Of the three, Abraham is known as the one who acquires his virtue by teaching. Philo further describes Abraham as one who was 'filled with zeal for piety, the highest and greatest of virtues' and as being 'eager to follow God and to be obedient to his commands; understanding by commands not only those conveyed in speech and writing but also those made manifest by nature with clearer signs' (*Abr.* 60).

Abraham was one of those who obeyed the natural law and whom the later Mosaic Law copied. Abraham was himself a law, 'the law of Moses derives its specifications from those specific things which Abraham (and other patriarchs) did'.[90] Philo ends his discussion of Abraham in *De Abrahamo* by saying,

85. V. Nikiprowetzky, *Commentaire*, pp. 117–31.
86. Wolfson, *Philo*, vol. II, p. 179.
87. Williamson, *Philo*, pp. 201–202.
88. Wolfson, *Philo*, vol. II, p. 180.
89. *Place*, p. 108.
90. Sandmel, *Place*, p. 107.

[T]o these praises of the Sage… Moses adds this crowning saying, 'that this man did the divine law and the divine commands'. He did them, not taught by written words, but unwritten nature gave him the zeal to follow where wholesome and untainted impulse led him… Such was the life of the first, the founder of the nation, one who obeyed the law, some will say, but rather, as our discourse has shown, himself a law and an unwritten statute (*Abr.* 275–276; cf. Gen. 26.5).

e. *Abraham and the Law in the Allegory of the Law*
By interpreting Gen. 12.4, Philo describes Abraham as obedient to the law in *De migratione Abrahami*:

We are told next that 'Abraham journeyed even as the Lord spoke to him'. This is the aim extolled by the best philosophers, to live agreeably to nature; and it is attained whenever the mind, having entered on virtue's path, walks in the track of right reason and follows God, mindful of His injunctions, and always and in all places recognizing them as valid both in action and in speech. For 'he journeyed just as the Lord spoke to him': the meaning of this is that as God speaks – and He speaks with consummate beauty and excellence – so the good man does everything, blamelessly keeping straight the path of life, so that the actions of the wise man are nothing else than the words of God. So in another place He says, 'Abraham did "all My law"' (*Migr. Abr.* 129–130; cf. Gen. 26.5).

In the context of *De migratione Abrahami* the patriarch has been on the upward path to perfection and the rational part of his soul has triumphed. He walks on the path of right reason. Abraham follows God and is mindful of His injunctions. Since the injunctions are right reason, the verse 'Abraham did all my law' means that Abraham acted according to divine reason. The actions of Abraham are the words or the *logoi* of God.[91]

i. *Circumcision in Philo*. Philo usually gives circumcision an allegorical meaning. For example, in *Quaest. et Gen.* 3.46 he states, 'For that which is…male in us is the mind, whose superfluous growths it is necessary to cut off and throw away in order that it may become pure and naked of every evil and passion, and be a priest for God.'[92] He understands Abraham's physical circumcision in Gen. 17 allegorically as pruning off the appetites of the body.'[93]

In the section in *Quaest. in Gen.* 3.49 in which he addresses Abraham's circumcision, Philo contends that the nation which was 'given the command to circumcise (children) on the eighth day is called "Israel" in Chaldaean, and in Armenian (this means) "seeing God".'[94] Thus, circumcision is a sign of those who 'see God', meaning Israel.

While he discusses circumcision from an allegorical and etymological standpoint, this does not mean that Philo perceives that the literal practice is unimportant. One indication of the importance of the practice to Philo is his discussion of circumcision at the beginning of *De specialibus legibus*. In this work, Philo

---

91. Sandmel, *Place*, 166; Cf. *Migr. Abr.* 128–129 and *Abr.* 5, above.
92. Cf. *Quaest. in Gen.* 3.51.
93. *Quaest. in Gen.* 3.46–52.
94. R.P. Marcus notes that here the Armenian translator substitutes 'Armenian' for 'Greek'. *Quaest. in Gen.* p. 249 n. *b*.

subordinates a discussion of Jewish practices and laws under ten headings that are based upon the Ten Commandments. Mendelson states, 'In this one case, instead of subordinating the topic [circumcision] to one of the commandments, Philo inserts it very prominently at the beginning of the first book of *De speciali-bus legibus, before* his treatment of the first commandment'.[95]

Philo appears to see circumcision as a central issue; he responds to both Jewish and non-Jewish detractors. For the Jews he does not want to deny the symbolic importance of the rite, but he still believes that the literal sense should not be forsaken for the symbolic meaning: 'It is true that receiving circumcision does indeed portray the excision of pleasure and all passions, and the putting away of the impious conceit, under which the mind supposed that it was capable of begetting by its own power: but let us not on this account repeal the law laid down for circumcising' (*Migr. Abr.* 92). He particularly points to the parents as deserving a severe penalty for not circumcising their sons and thereby presumably showing contempt for the Torah and jeopardizing the survival of Judaism (*Quaest. in Gen.* 3.52).[96]

Philo defends circumcision in response to Gentile detractors who maligned the practice.[97] Yet he is more lenient with Gentile proselytes to Judaism than with Jewish parents who do not circumcise their children. For both Gentile proselytes and those Jews who were not circumcised as infants, their uncircumcision is not a disgrace based upon the example of the uncircumcised Hebrews who lived in Egypt at the time of Moses with 'self-restraint and endurance' (*Quaest. in Exod.* 2.2).

For Philo, circumcision was a central issue to his understanding of Jewish orthopraxy. As Mendelson asserts, 'His writings on the subject have a sense of urgency, for he saw circumcision not only attacked from without, but also undermined from within.'[98] And for Philo Abraham provides a prime example of one for whom circumcision symbolizes conquering passions, but who obeys the rite not only in his circumcision of his son Isaac but in the institution of the practice as well (*Quaest. in Gen.* 3.45–50).[99]

4. Conclusion: The Function and Significance of Abraham in the Works of Philo

Just as the author of *Jubilees*, Philo uses the major tradition about Abraham in which he seeks for and apprehends the one God. Abraham's reasoning is couched in the philosophical language of the day: he sees that the One Cause, the Intelligible and the Creator exists apart from his creation.

Abraham, as we have seen, is also the prototype of the proselyte. This is because he is said to be the first who believed in God (Gen. 15.6), meaning

95. Mendelson, *Identity*, p. 54.
96. Mendelson, *Identity*, p. 58.
97. For example, see 3.62; *Spec. Leg.* 1.9.
98. Mendelson, *Identity*, p. 58.
99. *Quaest. in Gen.* 3. 52.

monotheistic faith, and the first to leave behind idolatry in the form of astro-logical determinism. The tradition of Abraham as the first to discern or 'see' God provides evidence for the etymology of Israel as the nation that 'sees' God. As was discussed earlier, this title was distinctive to the nation of Israel. It appears reasonable to assume that the belief in one God based upon the figure of Abraham who was the first to 'see' the one, true God was not only a tradition distinctive to the nation of Israel but also a tradition which, to some extent, defined that nation.

It was also shown that a tradition of Abraham found in Philo was that he followed the law, albeit the natural law. For Philo, the natural law was the basis for the later Mosaic Law. Abraham was actually a living law. Again, this tradi-tion of Abraham following the law has already been seen in earlier chapters. This is particularly true of *Jubilees* where Abraham was depicted as obeying literal aspects of the law contained in the heavenly tablets before the Mosaic Law was actually given.

The question that remains, however, is how is the reader to respond to the depiction of Abraham found in the works of Philo? If Abraham signifies what the Jew is supposed to be, what is it that the Jew in Alexandria is supposed to do? One of the most telling depictions of Abraham in this regard was his relationship with his nephew. In the story of Abraham and Lot, we find that Lot honours fleet-ing things: wealth, reputation, office and good birth (e.g., *Migr. Abr.* 13). On the other hand, Abraham not only honours the four cardinal virtues, but he ultimately puts his faith in God, who alone is worthy of that faith. Earlier it was shown how status in the Hellenistic world became increasingly important to the Jew of Alexandria. In this Alexandrian context, Philo is telling his Jewish readers not to put too much faith in the accoutrements of status acquired in the Hellenistic world. The true Jew is to put his or her faith in the one God who alone is worthy of that faith.

Gentile readers should see that although Abraham eschewed some aspects of contemporary philosophy that gave the creation divine attributes which belonged to the Creator alone, Abraham's discernment of God was according to respected philosophical practices of the day. Abraham discerned the existence of God via the natural phenomena in a way similar to the discernment of God by the Stoics. Also central to the portrayal of Abraham in Philo was Abraham's discernment of the one God based upon the Stoic paradigm of the parallel between the mind that governs the body and the mind that governs the universe. In these ways, Abraham discerns God in a way that is very respectable to the Hellenistic Gentile reader.

The true Jew is to obey the literal law. Abraham, who did not have the Mosaic Law, was able to obey the natural law. The Mosaic law of the Jews is based upon the natural law, and the God of the Jews is Creator of both. In essence, Philo is telling the Jews of Alexandria that they have an easier task than Abraham did, since the law is now in written form. Furthermore, he is telling Jews who may be on the verge of apostasy that their law is valid and worthy of obedience.

However, Philo is speaking to Gentiles here as well. They are to see that the Creator who is responsible for the natural law produced the law of the Jews. In essence, according to Philo, the law of the Jews is the only written law that is valid because it is the only law which was revealed by the Creator God. Gentiles, then, will be following the revealed, natural law of God if they will but follow the Jewish law.

In the works of Philo, Abraham stands for those things which make the Jews distinctive from their Gentile neighbours in Alexandria: monotheistic faith and obedience to the Mosaic law. However, according to Philo, monotheism was the foundational tenet by which one was either included in or excluded from the Jewish community. As we have seen, Abraham functioned to portray the foundational monotheist, and thus the first member of Israel.

As we also have seen, Abraham functioned as the first Gentile to leave behind notions of idolatry in order to follow the one God. In this way, he became a model for Gentile proselytes to Judaism. However, for Philo, being a true Jew meant more than believing in one God. Being a true Jew also entailed worshipping God through obedience to the law. Abraham models this paradigm of monotheism plus obedience for his Gentile readers very well. However, in order for one to be a member of the people of God, monotheism is foundational.

Assuming that Philo wrote most of his works previous to the problems under Flaccus and the embassy to Rome, his works may have been produced and read at a time when, although the tension between Jews and Greeks had not yet resulted in clashes in violence, it called for an apologetic by a Jew who understood his Hellenistic environs. His work provides an apologetic for Gentiles and shows them the superiority of Jewish Scriptures by the indwelling Greek philosophy. Those Gentiles who aspire to join the mystical 'Israel' can do so if they see God. Those Gentiles who want to join the community of Jews – the *politeuma* – can do so by leaving behind idolatry for faith in God and adherence to the law. Those Jews who read Philo's work find a sophisticated apologetic for their religion. However, for both Israel and the Jews, the dividing line, the line from which Philo will not budge is monotheistic faith. This ultimately is what allows for membership in God's people and those who cannot embrace this tenet are thereby excluded. As we have seen, Abraham is the premiere example of this foundational tenet of the people of God.

Chapter 4

ABRAHAM AS THE FIRST MONOTHEISTIC LEADER
IN PSEUDO-PHILO'S *BIBLICAL ANTIQUITIES*

1. *Introduction: The* Biblical Antiquities

The *Liber Antiquitatum Biblicarum* or *Biblical Antiquities* of Pseudo-Philo can be classified as another example of rewritten Bible. Although the work covers the material from Adam up to the death of Saul, the author of the *Biblical Antiquities* structures his composition around the same theological centre as that found in the biblical text of Judges. The theological centre of both the *Biblical Antiquities* and Judges is the cycle of sin, divine punishment by means of an enemy, repentance and salvation through a divinely appointed leader.[1]

The author of the *Biblical Antiquities* structures the composition around great Israelite leaders, most of whom come to rescue Israel from sin and the onslaught of national enemies. In the presentation of the cycle, it is clear that the author is concerned about whether or not Israel will survive the political instability of his own day. Pseudo-Philo answers in the affirmative based upon Israel's status as God's chosen covenant people: as leaders have arisen to save Israel in the past, so they will in the present. For reasons which will become clear later in the chapter, I am using the term 'leader' as defined by G.W.E. Nickelsburg to refer to one who acts based upon trust in God rather than Frederick J. Murphy's definition of a leader as one who holds public and political office.[2]

In keeping with our intention to concentrate upon the traditions of Abraham's association with monotheism and the law in early Jewish literature, we will focus upon these themes as we discuss the *Biblical Antiquities*. Although Pseudo-Philo's account of Abraham's sacrifice of Isaac (*LAB* 32.2–4) demonstrates Abraham's obedience, we will not discuss this pericope because in it Abraham is not associated with Mosaic Law as such.[3]

---

1.   G.W.E. Nickelsburg, 'The Bible Rewritten and Expanded', in Michael E. Stone (ed.), *Jewish Writings of the Second Temple Period* (CRINT, 2.2.; Assen: Van Gorcum, 1984), pp. 89–156 (107).

2.   See G.W.E. Nickelsburg, 'Good and Bad Leaders in Pseudo-Philo's Liber Antiquitatum Biblicarum', in G.W.E. Nickelsburg and J.J. Collins (eds.), *Ideal Figures in Ancient Judaism* (SCS, 12; Chico, CA: Scholars Press), pp. 49–65; Frederick J. Murphy, *Pseudo-Philo: Rewriting the Bible* (New York: Oxford University Press, 1993), p. 234.

3.   On the sacrifice of Isaac, see Daly 'The Soteriological Significance of the Sacrifice of Isaac', *CBQ* 39 (1977), pp. 47–75; B.D. Chilton and P.R. Davies, 'The Aqedah: A Revised Tradition History', *CBQ* 40 (1978), pp. 514–46.

We find that Pseudo-Philo stresses the greatness of the law (*LAB* 9.8). The law and the covenant belong to Israel, and are said to be eternal (11.1, 5). In contrast to *Jubilees,* in which the law is said to have been instituted at creation and written in the heavenly tablets or the works of Philo in which the Mosaic Law is a codification of the natural law, Pseudo-Philo describes the law as having been prepared at creation, calling it a 'foundation of understanding' (32.7) which 'will not pass away' (11.5).[4]

However, for the author of the *Biblical Antiquities*, faith in God is central. As Jacobson points out, 'For LAB there is one central virtue, ideal and obligation, aside from the necessity to obey God's Law. That is to have absolute and unyielding faith in God and God alone.'[5] As a result, for Pseudo-Philo idolatry is the root of all evil (44.6) and is the cause of the sinful behaviour of the tribes (25.9–13). Aod (ch. 34), Gideon (36.3), Jair (ch. 38) and Micah (44.1–5) all lead the people astray by idolatry.

While the majority of scholars agree that Pseudo-Philo composed the *Biblical Antiquities* sometime shortly before or after the destruction of the temple in 70 CE, it is difficult to date the text more specifically.[6] The Latin text of the *Biblical Antiquities* was probably composed originally in Hebrew and later translated into Greek.[7] For his biblical text, Pseudo-Philo seems to have used what may be called a 'Palestinian' text type that may provide evidence for a Palestinian provenance.[8]

A consideration of the characteristics of the text of the *Biblical Antiquities* may be helpful at this point. As mentioned above, the compositional structure of the *Biblical Antiquities* is based on themes similar to those found in Judges in which a sinful people is saved by means of a divinely appointed leader. Pseudo-Philo has intentionally pulled this paradigm out of Israel's past. By using a theological paradigm from Judges, Pseudo-Philo chose a period when Israel was living in the land but was dominated by foreigners.[9] He lived in an age when the nation of Israel sought a leader.

4. All quotations of the *Biblical Antiquities* are from D.J. Harrington, 'Pseudo-Philo: A New Translation and Introduction', *OTP*, vol. II, pp. 297–377.

5. *A Commentary on Pseudo-Philo's Liber Antiquitatum Biblicarum with Latin Text and English Translation* (AGJU, 31; Leiden: E.J. Brill, 1996), vol. I, p. 245.

6. Bruce Norman Fisk, *Do You Not Remember? Scripture, Story and Exegesis in the Rewritten Bible of Pseudo-Philo* (JSPSup, 37; Sheffield: Sheffield Academic Press, 2001), pp. 34–40; M.R. James, *The Biblical Antiquities of Philo* (New York: KTAV, reprint, 1971), p. 32; Nickelsburg, 'Bible Rewritten', p. 109; Murphy, *Rewriting*, p. 6.

7. D.J. Harrington, 'The Original Language of Pseudo-Philo's Liber Antiquitatum Biblicarum', *HTR* 63 (1970), pp. 503–14; *The Hebrew Fragments of Pseudo-Philo's Liber Antiquitatum Biblicarum Preserved in the Chronicles of Jerahmeel* (SBLTT Pseudepigrapha 3; Missoula, MT: Scholars Press, 1974), p. 5.

8. D.J. Harrington, 'The Biblical Text of Pseudo-Philo's Liber Antiquitatum Biblicarum,' *CBQ* 33 (1971), pp. 1–17; 'Palestinian Adaptations of Biblical Narratives and Prophecies', in R.A. Kraft and G.W.E. Nickelsburg (eds.), *Early Judaism and Its Modern Interpreters* (SBLBMI, 2; Atlanta, GA: Scholars Press, 1986), pp. 239–58 (241).

9. F.J. Murphy, 'Retelling the Bible: Idolatry in Pseudo-Philo', *JBL* 107 (1988), pp. 275–87 (286).

The emphasis on the necessity of good leaders would have been especially appropriate during the period of the Jewish wars (66–70 CE) or shortly after when the Jews would have been looking for a leader to rescue them from powerful Gentile opposition and conquest.[10] During the years of the war with Rome, a variety of Jewish factions had revolted against the Roman government.[11] These revolutionary factions never became united into one anti-Roman force, even at the end of the wars. With a commitment to national freedom from the Romans, they fought believing that God was on their side. At least Simon bar Giora, if not the others, may have understood his actions in terms of waging a holy war against God's hated enemies.[12] Some even believed that by killing Jewish authorities who had contact with Gentile leaders they were cleansing the land of those who refused exclusive allegiance to God and were thereby saving their people from further moral degradation.[13]

In the section of the *Biblical Antiquities* that is fashioned upon the biblical account of Deborah, Pseudo-Philo portrays the people of Israel voicing their concern after the humiliation of Israel by the armies of Sisera. Here, Pseudo-Philo is putting words into the mouths of the Israelites who lived long ago in order to voice the concerns of his day. Evidently concerned about the oppression by their enemies, they simultaneously look for deliverance from their God:

> We say that we are more blessed than other nations, and behold now we have been humiliated more than all peoples so that we cannot dwell in our own land and our enemies have power over us. And now who has done all these things to us? Is it not our own wicked deeds, because we have forsaken the Lord of our fathers...perhaps God will be reconciled with his inheritance so as not to destroy the plant of his vineyard? (30.4).

In the *Biblical Antiquities*, Pseudo-Philo uses the speeches of leaders of Israel from the past to voice and to respond to the concerns of Jews who are his contemporaries. This is particularly true in the case of Deborah, where the author depicts her as saying:

> And...the Lord will take pity on you today, not because of you but because of his covenant that he established with your fathers and the oath that he has sworn not to abandon you forever... On account of this the Lord will work wonders among you and hand over your enemies into your hands. For our fathers are dead, but the God who established the covenant with them is life (30.7).

10. Nickelsburg, 'Leaders', pp. 49–65; L.H. Feldman, 'Josephus' *Jewish Antiquities* and Pseudo-Philo's *Biblical Antiquities*', in Louis H. Feldman and Gohei Hata (eds.), *Josephus, the Bible and History* (Detroit, MI: Wayne State University Press, 1989), pp. 59–80.

11. David M. Rhoads, *Israel in Revolution: 6–74 C.E.* (Philadelphia: Fortress Press, 1976), pp. 94–149; See also E. Schürer, *The History of the Jewish People in the Age of Jesus Christ* (4 vols.; repr. Edinburgh: T. & T. Clark, rev. edn, 1987), vol. I, pp. 484–513.

12. Rhoads, *Revolution*, p. 180.

13. Rhoads, *Revolution*, p. 180; see also R.A. Horsley and John S. Hanson, *Bandits, Prophets, and Messiahs: Popular Movements at the Time of Jesus* (San Francisco: Harper & Row, 1988), pp. 200–216, cf. pp. 190–99; Josephus, *War*, 2.254–56.

The hope of deliverance is expressed in Deborah's speech. The foundation of their hope is the covenant God made with their fathers. In the midst of catastrophe, Pseudo-Philo assures the people of God through the voice of Deborah that God will be faithful based upon his covenant in spite of their sin and in spite of the present circumstances. As God provided a leader who saved them in the person of Deborah, he will provide another leader who will save them from their current cycle of sin.

By structuring his composition around the theme of good and bad leaders, Pseudo-Philo is searching for a way out of foreign oppression by the enemies who in this case are the Romans. Taking his cue from Judges, he writes about righteous leaders who have risen up in the past and implicitly about one who might rise up to lead the nation of Israel to victory over its Roman oppressors. In order for the nation to be saved from its enemies, it must repent and return to single-minded devotion to its God and his law. Yet, their victory is not as dependent upon their repentance and devotion to God as it is upon God's faithfulness to his covenant with their ancestors.

2. *The Interpretation of Abraham in the* Biblical Antiquities

The most extensive portrayal of Abraham in the *Biblical Antiquities* is found in ch. 6. Pseudo-Philo gives the Abraham story a unique slant by including Abraham in the story of the Tower of Babel. In the chapters leading up to this point the reader has already been prepared for the story of Abraham. According to the *Biblical Antiquities*, Abraham was born in the lineage of the sons of Shem. Melcha, the wife of one of Shem's descendants, gives birth to Serug, who will become Abraham's great-grandfather. On the day of her delivery she prophesies, 'From him there will be born in the fourth generation one who will set his dwelling on high and will be called perfect and blameless; and he will be the father of nations, and his covenant will not be broken, and his seed will be multiplied forever' (4.11). How this prophecy of the unbroken covenant with Abraham comes true will be shown later in the *Biblical Antiquities*.

a. *Abraham's Refusal to Practise Idolatry*
Soon after the prophecy, the author sets up a conflictual relationship between the family of Serug, to which Abraham belongs, and the rest of the inhabitants on earth. The others foretell the future by observing the stars and performing divinations (4.16), while Serug's family is devoted to the one God. The other people on earth also had their children 'pass through the fire' which is another pagan practice in which parents burned their children in fire as sacrifices to pagan gods (4.16).[14] It is clear that Serug and his sons were different, because they 'did not act as these did' (4.17).

A comparison between the tradition of the ancestors of Abraham in the *Biblical Antiquities* and in *Jubilees* is necessary here. In *Jubilees* Serug, who

---

14. See also Deut. 12.31; 18.10; 2 Kgs 16.3; 17.17, 31; 21.6; 23.10; Jer. 7.31.

dwells in Ur, is said not only to worship idols, but to practise astrology and divination as well (11.1–8). Abraham is strikingly different from his family because of his worship of one God (*Jub.* 11.16–17). However, in the text at hand, it is the family of Abraham that is different from those outside. Pseudo-Philo rejects the story that Terah, Abraham's father, was an idolater. This contrast between the portrayal of Abraham's family found in *Jubilees* and the *Biblical Antiquities* helps to emphasize the contrasting purposes behind the portrayal of Abraham in these texts. In the portrayal of Abraham in *Jubilees* as seen in chapter two, the author was more concerned to contrast faithful with unfaithful Jews. Given the historical context of assimilationist and nationalistic Jewish factions within the Judaism that he addresses, this concern is understandable. Abraham stood for the faithful Jews. Pseudo-Philo, however, is more concerned to contrast the Jewish people with those outside. Murphy points out that as described in the *Biblical Antiquities* 4.16, '*All* humanity is characterized as idolatrous… Abraham comes from a family which alone, of *all* the inhabitants of earth, distinguishes itself by its rejection of idolatry.'[15]

In Pseudo-Philo's account of Abraham in Babylon, he is given an opportunity to add a brick with his name written upon it to the Tower of Babel. The purpose of building the tower is so that those building it can make a name for themselves and a glory upon the earth.[16] Abraham and eleven men refuse to participate in this building scheme. When asked why they will not participate, they answer, 'We know the one Lord and him we worship. Even if you throw us into the fire with your bricks we will not join you' (6.4). They apparently believe that by contributing to the tower they would deny their monotheistic faith.

How contributing bricks to a tower could be understood as idolatry is not apparent at first glance. However, given that the author has already set up an antithesis between the Jewish nation and the Gentiles, any kind of participation in a project in which they assimilated to Gentile persuasion and which glorified anyone other than their God could ostensibly be perceived as idolatry. The twelve are so devoted to their God that they suggest to the leaders of the land that they should be thrown into the fire with the bricks because they will not participate in Gentile idolatry (6.4).

It is interesting that Jacobson argues that chapter 6 is not about idolatry, but about an act of rebellion against God in building the tower.[17] However, in order to make his point Jacobson has to deny that the response of the twelve men to the command to add their name to the bricks is monotheistic: 'We know the one Lord, and him we worship' (6.4). Jacobson maintains that although the statement seems naturally to be a monotheistic protest, it comes primarily from other texts like the Palestinian Targum of Deut. 6.4 that emphasize Abraham's connection with idolatry and does not suit the context of rebellion in *LAB* 6.[18] However, it would seem that Pseudo-Philo's use of the monotheistic statement here is sig-

15. Murphy, 'Retelling', p. 276.
16. Cf. Gen. 11.4.
17. Jacobson, *Commentary*, p. 356.
18. Jacobson, *Commentary*, p. 358.

nificant especially since idolatry is a prominent theme in the *Biblical Antiquities* as a whole. It is thus the case that while rebellion is a theme in ch. 6, idolatry is the form that this rebellion takes.

In ch. 23, Pseudo-Philo provides a rewritten account of the covenant renewal by Joshua at Shechem. In 23.5 the author uses Josh. 24.2 which states: 'And Joshua said to all the people, "Thus says the lord, the God of Israel: Long ago your ancestors – Terah and his sons Abraham and Nahor – lived beyond the Euphrates and served other gods"'. Pseudo-Philo paraphrases Josh. 24.2 to make Abraham look as if he had never been involved in idolatry: 'And when those inhabiting the land were being led astray after their own devices, Abraham believed in me and was not led astray with them'. This would indicate that not only was Pseudo-Philo trying to cleanse Abraham's name, but he was also refer-ring back to ch. 6 in which Abraham did not participate in the idolatry of the tribes around him when they built the tower. Thus, Abraham's rejection of idolatry seems to be a key element in *LAB* 6.

After their refusal to participate in the building of the tower, the twelve men are threatened with being thrown into the fire. Joktan, who is a 'chief of the leaders' (6.6), announces a proviso: the twelve will be given seven days to repent and cast in bricks. In the meantime, Joktan plans to take the twelve into the mountains to hide. Eleven of the men agree; only Abraham refuses to escape. He is willing to take his chances and face death if necessary. He states, 'as he in whom I trust lives, I will not be moved from my place where they have put me. If there be any sin of mine so flagrant that I should be burned up, let the will of God be done' (6.11).

Joktan, who is characterized as a descendant of Shem (5.1, 6) who serves God (6.6), trusts that God will save those who escape to the hills (6.9). From the text, it appears that the eleven attribute their rescue to Joktan (6.10); they make no mention of being delivered by God. A major theme of Pseudo-Philo is that the plans of human beings are fated to be mistaken or evil unless they are completely dependent upon divine guidance.[19] In contrast to Joktan who devises his plan by his own wits rather than through dependence on God and to the eleven who submit to his plans, Abraham depends upon the God in whom he trusts.

Subsequently, Joktan's plan does go wrong. After seven days, Abraham is taken and thrown into the fire with the bricks. The narrator explicitly tells the reader of Joktan's intense emotional conflict as he throws Abraham into the fire. He is caught between those whose evil plans he must pretend to endorse publicly and the one whose loyalty to God he supports.[20] Instead of revealing his devotion to God to those around him, Joktan throws Abraham into the fire. However, God himself comes to Abraham's rescue; an earthquake occurs which causes all of those around the furnace to be burned (83,500). Abraham is not the least bit injured (6.17). Abraham finds the eleven men in the mountains who come down after hearing his report and the place of the furnace is named in honour of Abraham (6.18).

19. Murphy, *Rewriting*, p. 251.
20. Murphy, *Rewriting*, p. 48.

Abraham is depicted as one whose trust in God leads him to defy death. By placing Abraham in the fiery furnace, Pseudo-Philo not only explains how it is that Abraham escapes from the 'Ur' of the Chaldees ('Ur ' sounds like the Hebrew word for fire), but makes the account very much like that found in Dan. 3.[21] Nickelsburg points out that in Dan. 3 all three protagonists commit themselves to a common death in the furnace of blazing fire (vv. 16–18). Although in this text all twelve resist the pressure to commit idolatry, Abraham is the only one of them who refuses to follow Joktan's plan and accepts the possibility of death.[22] Pseudo-Philo conveniently provides the reader with a foil to Abraham's faith in the character of Joktan who, while he sounds as if he is a true servant of God, in the end chooses to please those who endorse idolatry while allowing for the death of the servant of God. As Murphy states, 'The tower episode shows that Israel has its origins in Abraham, the one who resisted human evil and trusted in God'.[23]

Another concern of Abraham's was how he and his God would appear to the citizens of Babylon. Abraham states, 'Behold, today I flee to the mountains… we will be found fleeing from the people of this land but falling in our sins' (6.11). The twelve had already confessed that they knew the one Lord (6.4). A lack of trust in God's action on their behalf would certainly be evident from their escape. Abraham is the one who manifests this trust by his willingness to die in order to prove the triumph of his God over the idolatrous plans of the Gentiles. The result of Abraham's deliverance from the fire is the same as that of the deliverance of Shadrach, Meshach and Abednego in Dan. 3: the God whom they serve is glorified.

Abraham appears as the prototypical good leader in the *Biblical Antiquities*. Like the other good leaders, Abraham's trust is put into action. Unlike the other leaders, he explicitly states that he trusts in God (6.11). As a consequence, trust in God is most apparent in the account of Abraham.

However, unlike the Abraham depicted in *Jubilees*, in the *Biblical Antiquities* Abraham does not obey the Mosaic Law as such. For example, circumcision is not connected with Abraham in the *Biblical Antiquities*, but with Moses (cf. 9.13). However, by turning from idolatry he is in effect obedient to the first commandment even before it is given (cf. 11.6).

Because of Abraham's opposition to idolatry, God elects him to receive land, his eternal covenant (7.4) and descendants (7.4; 8.3). Abraham separates from Babylon when he heads for the land promised to him (8.1). Murphy sums up the story by stating, 'Israel begins with Abraham's rejection of idolatry and the choice to serve God. Such service separates Israel from the rest of humanity. This alerts us to the converse, viz., mixing with the nations leads to disloyalty to God'.[24]

21. Cf. Gen. 15.7.
22. Nickelsburg, 'Leaders', p. 52.
23. Murphy, *Rewriting*, p. 230.
24. Murphy, 'Retelling', p. 276.

48 *Paul, Monotheism and the People of God*

b. *Abraham the Good Leader in Contrast to Bad Leaders*

In the *Biblical Antiquities*, Abraham was portrayed as the first good leader. He trusted in God and acted upon that trust to the extent that from among his compatriots, he alone was willing to face death. His faith in the one God was so strong that he would rather die in flames than practise idolatry. As the first to spurn idolatry and maintain allegiance to the true God, Abraham set the pattern for the leaders to come. Those who were good leaders such as Kenaz and Amram were those who maintained devotion to the one God. In contrast, the bad leaders were most often known for practising idolatry, and often this idolatry was a result of assimilation to the beliefs of Gentile neighbours (cf. 34.5; 41.3; 44.6).

For example, one of the bad leaders, Jair, built a sanctuary to Baal and attempted to burn those who would not worship Baal in the fire. Nathaniel, the 'angel who was in charge of the fire' (38.3) came and extinguished the fire, saving those devoted Jews who would not participate in Baal worship. Instead, it is Jair who is burned with the fire, and who is told by God, those 'who were burned with corruptible fire, now are made alive with a living fire and are freed; but you die…and in the fire in which you will die there you will have a dwelling place' (38.4). Jair, Baal and 1000 others are destroyed. The story of Abraham has paradigmatic value for Pseudo-Philo in the account of Jair. Jair, who worshipped idols, is killed by the very flames that he intended for those who were true to God. Abraham, in contrast, was saved from the flames because of his refusal to participate in idolatry.[25]

What emerges from much of the *Biblical Antiquities* is that idolatry is the root of sin. It symbolizes abandonment of God and his claim on his people. God's people break every command by making idols (*LAB* 44.6–10). Thus, Abraham's example of rejecting idolatry for faith in the one God provides the ultimate foundation for the identity of the people of God. Even before God's commandments comes allegiance to him.

c. *Abraham and the Faithfulness of God*

Pseudo-Philo appeals to the figure of Abraham in references to God's faithfulness to his people based upon his eternal covenant. One illustration of this covenant fidelity theme occurs in the depiction of Amram, Moses' father, when the Egyptians are killing the Israelite boys by throwing them into the river and keeping the Israelite girls to give to their slaves as wives (*LAB* 9.1). The Israelite people mourn their misfortune and plan to have no more offspring because it is likely that their daughters will marry Gentiles and become idolaters (9.2). Amram reassures them that the race of the sons of Israel is eternal and 'there will be fulfilled the covenant that God established with Abraham' (9.3). Amram recalls God's covenant with Abraham to encourage his compatriots to trust in their God, especially concerning the promise of descendants. Amram is like Abraham because he trusts in God, defies the authorities and maintains faith when his compatriots are in despair.[26]

25. See also Murphy, *Rewriting the Bible*, pp. 161–62, see also pp. 174–75.
26. Nickelsburg, 'Leaders', pp. 52–53.

Because of Abraham and others, God is continually faithful to Israel even when they have not been obedient to God's law. For example, in 35.3, Gideon is depicted as saying, 'you have not been mindful of the commandments of God that those who were before you commanded you, so that you have come into the displeasure of your God. But he will have mercy, as no one else has mercy, though not on account of you but on account of those who have fallen asleep'. Similarly, in 30.7 Deborah states, 'And behold now the Lord will take pity on you today, not because of you but because of his covenant that he established with your fathers'.

In fact as spoken later by Deborah, God's rescue of Abraham from the fire is equated with Israel's election: 'And [God] chose our nation and took Abraham our father out of the fire and chose him over all his brothers and kept him from the fire and freed him from the bricks destined for building the tower' (32.1). Of course, Abraham's rescue was based upon his faith in God and his refusal to participate in idolatry. Because of this faith and obedience, God will remain faithful to Abraham's descendants, the nation of Israel.

3. *Conclusion: The Function and Significance of Abraham in the* Biblical Antiquities

In the *Biblical Antiquities*, Abraham's rejection of idolatry and his trust in the one God were his most notable functions. Because of his monotheistic faith, God bestowed a covenant and many blessings upon Abraham and his descendants for all time.

How does Abraham function as a prototype for the Jewish people in the late first-century CE context of the *Biblical Antiquities*? The idolatry in which Abraham refused to participate was not the worship of a tangible idol, but the participation in the activities of those who were idolaters and who intended to glorify and make a name for themselves. Abraham would not assimilate to the self-aggrandizing intentions of idolatrous people because he saw this assimilation as idolatry. Because of his monotheistic faith, Abraham functioned to separate Israel from their Gentile neighbours. As Murphy states, 'Beginning from Israel's ancestor Abraham and continuing throughout the *Biblical Antiquities*, Israel differs from the nations because it worships God. The Gentiles are idolaters and so cannot please God'.[27]

Through Abraham, Pseudo-Philo may be telling his readers that assimilation with the self-aggrandizing plans of the Romans is idolatry. To be like their forefather Abraham, the Jewish people had to maintain unstained devotion to their God through complete non-assimilation with Gentiles. Not only that, but to be like Abraham meant that devotion to the one God was so paramount that they should be willing to face death rather than assimilate to Gentile ways.

Thus to be identified with God's people meant unswerving allegiance to God. Assimilation with outsiders would bring with it opportunities for idol-worship

---

27. Murphy, *Rewriting*, p. 230.

and the subsequent diluting of obedience to God's commands and eventual exclusion from God's people. Those who did assimilate risked bringing God's wrath upon themselves. Abraham provides the prototype of one who maintains faithfulness to God and separates from those things that might deter him from monotheistic devotion. In this way did one remain within God's covenant and therefore his people.

Chapter 5

ABRAHAM THE HELLENISTIC PHILOSOPHER
IN JOSEPHUS' *ANTIQUITIES OF THE JEWS*

1. *Introduction: Josephus' Life and Work*

a. *Josephus*

Josephus was a member of an aristocratic priestly family who could trace their roots back to the era of the Hasmonaeans under the rule of John Hyrcanus.[1] During his upbringing, he studied Jewish law and traditions and, as a member of the Jewish aristocracy, he probably received instruction in rudimentary elements of a Greek education.[2]

Although Josephus claimed to be supportive of Jewish law and practice, he also had the characteristics of many prominent Jews of the time in his acceptance of Roman power and his mixing with Greeks.[3] When he did become involved in the war against the Romans, he received a military assignment, the nature of which remains contested (*War* 2.568–646; *Life* 28–413).[4] Vespasian defeated the Galileans in the spring of 67 CE and any authority that Josephus may have had ended with the fall of the fortress of Jotapata (*War* 3.328).

The motivation behind Josephus' behaviour after the fall of the fortress has been a point of contention for centuries among Josephus scholars. For two days after the Roman victory, Josephus hid in a cave along with 'forty persons of distinction' (*War* 3.342).[5] Believing himself to be an interpreter of dreams and 'skilled in divining the meaning of ambiguous utterances of the Deity' Josephus claimed to have remembered nightly dreams in which God had told him of the 'impending fate of the Jews and the destinies of the Roman sovereigns' (*War* 3.352). When he announced that he intended to surrender, his compatriots sur-

---

1. E. Schürer, *The History of the Jewish People in the Age of Jesus Christ* (4 vols.; repr.; Edinburgh: T. & T. Clark, rev. edn, 1987), I, p. 44. See also *Life* 1–6.
2. H.W. Attridge, 'Josephus and His Works', *Jewish Writings of the Second Temple Period* (CRINT, 2.2; Assen: Van Gorcum, 1984), pp. 185–232.
3. Tessa Rajak, *Josephus: The Historian and His Society* (Philadelphia: Fortress Press, 1984), p. 4; M. Goodman, *The Ruling Class of Judaea* (Cambridge: Cambridge University Press, 1987), pp. 20–21; cf. *Life* 12.
4. Per Bilde, *Flavius Josephus between Jerusalem and Rome: His Life, his Works, and their Importance* (Sheffield: JSOT Press, 1988), pp. 44–45; H. Attridge 'Works', pp. 185–90.
5. Translations of Josephus used in this chapter are taken from *Josephus in Nine Volumes* (LCL; London: Heinemann, 1926–1965).

rounded him and accused him of being a traitor. A suicide scheme was devised whereby they should draw lots for the order in which they would slay one another (*War* 3.387–390). The lots were cast in such a way that all others died before Josephus and one other. At that point, Josephus persuaded his compatriot that they both should remain alive (*War* 3.391).

It was only after the group was betrayed that Josephus faced the Roman tribunes (*War* 3.344). According to Josephus' account, when he was led before Vespasian he predicted the future emperor's elevation to the throne (*War* 3.399–408). Because of the prediction, Josephus' life was spared. Two years later, the prophecy was fulfilled and Vespasian was proclaimed emperor. Vespasian granted Josephus his freedom as a mark of gratitude (*War* 4.622–629).

As a result of these actions, scholars have both maligned and exalted the character of Josephus. For example, writing from the standpoint that Josephus' motivations were less than commendable, Schalit contends that 'Josephus artfully cast the lots, deceitfully managing to be one of the two last men left alive, and then persuaded his companion to go out with him and surrender to the Romans… To convince the Romans, Josephus attributed to himself the qualities of a diviner'.[6] Thackeray calls Josephus an 'egoist…[a] flatterer of his Roman patrons… He was not one to sacrifice his life in a great cause: no warlike liberator of his country like Judas Maccabaeus'.[7]

In more recent years, authors of works on Josephus have given him the benefit of the doubt, if not outright praise. Tessa Rajak presents a more generous appraisal of Josephus' actions: 'What happens to him is still, in part, a reflection of his class position and attitudes; but we have also to reckon…with individual, personal attributes. Ingenuity, quick thinking, unscrupulousness and good fortune all contributed to the way he came out of the affair.'[8] In his appraisal of Josephus' actions at Jotapata, Per Bilde goes so far as to say that in keeping with important themes in the *Jewish Wars* as a whole, 'this incident depicts Josephus as a prophet unappreciated and persecuted by his own people…who…is saved solely by the hand of God…as one who acted solely on God's word and as his servant, because God gave him a message to bring to both Vespasian (Rome) and to his own people'.[9] Cohen probably comes closest to the truth when he says that Josephus 'considered himself much too important for a death in a cave near an obscure fortress in the country district of a small province'.[10]

b. *The* Jewish Wars *and the* Antiquities of the Jews
However one appraises Josephus' true motivations, his actions during the Jewish war affected the rest of his life and his writings. His first work, the *Jewish War*

6. A. Schalit, 'Josephus Flavius', in Cecil Roth and Geoffrey Widoger (eds.), *Encyclopaedia Judaica* (16 vols.; Jerusalem: Macmillan, 1971), vol. X, pp. 251–66 (253).
7. H. St. John Thackeray, *Josephus: The Man and the Historian* (New York: KTAV, 1967), p. 19.
8. Tessa Rajak, *Society*, p. 168.
9. Per Bilde, *Jerusalem*, p. 52.
10. Shaye J.D. Cohen, *Josephus in Galilee and Rome: His Vita and Development as a Historian* (Leiden: E.J. Brill, 1979), p. 230.

covers Jewish history from the Hasmonean period through the siege and conquest of Jerusalem until the aftermath of the war, down to the destruction of the last remaining revolutionaries. He completed the work under Vespasian's patronage.[11] The degree to which Josephus felt obligated to the Roman emperor as he wrote his history and how much this influenced his work is debatable.[12] Yet, that Josephus wrote the *Jewish War* from an apologetic standpoint against those who would malign Jews and Judaism is supported by his statement in *Ant.* 1.4, 'For, having known by experience the war which we Jews waged against the Romans... I was constrained to narrate it in detail in order to refute those who in their writings were doing outrage to the truth'.

Josephus' *Antiquities of the Jews* is most germane for our concerns. Written in 93–94 CE, the twenty-volume work covers the story of the Jewish people from creation until the administration of the last procurators before the war with Rome. The *Jewish Antiquities* bears similarities to literature characterized by a style best described as 'rewritten Bible,' much like the works treated in the previous chapters. As we shall see, many of the non-scriptural details in Josephus' rendition of the biblical text are paralleled in various re-writings of Scripture from the Second Temple period, such as *Jubilees* and the *Liber Antiquitatum Biblicarum*. It may be that Josephus relied on extra-biblical traditions from his Palestinian Jewish upbringing or from his Diaspora context.

What were Josephus' purposes when writing the *Antiquities*? Many have argued that his main purpose was to provide an apologetic for Judaism for a Gentile audience.[13] For example, Josephus states, 'I have undertaken this present work in the belief that the whole Greek-speaking world will find it worthy of attention; for it will embrace our entire ancient history and political constitution translated from the Hebrew records' (*Ant.* 1.5). He later states in *Against Apion,* 'In my history of our *Antiquities*... I have...made sufficiently clear to any who may peruse that work the extreme antiquity of our Jewish race, the purity of the original stock, and the manner in which it established itself in the country which we occupy today' (*Apion* 1.1).

Steve Mason argues that Josephus wrote the *Antiquities* neither as a vague apologetic for Gentiles nor as a work intended for a Jewish readership.[14] Instead, he maintains that Josephus wrote for 'a Gentile audience in Rome that is keenly interested in Jewish matters...the book has a coherent and powerful message... his audience desires a comprehensive but readable summary of the Judean constitution and philosophy: origins, history, law and culture'.[15]

Mason's main point makes good sense: it is difficult to imagine Gentiles who were only marginally interested in Judaism sitting 'patiently through...20 vol-

11. *Life* 422–423.

12. See discussions by Steve Mason, *Josephus and the New Testament* (Peabody, MA: Hendrickson, 1992), p. 64; Rajak, *Society*, pp. 196–97, 203; Bilde, *Jerusalem*, p. 76.

13. For example, see L. Feldman, *Studies in Josephus' Rewritten Bible* (Leiden: E.J. Brill, 1998).

14. Steve Mason, ' "Should Any Wish to Enquire Further" (Ant. 1.25): The Aim and Audience of Josephus's *Jewish Antiquities/Life*', in Steve Mason (ed.), *Understanding Josephus: Seven Perspectives* (JSPSup, 32; Sheffield: Sheffield Academic Press, 1998), p. 95.

15. Mason, 'Should Any', p. 101.

umes on Judean history and culture'.[16] It would seem likely that Josephus aimed primarily for an audience of Gentiles who probably resided in Rome and who were interested in Judaism.[17] Many Gentiles were interested in Judaism in Rome and elsewhere (cf. Tac., *Hist.* 5.5; *Ant.* 18.81–85). Such individuals could be located on a continuum comprising those who followed a few Jewish laws to those who became full proselytes.

However, what about Jewish readers? Some scholars have focused on Josephus' attempts to provide an apologetic for the Jewish community among whom he was dubbed a traitor even early in his military career.[18] Recently Steve Mason has argued that if the *Antiquities* were written for Jews, Josephus would not need to explain so much about Jewish life and heritage for his audience.[19] However, does this necessarily mean that he had no Jewish readers in mind at all? Sterling, among others, has argued that the *Antiquities* were written not only for a Gentile readership but for a Jewish audience as well.[20] One reason is that Josephus himself mentions his fellow Jews that may be reading his book when he apologises for collecting the laws systematically in the *Antiquities*. He says 'I have thought it necessary to make this preliminary observation, lest perchance any of my countrymen who read this work should reproach me at all for having gone astray' (*Ant.* 4.197; cf. *War* 6.107).

Given that Jews in the Diaspora were highly Hellenized, one cannot rule out the idea that in his history of the Jews Josephus presents Judaism in such a way as to be attractive to them. As we have seen, Philo wrote to both Jews and Gentiles in his highly Hellenized accounts. While it may be that the assimilation of Roman Jews to pagan culture was not as widespread as assimilation among Alexandrian Jews, one cannot totally rule out some assimilation.[21] Mason mentions that high-profile Jews like Agrippa II and Berenice may have acted as types of literary patrons for Josephus.[22] As Barclay notes, both were probably highly assimilated to

16. Mason, 'Should Any', p. 68.

17. See also the discussion in N.L. Calvert, 'Abraham Traditions in Middle Jewish Literature: Implications for Galatians and Romans' (PhD dissertation, University of Sheffield, 1993), pp. 343–48.

18. Mireille Hadas-Lebel, *Flavius Josephus: Eyewitness to Rome's First-Century Conquest of Judea* (trans. Richard Miller; New York: Macmillan Publishing Company,1993), p. 73.

19. Mason, 'Should Any', pp. 66–68.

20. Gregory E. Sterling, *Historiography and Self-Definition: Josephos, Luke–Acts and Apologetic Historiography* (NovTSup, 64; Leiden: E.J. Brill, 1992), p. 306; See also Paul Spilsbury, *The Image of the Jew in Flavius Josephus' Paraphrase of the Bible* (Texte und Studien zum Antiken Judentum, 69; Tübingen: Mohr Siebeck, 1998), p. 21; Nancy Calvert-Koyzis, 'Josephus Among His Contemporaries: Abraham the Philosopher and Josephus' Purposes in Writing the *Antiquities of the Jews*', in John Kessler and Jeff Greenman (eds.), *Teach Us Your Paths: Studies in Old Testament Literature and Theology* (Toronto: Clements Publishing, 2001), pp. 89–110.

21. For example, see John M.G. Barclay, *Jews in the Mediterranean Diaspora: From Alexander to Trajan* (323 BCE–117 CE) (Edinburgh: T. & T. Clark, 1996), pp. 316–19, 320–35; Graydon F. Snyder, 'The Interaction of Jews with Non-Jews in Rome', in Karl P. Donfried and Peter Richardson (eds.), *Judaism and Christianity in First Century Rome* (Grand Rapids, MI: Eerdmans, 1998).

22. Mason, 'Should Any', p. 78.

the culture around them.[23] One might argue that while supporting Josephus' work they also took the opportunity to consider his views concerning what it meant to be a Jew in a Hellenized world not long after the destruction of the Temple. Josephus' fairly rudimental explanations of Judaism would be for his primarily Gentile readership.

Thus while a major reason that Josephus wrote his *Antiquities of the Jews* may have been his desire to convince interested Gentiles of the superior philosophy of the Jews, this was almost certainly not his only reason. Josephus seems also to have written for his compatriots, some of whom may have dubbed him a traitor in earlier years, but who now attempted to reconcile their own questions about Judaism in light of their own assimilation. In this case, Josephus explains aspects of Judaism not only for Gentiles but for his assimilationist Jewish readers as well.

Jewish readers probably would have recognized Josephus' dependence upon biblical books, especially in the early parts of the *Antiquities* where he describes the foundation of the Israelite nation. He states repeatedly that he uses the Hebrew scriptures as a major source, sometimes with statements such as 'I have recounted each detail here told just as I found it in the sacred books' (*Ant.* 2.347) or '[t]he precise details of our Scripture records will...be set forth...I have promised to follow [them] throughout this work, neither adding nor omitting anything' (*Ant.* 1.17).

However, when one reads the work it is obvious to a twenty-first century eye that he indeed has added and omitted several sections of the biblical text. Bilde points out that biblical translation at the time of Josephus, was 'more a question of rendering the essential contents of a text as it was understood by the translator rather than literally transposing it from one language to another'.[24] For Josephus, these sacred books contain the evidence of the antiquity and nobility of the Jewish nation. Josephus 'translated' the books, according to Bilde, 'by virtue of his Hellenistic transformation and modernization of their form'.[25] An example of this Hellenistic transformation is his use of Hellenistic political language to describe aspects of Judaism, such as his using the term 'constitution' in reference to the Jewish law.[26] In this way, he provided a comprehensible version of the foundation of Israel for his Hellenistic contemporaries to accept or reject.

In contrast to those of previous decades, more recently Josephus scholars have pointed out that not only is Josephus providing an apologetic for the history of the Jews, but also for their religion – in other words, Josephus' work is both historical and theological. This theology, according to Paul Spilsbury, revolves around the 'description of God as one who exercises providence...over his creation, an activity which entails alliance with those who exercise piety and retribution on

23. Barclay, *Diaspora*, pp. 323, 328.
24. *Jerusalem*, p. 96.
25. *Jerusalem*, p. 97.
26. For example, see *Ant.* 1.5 and further, H. Attridge, *The Interpretation of Biblical History in the Antiquitates Judaicae of Flavius Josephus* (HDR, 7; Missoula, MT: Scholars Press, 1976), pp. 62–63; Mason, 'Should Any', pp. 80–87.

those who do not. Secondly, and as a logical consequence of this conception of God, Josephus emphasizes the moral and religious qualities of his principal characters'.[27]

Much like Dionysius of Halicarnassus upon whose work Josephus modelled several aspects of the *Antiquities,* Josephus is attempting to educate his reader on the subject of personal morality (Cf. *Ant.* 1.23–24; *Ant. Rom.* 1.5.1–3) while also providing an explanation and a defence of his national traditions.[28] For Josephus, those who hold to the doctrines given by the Lawgiver participate in the virtue of God and can expect to be rewarded; those who do not can expect otherwise (*Ant.* 1.14–15). Josephus also believes that the law given by God is 'set forth in keeping with the nature of the universe' (*Ant.* 1.24).

Thus, most scholars seem to agree that central to this religion, as seen by Josephus, is the Jewish constitution, or the Mosaic Law, and then Jewish philosophy – primarily the philosophy of God. Per Bilde points out that, 'Josephus describes Judaism as an attractive religion centred around a sublime conception of God and around moral capability and virtue'.[29] For Bilde, the most important point in the Jewish concept of the divine is faith in God's providence and guidance.[30] Although Steve Mason does not explicitly focus on Josephus' presentation of Jewish religion, he does understand Josephus as providing a comprehensive but readable summary of the Judean 'constitution and philosophy' which, of course, refers to their law and their idea of God – the essence of their religion.[31] Schrekenberg sees Josephus as defending the Jewish religion not only as a religion of venerable age and as satisfying even the most demanding expectations and whose laws bring happiness to mankind, but as a religion far superior to pagan polytheism.[32]

In the *Antiquities,* Josephus cites numerous Roman documents that testify to the privileges granted to the Jewish people (*Ant.* 14.185–267). Apparently, many people had refused to believe that the documents were authentic (*Ant.* 14.187). Josephus gives his motivation for citing these decrees in order to show that in former times the Jewish people 'were treated with all respect and were not prevented by…rulers from practising any of [the] ancestral customs but, on the contrary…had the co-operation in preserving…religion and [their] way of honouring God' (*Ant.* 16. 174).

He states that he mentions the decrees in order 'to reconcile the other nations to us and to remove the causes for hatred which have taken root in thoughtless

---

27. Spilsbury, *Image,* p. 17; see also Paul Spilsbury, 'God and Israel in Josephus: A Patron-Client Relationship', in Steve Mason (ed.), *Understanding Josephus: Seven Perspectives* (JSPSup, 32; Sheffield: Sheffield Academic Press, 1998), pp. 172–91 (186–87).

28. Attridge, *Interpretation,* p. 56.

29. Bilde, *Jerusalem,* p. 101.

30. Bilde, *Jerusalem,* p. 186.

31. Mason, 'Should Any', p. 101.

32. Heinz Schreckenberg, 'Preliminaries to the Early Christian Reception of Josephus', in Heinz Schreckenberg and Kurt Schubert (eds.), *Jewish Historiography and Iconography in Early and Medieval Christianity* (CRINT, III.2; Assen/Maastricht, Minneapolis: Van Gorcum, Fortress Press, 1992), pp. 17–50 (25).

persons among us as well as among them' (*Ant.* 16. 175). Bilde maintains, 'It is equally clear – first by citing the pro-Jewish decrees, but secondly also with *Ant.* in its entirety – that the purpose is to defend the Jewish people and their rights in the Roman Empire'.[33] In the *Antiquities*, Josephus, then, is apologetic not only in the way that he presents the validity of the Jewish religion and the antiquity of their people, but also in his concern to assist the Jewish people in their political relationship with Rome. Although the apologetic motif is foremost in his mind, he is also offering his compatriots assistance. Given his education and his connections in Rome, he is well placed to offer assistance in this way. Although reconciliation with those among his fellow Jews who considered him such a traitor may not be possible, this treatment of Judaism may have helped his reputation among Jews. In any event, he offers a work to the educated world that not only supports better treatment of the Jewish people, but also provides an account of their history in such a way that it could only be admired by its Hellenistic readers.

2. *The Interpretation of Abraham in Josephus'* Antiquities

a. *Josephus' Portrayal of Abraham the First Monotheist*
Scholars of Josephus have traditionally seen him in a negative light and have related this judgement to his literary works. Sandmel, for example, believed that Josephus' works were devoid of originality and his depiction of Abraham lacked coherence.[34] In contrast to such an approach, I maintain that, using traditions about Abraham from a variety of oral and written sources, Josephus provides his reader with a politically expedient, coherent reworking of the life of Abraham.[35] We will not consider Josephus' entire description of Abraham here, but only those aspects which portray Abraham as following what Josephus calls the Jewish 'constitution' and his portrayal of Abraham as the prototypical monotheist and premier philosopher.

Josephus describes Abraham this way:

> He was a man of ready intelligence on all matters, persuasive with his hearers, and not mistaken in his inferences. Hence he began to have more lofty conceptions of virtue than the rest of mankind, and determined to reform and change the ideas universally current concerning God. He was thus the first boldly to declare that God, the creator of the universe, is one, and that, if any other being contributed aught to man's welfare, each did so by His command and not in virtue of its own inherent power. This he inferred from the changes to which land and sea are subject, from the course of sun and moon, and from all the celestial phenomena; for, he argued, were these bodies endowed with power, they would have provided for their own regularity, but since they lacked this last, it was manifest that even those services in which they cooperate for our greater benefit they render not in virtue of their own authority, but through the

33. *Jerusalem*, pp. 100–101; see also Schreckenberg, 'Preliminaries', p. 18.
34. *Philo's Place in Judaism: A Study of Conceptions of Abraham in Jewish Literature* (New York: KTAV, 1971), p. 75.
35. See also Louis H. Feldman, *Josephus' Interpretation of the Bible* (Berkeley: University of California Press, 1998), p. 223.

might of their commanding sovereign, to whom alone it is right to render our homage
and thanksgiving (*Ant.* 1.154–156).

According to Josephus' description of Abraham discerning the existence of
the one, Creator God from the changes of the land and sea, the course of the sun
and moon, and all the heavenly conjunctions, Abraham is a superior theologian
and philosopher.[36] Because Abraham is the first to promulgate a monotheistic
view of God, he upstages later Greek philosophers who also held this view.[37] As
Feldman states, his 'proof is in the form of the proofs for the existence of G-d
promulgated by the Greek philosophic schools, notably the Stoics…who first presented the teleological argument that the orderly state of the universe manifests a
design perfected by the rational power of an infinite mind'.[38] However, in opposition to most teleological arguments that are based on the regular movements of
the stars and planets, Abraham reasons inversely that since their movement is
irregular, then there must be a 'commanding sovereign' or a God. The phrase
Josephus uses to describe these celestial phenomena – 'those services in which
they cooperate for our greater benefit' – sounds like a description of the theory
behind astrology, in which the stars and planets cooperated together in determin-
ing the steps of human beings.[39]

Concerning the astrology of the Chaldaeans, Philo states,

> The Chaldeans have the reputation of having…elaborated astronomy and the casting
> of nativities… Following as it were the laws of musical proportion, they have exhib-
> ited the universe as a perfect concord or symphony produced by a sympathetic affinity
> between its parts… These men imagined that this visible universe was the only thing
> in existence, either being itself God or containing God in itself as the soul of the whole.
> And they made Fate and Necessity divine, thus filling human life with much impiety,
> by teaching that apart from phenomena there is no originating cause of anything
> whatever, but that the circuits of sun and moon and of the other heavenly bodies
> determine for every being in existence both good things and their opposites (*Migr.
> Abr.* 178–179).

Philo attests to a similar tradition of Abraham discerning God from nature in *De
Abrahamo*:

> The Chaldeans were especially active in the elaboration of astrology and ascribed every-
> thing to the movements of the stars. They supposed that the course of the phenomena
> of the world is guided by influences contained in numbers and numerical propor-
> tions…they glorified visible existence, leaving out of consideration the intelligible and
> invisible. But while exploring numerical order as applied to the revolution of the sun,
> moon, and other planets and fixed stars, and the changes of the yearly seasons and the
> interdependence of phenomena in heaven and on earth, they concluded that the world
> itself was God, thus profanely likening the created to the Creator. In this creed

36. T.W.S. Franxmann, *Genesis and the Jewish Antiquities of Flavius Josephus* (BibOr, 35; Rome:
Biblical Institute Press, 1979), p. 119.

37. Carl R. Holladay, *Theios Aner in Hellenistic Judaism: A Critique of the Use of this Category
in New Testament Christology* (SBLDS, 40; Missoula, MT: Scholars Press, 1977), p. 73.

38. Feldman, 'Abraham the Greek Philosopher in Josephus', *TAPA* 99 (1968), p. 143–56 (146);
see also *Josephus's Interpretation of the Bible* (Berkeley: University of California Press, 1998), pp.
228–34, 288.

39. See Feldman, 'Greek Philosopher', p. 147; Franxmann, *Genesis*, p. 119.

Abraham had been reared and for a long time remained a Chaldean. Then, opening the soul's eye as though after profound sleep...he followed the ray and discerned...a charioteer and pilot presiding over the world and directing in safety his own work, assuming the charge and superintendence of that work, and of all such parts of it as are worthy of the divine care (*De Abr.* 68–70).

Although in Philo's work Abraham notices the *orderly* movement of the heavenly bodies and discerns that there is a God beyond them, both Josephus and Philo thus depict Abraham as discerning the existence of God and his care for the world from the phenomena of the natural world around them. In Philo's work, it is clear that Abraham had been reared in the practice of astrology. Through the teleological argument, Abraham is able to infer that the one Creator God exists and acts on behalf of all humankind.

If we contrast the attitude towards Abraham's practice of astrology in *Jubilees* with Josephus' attitude towards astrology in the *Antiquities,* a significant difference of opinion is noticeable. In *Jubilees,* the author rejects the practice of astrology outright through his example of Abraham. In the *Antiquities,* Josephus does not so much condemn the practice as some of the presuppositions that exist behind the practice. It is not the stars that act by virtue of their own power for the benefit of humankind, but the one Creator God who does so. Astrology in this passage is not necessarily equivalent to idolatry; idolatry in this passage is the non-recognition from the natural phenomena that one God exists and works for the benefit of humankind.

Josephus and the author of *Jubilees* are on opposite ends of the spectrum in reference to their attitude to the surrounding culture. Josephus represents the progressive Jew in terms of Hellenism; he has no problem portraying Abraham in the garb of an intelligent Hellenistic rhetorician who uses the philosophical proofs of the time to make his own deductions.

Josephus has turned Abraham into such a Hellenist that he even uses the word δημιουργός to describe Abraham's God. The word δημιουργός originally meant 'artisan'. However, if 'δημιουργός is also used in [Greek] religion and philosophy for the power which fashions the world, this is because the δημιουργός τοῦ κόσμου has made the world out of existing material as the ordinary δημιουργός does his products out of his materials'.[40]

The word Josephus uses for the Creator, then, is consonant with a Hellenistic view of the creation of the world, that is, that the universe was created from already existing material. The δημιουργός made order out of disorder. In Abraham's proof, the stars and planets were irregular in their movements, and were unable to produce order or uniformity among themselves; thus, they could not be the Creator (δημιουργός). Josephus' Abraham has assimilated with the Hellenistic culture but come out using it successfully for the propagation of the idea that one Creator God exists.

In contrast, the author of *Jubilees* portrays Abraham as the explicitly law-abiding separatist Jew. Abraham's slogan is separation from all things Gentile. To the author of *Jubilees,* taking on the attributes associated with Hellenism is tanta-

---

40. W. Foerster, 'κτίζω', *TDNT*, III, pp. 1000–1035 (1025).

mount to taking on the idolatry upon which the degenerate Gentile ways are based.

However, that each author makes use of the same traditions to speak to their respective audiences, one from the standpoint of assimilationist Judaism and one from the standpoint of a more nationalistic Judaism, suggests the existence of a collection of either oral or written traditions about Abraham which had developed. While these traditions may be based upon information found in the Genesis account, the specific details they provide suggests their development. For example, while Abraham is depicted as meeting with God in Gen. 15 and 17, the traditions in both *Jubilees* and the works of Josephus emphasize Abraham as the first to recognize God who is 'one'. Although Abraham's descendants are foretold as being like the stars in Gen. 15.5, it is only in the developed traditions that Abraham uses the stars to reason that the one God exists.

While one can conclude from Josh. 24.2–3 that Abraham leaves idolatry when he leaves his homeland, the tradition is not explicit there or in the Genesis text. Josephus, however, tells us that after Abraham discerned the one Creator God, that the Chaldaeans rose against him for his opinions, after which Abraham emigrated to Canaan 'at the will and aid of God' and made a sacrifice to God in his new homeland (*Ant.* 1.157). Philo also portrays Abraham as leaving his homeland of Chaldaea with its astrological science so that he might better understand God (*Abr.* 71). In this way, Abraham's departure from his homeland becomes a symbol for his rejection of idolatry.

Thus, the extra-biblical traditions with which Josephus is familiar are that Abraham was the first to recognize that God was the Creator of the universe and that God indeed was one; that Abraham recognized the one Creator God from his observation of the natural phenomena; and that in leaving his homeland behind Abraham also leaves behind his former idolatry.

Josephus has made both Abraham and Judaism attractive to his Greco-Roman readers. The Greco-Roman world was used to a plurality of gods in a variety of forms. J.R. Bartlett suggests, 'Jewish refusal to accept such gods incurred the charges of atheism and misanthropy (*Apion* 2.14) and sometimes ridicule… Josephus denies the charge of atheism and challenges polytheism by affirming the superiority of Jewish monotheism, the origin of which he attributes to the Jewish patriarch and philosopher Abraham'.[41]

The monotheism that Abraham was the first to introduce is important in much of the rest of the Jewish *Antiquities*. For example, it is present in Josephus' description of the Ten Commandments (*Ant.* 2.91) where Moses instructs the people that 'God is one and that he only must be worshipped' (cf. *Ant.* 4.201). As Spilsbury notes, monotheism is brought out explicitly again in the account of the Midianite seduction when Hebrew youths acquiesce in polytheistic ways (*Ant.* 4.139) and when Elijah blames King Ahab for the misfortunes which he has brought in their country by introducing foreign gods and worshipping them while

41. John R. Bartlett, *Jews in the Hellenistic World: Josephus, Aristeas, the Sibylline Oracles, Eupolemus* (Cambridge Commentaries on Writings of the Jewish and Christian World 200 BC to AD 200, I.1.; Cambridge: Cambridge University Press, 1985), pp. 146–47.

abandoning the one true God (*Ant.* 8.335).[42] Elijah also challenges the people from Mount Carmel to decide which God they will serve, and if they believe him to be the only true God to follow him and his commandments (*Ant.* 8.337). At the conclusion of the episode, they fall down and worship the one God and acknowledge him as the only true and Almighty God while the other gods were only invented names (*Ant.* 8.343; cf. 8.350).

As with the rest of his work, Josephus attempts not to offend the sensibilities of his readers, in this case, their polytheism. Although in *Against Apion* Josephus portrays Moses as representing God as the one only true God (*Apion* 2.166–167) and the gods of the Greek sages as negative inventions (*Apion* 2.239–241), he maintains that Jews are not to blaspheme the gods recognized by others (*Apion* 2.237). Yet it is clear that although he attempts to be apologetic in his presentation, Josephus still supports monotheism and does not ultimately sympathize with the worship of foreign gods.[43] It is also clear that Abraham is the original source of this monotheism.

b. *Josephus' Ancient Sources*
In the *Antiquities* 1.158–160, Josephus writes about a number of the sources he used in his account of Abraham and the information they contain. According to Josephus, Berossus states, 'In the tenth generation after the flood there lived among the Chaldaeans a just man and great and versed in celestial lore' (*Ant.* 1.158; cf. *Praep. Ev.* 9.16). Josephus mentions that Berossus does not actually identify the man as Abraham; Josephus assumes from the information given that the man written about must be Abraham.

Berossus was a priest of Marduk in early third century BCE, Babylon. According to J. VanderKam, he wrote *Babyloniaca* 'in order to make the culture and antiquities of his Babylonian people available to Greek readers…he claimed to have based his presentation on very ancient sources'.[44] Because Babylonia was famous for the practice of astrology, the origin of the practice would have been important to Berossus. Josephus used the information from Berossus to support and perhaps clarify his story in which Abraham knew astrology and used this knowledge to prove the existence of God.

Other ancient authors not found in Josephus also attested to the tradition that Abraham was the founder of astrology. Artapanus, an Egyptian Jew who wrote before 100 BCE, maintained that Abraham taught Pharaoh astrology (*Praep. Ev.* 9.18).[45] Thus, to Artapanus, Abraham was responsible for an aspect of Egyptian culture. Eupolemus, or perhaps Pseudo-Eupolemus, also attests to the tradition that Abraham was the founder of astrology and the Chaldaean science in about the 2nd century, BCE (*Praep. Ev.* 9.17. 2–9; 9.18.2).[46] He later states that really

---

42. *Image*, p. 60.
43. Spilsbury, *Image*, p. 61.
44. *Enoch and the Growth of an Apocalyptic Tradition* (CBQMS, 15; Washington, DC: Catholic Biblical Association of America, 1984), p. 26.
45. Attridge, 'Historiography', *Jewish Writings of the Second Temple Period* (CRINT, 2.2; Assen: Van Gorcum, 1984), pp. 157–84 (168).
46. Whether or not the fragments in Eusebius are from Eupolemus is debated. See Attridge, 'His-

Enoch was the founder of astrology but that Abraham also taught astrology to the Phoenicians before passing on into Egypt (*Praep evang.* 9.17.8; 9.18.2). Considering that these historians share the same tradition that Abraham was connected in some way with astrology, it is not surprising that Josephus would assume that the subject of Berossus' tradition was Abraham.

Josephus attributes his second source to Hecataeus of Abdera, who is said to have left a book composed about Abraham (*Ant.* 1.159). This book, *Abraham and the Egyptians*, is actually by Pseudo-Hecataeus.[47] In a fragment from *Abraham and the Egyptians* that Clement of Alexandria cites (*Strom.* 5.14; cf. *Praep. Ev.* 13.13), Pseudo-Hecataeus lauds the truth of monotheism while deprecating the vanity of idol worship. The subjects of monotheism and the rejection of idolatry are associated with Abraham. Attridge contends that some of the non-biblical material about Abraham in Josephus may derive from this source.[48]

Josephus has furnished his reader with sources of some antiquity that make reference to Abraham's experience with astrology. Traditions about Abraham were obviously of enough importance to have an entire book devoted to them. By using sources of antiquity, Josephus is underlining the perceived importance of Abraham and thus the Jewish nation in history and in culture and the particular popularity of the tradition of Abraham and the advent of astrology.

c. *Abraham the Educated Hellenist*

As found in the biblical account, Abraham travels to Egypt because of a famine in the land (Gen. 12.10; *Ant.* 1.161). But according to Josephus, Abraham's foundational reason for travelling to Egypt was that he 'was of a mind to visit them, alike to profit by their abundance and to hear what their priests said about the gods; intending, if he found their doctrine more excellent than his own, to conform to it, or else to convert them to a better mind should his own beliefs prove superior' (*Ant.* 1.161). His journey of inquiry leads him to learn from the priests of the Egyptians like a student in a philosophical school. Feldman points out that one of the 'recurrent characteristics of the pre-Socratic philosophers as viewed in Hellenistic times, is that they visited Egypt to become acquainted with Egyptian science and other esoteric lore and to engage in discussions with Egyptian wise men'.[49] Abraham is a true philosopher; what he believes about God depends upon which doctrine is superior. As portrayed by Josephus, he apparently would have no problem converting to Egyptian beliefs should their arguments prove superior. Feldman further notes that this depiction of Abraham participating in true Hellenistic philosophical disputation has no parallel in any

toriography', pp. 165–66; Doran, 'The Jewish Historians Before Josephus', *ANRW* 2.20.1 (Berlin: W. de Gruyter, 1987), pp. 246–97 (263–74).

    47. Stern, *Greek and Latin Authors on Jews and Judaism* (2 vols.; Jerusalem: The Israel Academy of Sciences and Humanities, 1974), p. 22.

    48. Attridge, 'Historiography', p. 170.

    49. Feldman 'Greek Philosopher', p. 151.

other account of Abraham. Only here is Abraham depicted as willing to convert if he is defeated in argumentation.[50]

In the *Antiquities* (1.163–165), as in the biblical account of Abraham and Sarah in Egypt (Gen 12.10–20), Abraham fears the Egyptian reprisals because of Sarah's great beauty. Abraham pretends to be her brother and instructs Sarah to play the part of his sister. Everything happens as Abraham predicted (1.163): Pharaoh takes Sarah but his desire for her is thwarted by an outbreak of disease and political disturbances (1.164) sent by God. Pharaoh's priests notify him that these calamities were due to his desire for Sarah, after which he goes to Abraham with a defence. He confesses that he had believed her to be Abraham's sister and he had wished to contract a marriage alliance. Pharaoh gives Abraham abundant riches.

According to Franxman's study of the account of Abraham and Sarah in Egypt in the *Antiquities* in comparison with that found in Genesis, Josephus uses information from both the accounts of Abraham and Sarah in Egypt (Gen. 12.10–20) and in Gerar (Gen. 20.1–18).[51] What is most striking about Josephus' adaptation is his omission of the king's complaint against Abraham (Gen. 12.18–19; 20.9–10). Abraham and Sarah come out looking blameless of anything.

But foremost in Josephus' mind is not purifying Abraham's character but how to make Abraham look increasingly like someone worth the admiration of his Gentile readership. The story of Abraham in Egypt is merely embedded in his account of Abraham the supreme Hellenist. Josephus continues,

> Abraham consorted with the most learned of the Egyptians, whence his virtue and reputation became still more conspicuous. For, seeing that the Egyptians were addicted to a variety of different customs and disparaged one another's practices and were consequently at enmity with one another, Abraham conferred with each party and, exposing the arguments which they adduced in favour of their particular views, demonstrated that they were idle and contained nothing true. Thus gaining their admiration at these meetings as a man of extreme sagacity, gifted not only with high intelligence but with power to convince his hearers on any subject which he undertook to teach, he introduced them to arithmetic and transmitted to them the laws of astronomy. For before the coming of Abraham the Egyptians were ignorant of these sciences, which thus travelled from the Chaldaeans into Egypt, whence they passed to the Greeks (*Ant*. 1.165–168).

In the *Antiquities*, Abraham becomes the Hellenistic philosopher without equal. The trip to Egypt ends with Abraham participating in the debate foretold at its beginning (*Ant.* 1.161). Apparently, Abraham was not at all convinced by their arguments, and was even able to show how empty they were of truth in the fashion of a Hellenistic philosopher.[52] Abraham is portrayed as such a convincing teacher that he was able to persuade his hearers on any chosen subject. If we again refer back to the introduction to the trip to Egypt, we find that Abraham intended to discuss their respective doctrines about the gods (*Ant.* 1.161). And

---

50. *Judean Antiquities: Translation and Commentary* (vol. 3 of *Flavius Josephus: Translation and Commentary*, ed. Steve Mason; Leiden: E.J. Brill, 2000), p. 61 n. 517.

51. *Genesis*, pp. 129–31.

52. 'Greek Philosopher', p. 153.

if we again consider Josephus's statements that Abraham was determined to 'reform and change the ideas universally current concerning God' (*Ant.* 1.155, see also above), one might conclude that one of the subjects in which Abraham was convincing was his doctrine of monotheism.

Yet Abraham's teaching the Egyptians about monotheism is not explicit in this text. Feldman maintains, 'Josephus does not portray Abram as teaching the Egyptians about his monotheism, presumably because this would expose Josephus to the charge of seeking to proselytise – a charge [about which] the Romans were particularly sensitive'.[53] Thus, any missionary zeal that may have been detected in Abraham's desire to 'reform' peoples' minds about God is curtailed. It is also noteworthy that Abraham is said to be willing to convert to the Egyptian views of God 'if he found their doctrine more excellent than his own' (*Ant.* 1.161). Of course, this does not happen either, allowing Josephus to imply that Abraham's notions about God were indeed superior to those espoused by the Egyptians.

Josephus depicts Abraham as gifted in the very areas most cultivated by the Hellenistic Greeks: rhetoric, philosophy and science. Through the depiction of Abraham exposing empty arguments and teaching in such a manner that he always convinced his listeners, Josephus portrays Abraham as the supreme logician and rhetorician. His mastery of philosophy was found in his proof for the existence of God. Finally, by teaching the Egyptians arithmetic and astrology Josephus portrays Abraham as gifted in the sciences. Abraham's virtue, announced earlier (e. g. *Ant.* 1.14–15, 154, 165), has now become conspicuous. Because virtue could refer to 'excellence of achievement, to mastery in a specific field…or to endowment with higher power…or often both' Abraham's mastery of several fields and his extreme wisdom and intelligence as portrayed by Josephus provide the evidence for his virtue.[54]

Obviously, Josephus portrays Abraham purposefully. At the end of the section he reminds us that before Abraham the Egyptians were ignorant of astronomy and arithmetic which were then passed on to the Greeks. Not only is Abraham a well-educated Hellenist, but he is also responsible for important aspects of culture being given to the Egyptians and the Greeks. Ultimately, even Roman readers owe this scientific knowledge to Abraham himself.

In *Against Apion,* Josephus specifies some of the charges against the Jews with which he must deal. He states that Apollonius Molon has been 'reviling us…as atheists and misanthropes… He adds that we are the most stupid of all barbarians and are consequently…the only people who have contributed no useful invention to civilization' (*Apion* 2.147–149). Apollonius was not alone in his anti-Jewish sentiments. Because the Jews would not participate in the worship of Hellenistic gods, this exclusivity even led to the charge that the Jews were actually atheists.[55] In his portrayal of Abraham, Josephus has created a narrative based on Genesis that defends the Jews against such accusations. Abraham was no atheist; in fact,

53. Feldman, *Commentary*, p. 63 n. 537.
54. O. Bauernfeind, 'ἀρετή', *TDNT*, I, pp. 457–61 (458).
55. Jerry L. Daniel, 'Anti-Semitism in the Hellenistic–Roman Period', *JBL* 98 (1979), pp. 45–65 (61).

he was the first to believe in the one God. The Jews are not misanthropes; their forefather Abraham was the first to teach the Egyptians arithmetic and astronomy, which in ancient thought was tantamount to astrology.[56] The Greeks and Romans should be thankful for all of Abraham's instruction.

d. *Abraham and the Law*

i. *Conforming to God's Will.* Near the beginning of Josephus' rendition of the story of Abraham is his portrayal of Sarah as Abraham's niece rather than his half-sister as found in the Genesis account (Gen. 20.12). The tendency to 'whitewash' important people from Israel's past is common in rewritten Bible literature. Marrying one's sister or half sister was considered to be an abomination according to Mosaic Law (Lev. 20.17). Josephus' intention here is to show Abraham as law-abiding; marrying one's niece was well within the law (Lev. 18.12–14; 20.19–21). This is especially important given that one of his themes in the *Antiquities* noted earlier, namely, that those who live virtuously can expect to 'prosper in all things beyond belief, and for their reward are offered by God felicity' (*Ant.* 1.14).[57] For Josephus, the Mosaic Law was a guide to virtuous living. Abraham, the father of the Jewish nation, becomes a model of this law.

In respect to Abraham and the law, the vocabulary used in the account of the birth and sacrifice of Isaac by Josephus is of special significance. Both Isaac and Abraham are described as having θρησκεία or devotion towards God. According to Attridge, the word as used here 'encompasses the whole response of the religious individual to God. While it does have cultic overtones, it is almost synonymous with "εὐσέβεια" [piety]' which, in the *Antiquities,* 'is the proper human response to the fact of God's providence'.[58] It is Abraham's devotion that God is testing.

Faced with the destruction of his son, whom he had received as his reward for his conduct in battle (*Ant.* 1.183) and in whom he has such an emotional stake, Abraham decides to sacrifice him without any indication of hesitation. As Feldman states, 'by eliminating…the direct command of G-d to Abraham, as well as Abraham's laconic response "Here I am", and by putting the whole scene in indirect discourse, Josephus…indicates that Abraham took all this in his stride'.[59] According to Josephus, Abraham considered that 'nothing would justify disobedience to God and that in everything he must submit to his will since all that befell His favoured ones was ordained by His providence [πρόνοια]' (*Ant.* 1.225). God exercises πρόνοια, which may be understood as 'watchful, concerned forethought and consideration…Abraham agreed to sacrifice his son because of his belief that whatever came the way of those favored by God came through his providence'.[60]

---

56. H.I. Marrou, *A History of Education in Antiquity* (New York: Sheed and Ward, 1956), p. 182; H. Koester, *History, Culture, and Religion of the Hellenistic Age* (Philadelphia: Fortress Press, 1982), p. 157.

57. On *Ant.* 1.14, see above, p. 56.

58. *Interpretation*, p. 89 n. 2 and p. 116, respectively.

59. 'Josephus' Version of the Binding of Isaac', *SBL Seminar Papers, 1981* (*SBLSP* 21; Chico, CA: Scholars Press, 1982), pp. 113–28 (113).

60. Attridge, *Interpretation*, pp. 71–72.

The idea that providence (πρόνοια) ruled the world was a popular Stoic concept. Stoics believed that they could show that the whole world was 'the planned and providential work of God, that human reason if correct must think in the same way as the divine reason, and that man should therefore accept willingly all that happens'.[61] Piety was the proper response to the providential work of the gods, as Epictetus writes, 'For piety (εὐσέβεια) towards the gods, know that the most important thing is this: to have right opinions about them – that they exist, and that they govern the universe well and justly – and to have set yourself to obey them'.[62] Abraham's pious response to the requirement of God that he sacrifice his son is in keeping with this Stoic concept.[63] And in response to Abraham's piety, God saved Isaac (*Ant.* 1.233–236). Thus, Josephus has succeeded in his intentions to show how those who conform to God's will and obey his laws are rewarded by God beyond belief (*Ant.* 1.14).

Additionally, Feldman rightly emphasizes Josephus' concern to play down the theological aspects of the account, especially those aspects having to do with theodicy, while playing up the virtuous character of Abraham.[64] To secure his depiction of Abraham as deserving the admiration of the Hellenist reader, Josephus concludes his portrayal of the life of Abraham saying, 'Abraham died, a man in every virtue supreme, who received from God the due need of honour for his zeal in His service (*Ant.* 1.256).

ii. *Abraham and Circumcision*. Josephus states, 'to the intent that his [Abraham's] posterity should be kept from mixing with others, God charged him to have them circumcised and to perform the rite on the eighth day after birth' (*Ant.* 1.192). Attridge contends that circumcision 'becomes a distinguishing feature of the offspring of Abraham, to keep them separate from their neighbors, but not a covenantal bond between the people and God'.[65] Perhaps in order to avoid charges of misanthropy, Josephus alludes to his expounding the reason for circumcision elsewhere in a volume he never wrote or we no longer possess.[66] In the *Antiquities*, Abraham acts without question.

Josephus states that eight days after Isaac's birth Abraham circumcises him, and 'from that time forward the Jewish practice has been to circumcise so many days after birth' (*Ant.* 1.214). Circumcising Isaac on the eighth day was in line with the command given by God and recorded earlier (*Ant.* 1.192; cf. Gen. 17.9–14). However, in the account of the birth and circumcision of Isaac, Josephus makes Abraham and Sarah the explicit model for subsequent generations, which the story of Isaac's birth in Genesis does not (cf. *Ant.* 1.214; Gen. 21.4). Through

61. F.H. Sanbach, *The Stoics* (New York: W.W. Norton, 1975), p. 69.

62. Whitney J. Oates (ed.), *The Stoic and Epicurean Philosophers: the Complete Extant Writings of Epicurus, Epictetus, Lucretius, Marcus Aurelius* (trans. P.E. Matheson; New York: Random House, 1940), p. 476.

63. Feldman, 'Binding', pp. 116–17.

64. 'Binding', p. 127.

65. Attridge, *Interpretation*, p. 80.

66. Feldman, *Commentary*, p. 72 n. 597.

this explicit model, Josephus explains the origin of the practice of circumcision to his non-Jewish readers.

In Josephus' rewriting of the Abraham account, no covenant promises exist. Even circumcision is unrelated to the covenant. Circumcision is instituted to prevent Abraham's descendants from mixing with the members of other nations (*Ant.* 1.192; cf. *Ant.* 1.214). In *Ant.* 12.241, when the Hellenizers appeal to Antiochus Epiphanes to build a gymnasium, he does so. In response the Hellenizers conceal their 'private parts in order to be Greeks even when unclothed, and giving up whatever other national customs they had, they imitated the practice of foreign nations'. Thus, circumcision is a symbol of Jews as a nation in contrast to those outside.

In *Ant.* 13.257–258, Hyrcanus is said to permit the Idumaeans to remain in their country as long as they were circumcised and observed the laws of the Jews. He states that the Idumaeans, 'submitted to circumcision and to making their manner of life conform in all other respects to that of the Jews'. He further states, 'And from that time on they have continued to be Jews'. Thus, one can become Jewish not only by descent from Abraham but also by taking on circumcision and the laws of the Jews.

In a well-known segment on circumcision, Josephus writes of King Izates who desires to convert to Judaism because his mother was enamoured with Judaism. Izates is ready to be circumcised so that he can be a genuine Jew but his mother attempts to stop him for fear of his life should his subjects discover his conversion (*Ant.* 20.38–40).

Izates goes to Ananias who agrees with Izates' mother. He said that the king could 'worship God even without being circumcised if indeed he had fully decided to be a devoted adherent of Judaism, for it was this that counted more than circumcision. He told him, furthermore, that God Himself would pardon him if, constrained thus by necessity and by fear of his subjects, he failed to perform this rite' (*Ant.* 20.41–42). Later Izates asks another Jew named Eleazer who had a reputation for being strict in matters of Jewish law. Eleazar urges Izates to carry out the rite of circumcision.

Feldman and others have considered how Josephus' story mirrors rabbinic arguments about the necessity of circumcision for proselytes.[67] Ananias' view that Izates could bypass circumcision and worship God without being circumcised is important. It is obvious that the foundational aspect of conversion – of being considered a Jew – was monotheism. But in order to truly follow Abraham's example, one needed to be circumcised.

3. *Conclusion: The Function and Significance of Abraham in the* Antiquities *of Josephus*

Whether or not Josephus wrote the *Antiquities* from a desire to clear his name with his compatriots is not ultimately discernible from the text. That he was well

---

67. *Jewish Antiquities Books XVIII–XX* (trans. Louis H. Feldman; LCL; Cambridge, MA: Harvard University Press, 1965), pp. 410–11, n.a.

acquainted with the Jewish law and that he knew Greco-Roman culture and literature, however, is evident. That he used this knowledge to write a timely apologetic for the Jews has been established.

That Abraham was part of this apologetic agenda is obvious. Josephus' portrayal of Abraham was that which would have spoken best to his Hellenistic, non-Jewish readers. Abraham is the first to proclaim monotheism, creatively using a popular philosophical proof of God. Abraham is able to refute empty arguments and persuade his audience convincingly on any topic he chooses. He graciously shares his scientific knowledge of arithmetic and astronomy with those in Egypt who in turn will pass it on to the rest of the then civilized world. Abraham is an example of the educated Hellenistic gentleman.

According to Josephus, those who hold to the doctrines given by the lawgiver participate in the virtue of God. Abraham was shown to obey particular Jewish laws, like circumcision and marriage to a niece rather than a half-sister. Based upon Abraham's willingness to submit to the will of God in the offering of Isaac, Abraham is granted felicity. Because Abraham was so highly virtuous before the law was given, he was simultaneously obedient to the essence of Jewish law.

Why did Josephus portray Abraham in such a way? First, he was providing an apologetic for Judaism for non-Jewish readers. Jews had been accused of atheism, misanthropy, offering nothing to civilization, and cowardice. In his portrayal of Abraham, Josephus is showing how the story of the forefather of the Jewish nation refutes all of these charges. In fact, Abraham is said to be 'in every virtue supreme' (*Ant.* 1.256). In Hellenistic society someone could be said to have virtue in reference to such qualities as morality, culture, achievement and knowledge. Abraham was shown to be virtuous in all of these.

Josephus also shows how it is that those who are morally virtuous are rewarded with a happy life. In spite of the dire consequences that were apparent to Abraham from a human perspective, he was willing to sacrifice his son Isaac, his only source of happiness, in obedience to God's providence. For this action, he was given his due in a life of bliss. The message to the Hellenistic reader is that living according to such virtue leads to a happy life. Additionally, since the Jewish law is in keeping with this virtue, the Jewish law is a highly reasonable code by which to live.

How does Abraham function in reference to Jewish identity and separation from others? First, he is the father of the Jewish race. However, this descent is not the only criterion for one to be considered Jewish. Even for Josephus who attempted to provide a highly inoffensive apologetic, the necessity of obedience to the law is still a factor of Jewish identity. For example, Josephus maintains that Abraham married his niece rather than his daughter and Abraham first practised circumcision, which was symbolic of the separation of Jews from Gentiles. Abraham is shown to be supportive of the 'constitution' before it is given.

However, the most distinctive element of Josephus' portrayal of Abraham is his monotheism. As Spilsbury states, 'The most profound implication of descent from Abraham is that the Jew is a monotheist.'[68] As portrayed by Josephus, this belief is based upon sound, reasonable philosophical principles. In contrast to the polytheistic tenor of the day, this made the Jews themselves distinctive. Abraham, the first monotheist, provides the foundation for this distinctive faith.

In contrast to the works of Philo in which Abraham also functions as the example of the proselyte to Judaism, in Josephus, Abraham has no real missionary function.[69] While his monotheistic faith is obvious, his role in the conversion of others to monotheism is not. So while Abraham does function to define foundationally what it means to be Jewish, it is not with the conversion of others in mind. Yes, the Jewish religion is shown to be superior to polytheistic faith, but the apologetic functions to provide a favourable account of the Jews, not to convert its readers.

Because Josephus shies away from describing the covenant or the election of the Jews, he never explicitly says that those who do not practise these things, particularly monotheistic faith, are not members of the people of God. Yet, if in his apologetic to an audience that is primarily Gentile he is trying to prove the attractiveness of these essential elements, it would follow that in order to be of the community of Jews, one would need to identify oneself in these ways. Circumcision and monotheism are described as the key elements in the story of Izates and it is Abraham that is the founder of each of these. Thus, these are ways to identify members of the people of God and provide boundary markers insofar as one is interested in taking on that new identity.

68. *Image*, p. 92.
69. Cf. Feldman, *Josephus's Interpretation of the Bible* (Berkeley: University of California Press, 1998), p. 162; see also pp. 157–59.

Chapter 6

ABRAHAM AS THE REJECTER OF IDOLATRY
IN THE *APOCALYPSE OF ABRAHAM*

1. *Introduction*

Although the work presently exists in Slavonic, it is commonly held that the *Apocalypse of Abraham* was originally written in Hebrew or Aramaic.[1] The date of composition appears to be soon after the destruction of the Temple in Jerusalem because that is the main event to which reference is made (*Apoc. Abr.* 27.1–3).[2] The apocalypse was probably composed in Palestine.[3]

Like the book of Daniel, the apocalypse is composed of two parts. Chapters 1 through 8 contain narratives concerning Abraham the seer, while chs. 9 through 32 give the account of the revelation to Abraham. While some have argued for different authors for the two sections, it is clear from the references back to the narrative in the revelatory section that even if different authors wrote the sections, it comprises a coherent literary piece. According to M.E. Stone, the stories of Abraham in the narrative section form 'a fitting preamble to the extensive vision which follows, since they culminate in Abraham's remarkable prayer in which he asks for knowledge of God'.[4]

The *Apocalypse of Abraham* belongs to the apocalyptic literary genre. In the apocalypse one finds the theme found in many Palestinian apocalypses, namely, how God's historic promises to the Jewish people would be fulfilled and how the Jews would be vindicated over their oppressors although in the present their future looked bleak.[5] A second concern of the author of the *Apocalypse of Abraham*, which is also a concern often found in apocalyptic literature, is how to

---

1. G.H. Box and J.I. Landsman, *The Apocalypse of Abraham* (London: SPCK, 1918), p. xv; M.E. Stone, 'Apocalyptic Literature', *Jewish Writings of the Second Temple Period* (CRINT, 2.2; Minneapolis, MN: Fortress Press, 1986), pp. 383–441 (415); R. Rubinkiewicz, 'The Apocalypse of Abraham: A New Translation and Introduction', *OTP*, vol. I, pp. 681–719 (682).

2. James R. Mueller, '*The Apocalypse of Abraham* and the Destruction of the Second Jewish Temple', *SBLSP* 21 (Chico, CA: Scholars Press, 1982), pp. 341–49.

3. Box, *Apocalypse*, p. xvi; Rubinkiewicz, 'Translation', p. 683.

4. Stone, 'Apocalyptic', p. 415.

5. E.P. Sanders, 'The Genre of Palestinian Jewish Apocalypses', in David Hellholm (ed.), *Apocalypticism in the Mediterranean World and the Near East: Proceedings of the International Colloquium on Apocalypticism* (Tübingen: J.C.B. Mohr [Paul Siebeck], 2nd edn, 1989), pp. 447–59 (456). See also John J. Collins, *The Apocalyptic Imagination: An Introduction to Jewish Apocalyptic Literature* (Grand Rapids, MI; Eerdmans, 2nd edn, 1998), p. 225.

understand the sometimes catastrophic events in his contemporary world, in his case the destruction of the Jewish Temple in Jerusalem, in light of a heavenly perspective.[6] A third major theme is the concentration in the *Apocalypse of Abraham* on the Gentiles as both the oppressors and the corrupters of the Jewish people. The comparatively subtle influences of Hellenistic culture were a challenge to the faith of the Jews because it forced them, in many regards, to conform. This is true especially in reference to idol worship in the *Apocalypse of Abraham.*

2. *The Narrative Section: Abraham Rejects Idolatry*

The narrative section of the apocalypse begins with Abraham guarding the gods of his father Terah and his brother Nahor, during which time he performs a number of tests in order to discover which god is the strongest. He enters the temple to sacrifice to the gods on behalf of Terah, and finds the stone god Marumath at the feet of the iron god Nakhin (*Apoc. Abr.* 1.3). Abraham runs to his father for assistance in replacing the heavy stone god. While the two are putting the god back in place, the head of the god falls from the idol accidentally. Terah calls to Abraham to bring him stone-cutting tools from the house. Terah solves the problem by carving a new Marumath (1.9).

The portrayal of Abraham's family in the *Apocalypse of Abraham* as not only those who participate in idolatry but as those who actually make idols is significant. Because he manufactures idols, Terah is actually a perpetrator of idolatry. Earlier in this book it was shown how the author portrayed Terah and his family as being idol worshippers (*Jub.* 11–12). As has been noted, these similar extra-biblical traditions may be based not only upon aspects of the Genesis narrative, but also upon Josh. 24.2.

Subtly woven into the text already is the idea that participation in the worship of idols is vanity. The name for the god Marumath comes from the Hebrew word for deceit.[7] Consequently, it is a sarcastic name given by the author; the idol that Abraham and his father attempt to lift back to its place is in reality a stone of deceit.

Terah subsequently makes five more gods, commanding Abraham to sell them outside on the road (*Apoc. Abr.* 2.1). Abraham encounters some Syrian merchants whose camel screams, scares Abraham's ass, and three of the gods are smashed. The merchants pay Abraham for the smashed and the intact gods; Abraham throws the smashed remains of the gods into the river and they disappear (*Apoc. Abr.* 2.1–9).

In chapter three, the author of the apocalypse gives the reader insight into the thought processes of the boy Abraham. Abraham reasons that actually the idols should worship his father, because it is Terah who brought them into being.

---

6.   C. Rowland, *The Open Heaven: A Study of Apocalyptic in Judaism and Early Christianity* (London: SPCK, 1982), p. 2; see also Collins, *Imagination*, p. 195.

7.   Box, *Apocalypse*, p. xv.

Marumath could not stand up in his own sanctuary, nor could the three smashed gods save themselves. Abraham wonders how such a god as Marumath could possibly 'save a man, or hear a man's prayer, or give him any gift?' (*Apoc. Abr.* 3.8).[8]

Abraham returns to his father's house with the money from the sale of the idols. Abraham tells his father, 'The gods are blessed in you, because you are a god for them, because you made them, for their blessing is their perdition and their power is vain. They did not help themselves; how then can they help you or bless me?' (*Apoc. Abr.* 4.3). Terah becomes furious with Abraham because of his statements against his gods.

Another cycle of the narrative begins when Terah calls to Abraham just as he did when he repaired Marumath (*Apoc. Abr.* 5.1–2). On this occasion, Terah asks Abraham to make him lunch, using the wooden chips left over from his carving idols. In the midst of the chips Abraham finds the god Barisat. Abraham leaves Barisat near the enkindling fire, commanding him to watch the fire so that it does not go out. When Abraham returns, Barisat's feet are burning in the fire. Abraham laughs while Barisat is eventually reduced to ashes. Abraham tells Terah of Barisat's sacrifice for his lunch. Terah replies, 'Great is the power of Barisat! I will make another today, and tomorrow he will prepare my food' (*Apoc. Abr.* 5.17).

Once again, the author of the *Apocalypse of Abraham* uses the name of a god to signify the worthlessness of idols. In this case, the name of Barisat probably comes from the Aramaic meaning 'son of the fire'[9]

Abraham wonders at the stupidity and ignorance of his father. He again argues with his father concerning Terah's worship of Marumath and Barisat. He contends that even Nahor's god, which is made partially of gold, will be renewed if it grows old (*Apoc. Abr.* 6.6–7). However, Marumath, who is made of stone, cannot be renewed. Abraham further argues that Nahor's gods, made of gold and silver, are at least of some value in the eyes of humanity (*Apoc. Abr.* 6.9). However, Terah's gods are only made of stone and wood that was once rooted in the earth. Barisat, who is made of this wood, has perished. As portrayed in this parody of idol worship, Abraham cannot understand how it is that his father can actually continue to worship perishable gods that he himself has made (*Apoc. Abr.* 6.1–19).

Chapter 7 contains the speech of Abraham in which through reason he deduces the existence of God from his creation. As Rubinkiewicz points out, this chapter is probably a much later redaction.[10] We will include a consideration of it here because of its emphasis on Abraham's recognition of God by virtue of his observations of the natural phenomena.

Two forms of the speech exist. In both forms, Abraham's basic argument is the same. In *Apoc. Abr.* 7.1–6, Abraham argues that one should not believe in the changeable, created, subduable things:

---

 8. All citations of the *Apocalypse of Abraham* are from R. Rubinkiewicz, 'Translation,' pp. 681–719.

 9. Box, *Apocalypse*, p. xv.

 10. Rubinkiewicz, 'Translation', pp. 686–87.

> Fire is more venerable in formation, for even the unsubdued (things) are subdued in it, and it mocks that which perishes easily by means of its burning. But neither is it venerable, for it is subject to the waters. But rather the waters are more venerable than it (fire), because they overcome fire and sweeten the earth with fruits. But I will not call them god either, for the waters subside under the earth and are subject to it. But I will not call it a goddess either, for it is dried by the sun (and) subordinated to man for his work.

In the remainder of ch. 7, Abraham uses an argument based upon the heavenly phenomena: beyond the planets and stars a Creator and God exists. Abraham reasons that although the sun illuminates the whole universe, it is obscured at night by the moon, and by clouds. However, the moon and stars are not gods, since they are also dimmed. Instead, Abraham encourages his father to worship the true God who creates and empowers the universe. In the conclusion of the chapter, Abraham prays for the true God to reveal himself:

> More venerable among the gods, I say, is the sun, for with its rays it illuminates the whole universe and the various airs. Nor will I place among the gods the one who obscures his course by means of the moon and the clouds. Nor again shall I call the moon or the stars gods, because they too at times during the night dim their light. Listen, Terah my father, I shall seek before you the God who created all the gods supposed by us (to exist). For who is it, or which one is it who made the heavens crimson and the sun golden, who has given light to the moon and the stars with it, who has dried the earth in the midst of the many waters, who set you yourself among the things and who has sought me out in the perplexity of my thoughts? If [only] God will reveal himself by himself to us! (*Apoc. Abr.* 7.7–12).

The speech made by Abraham to his father is based upon extra-biblical tradition in which Abraham rejects idolatry based upon his discerning from the natural world that the true God is not contained within the creation but instead creates and controls the cosmos. This tradition is familiar from our previous study of work by Philo (*De Abr.* 69–70) and the author of *Jubilees* (*Jub.* 12.16–18). Even if ch. 7 was inserted at a much later time, it provides evidence for the continued widespread popularity of the tradition in which Abraham discerns God from the natural phenomena. In addition, as in *Jubilees*, Abraham's speech in *Apoc. Abr.* 7 functions on more than the level of the narrative. The chapter also functions to instruct the reader or hearer of the chapter about the vanity of idolatry.

Abraham's abhorrence of idolatry is obvious from his arguments with his father. Terah nonsensically continues to worship his own creations. Abraham has reasoned successfully that neither the created elements of fire, water, earth nor the created heavenly bodies – the sun, moon, and stars – should be worshipped. Instead, the One who created them is to be worshipped and it is to this One that Abraham cries out for revelation (*Apoc. Abr.* 7.12).

3. *The Revelatory Section: Idolatry Brings Destruction*

a. *Preparation for Revelation*
The author of the *Apocalypse of Abraham* juxtaposes Terah's call of Abraham found in the narrative (*Apoc. Abr.* 1.7; 5.1) with God's call of Abraham. While

Abraham is pondering the subject of his speech, the voice of the 'Mighty One' comes down from the heavens in a stream of fire. God says, 'You are searching for the God of gods, the Creator, in the understanding of your heart. I am he. Go out from Terah, your father, and go out of the house, that you too may not be slain in the sins of your father's house' (*Apoc. Abr.* 8.3–4). A bolt from heaven burns up Terah and his house as Abraham leaves home (8.6).

Again, one finds similarities between the account of Abraham in *Jubilees* and in the *Apocalypse of Abraham*. In *Jubilees*, Abraham burns the house of idols in which Haran is killed (*Jub.* 12.12–14). In the *Apocalypse of Abraham*, God burns the house of the idol-maker and its owner. In each case fire is used as the punishment for idolatry. A word-play between the name of the city, 'Ur' and the Hebrew word for fire which sounds like 'Ur', may be intentional here, as it is in *Jubilees*. In Gen. 12.1, God calls Abraham from 'Ur' of the Chaldees. According to the *Apocalypse of Abraham*, he was called forth previous to the fire, having been forewarned of the catastrophe by God.

For the author of the *Apocalypse of Abraham*, the significant events from the rest of Gen. 15 are not God's promises of land and descendants (Gen.15.5–5–7) but the sacrifice and burnt offerings. After commanding Abraham to gather a heifer, she-goat, ram, turtledove and pigeon, God states,

> And in this sacrifice I will place the ages. I will announce to you guarded things and you will see great things which you have not seen, because you desired to search for me, and I called you my beloved…you shall set out for me the sacrifice which I have commanded you, in the place which I will show you on a high mountain. And there I will show you the things which were made by the ages and by my word, and affirmed, created, and renewed. And I will announce to you in them what will come upon those who have done evil and just things in the race of man (*Apoc. Abr.* 9.5–10).

The sacrifice is not used as an affirmation of a covenant made between God and Abraham as it is in Gen. 15 but as a basis for the revelation of God's mysteries, past and present, to Abraham. Abraham receives this revelation because he did not succumb to idolatry but searched for the true God. The revelation explains what happened when Abraham fell asleep in Gen. 15.12, 'As the sun was going down, a deep sleep fell upon Abram, and a deep and terrifying darkness descended upon him.' It is in this darkness that God reveals the future of Abraham's descendants (cf. Gen. 15.13–16; *4 Ezra* 3.13–14; *2 Bar.* 4.5).

As with many of the recipients of revelation described in apocalyptic literature, Abraham is overcome when he realizes that he has been listening to the voice of God (*Apoc. Abr.* 10.2–3). He hears God continue to speak when he sends his angel Iaoel 'of the same name'. Although the angel is not equal to God, the name of this figure is a combination of the well-known Hebrew terms for God, Yahweh and El. God's dwelling in Iaoel may be derived from Exod. 23.20–21, where God promises to send an angel to lead Israel to the place prepared for them, and warns the Israelites not to rebel against this angel, stating, 'for my name is in him'.[11] The angel is to consecrate and strengthen Abraham through the mediation of God's

---

11. L. Hurtado, *One God, One Lord* (London: SCM Press, 1988), pp. 79–80.

name. The angel appears in the 'likeness of a man' (*Apoc. Abr.* 10.4), and stands Abraham on his feet. The angel states twice that God loves Abraham (*Apoc. Abr.* 10. 6, 7). Iaoel's duties include restraining the cherubim from one another and teaching the song that is described in enigmatic language as carried 'through the medium of man's night of the seventh hour' (*Apoc. Abr.* 10.9). It is also revealed that Iaoel ordered Terah's house to be destroyed (*Apoc. Abr.* 10.12).

Iaoel declares that he has been sent to Abraham to bless him and the land prepared for him. He tells Abraham to stand up, be bold and rejoice, because God has prepared an eternal honour for him. He further commands Abraham, 'Go, complete the sacrifice of the command. Behold I am assigned (to be) with you and with the generation which is predestined (to be born) from you' (*Apoc. Abr.* 10.14–16).

Abraham fasts for forty days and nights in the presence of the angel. They come to Horeb, where Abraham questions how it is he will make the sacrifice if he has no animals. The angel points out that the animals needed are following them. The imagery here of the whereabouts of the sacrifice being questioned and of the divine provision of the sacrificial victims is similar to the imagery found in the offering of Isaac (Gen. 22.1–22).

The angel also instructs Abraham to slaughter the animals, dividing them into halves. The types of animals for sacrifice and the instructions are in accordance with those found in Gen. 15. Abraham is to give the sacrifices to the men who will then offer sacrifice to the 'Eternal One' (*Apoc. Abr.* 12.9). Abraham is not to cut the birds in half because they will be their vehicles to heaven. Consequently, the author of the *Apocalypse of Abraham* provides an explanation of why the birds of the sacrifice were not to be cut in half where Gen. 15.10 did not. Additionally, the birds function here as they did in many pagan traditions of the time, where birds or bird-like beings functioned as 'psychopomps'. Psychopomps were the guides or bearers of the soul to the next world.[12]

The similarity between Abraham's actions in *Apoc. Abr.* 12 and those of Moses and Elijah are striking.[13] Just as Elijah travels forty days until he reaches Mt. Horeb (1 Kgs 19.8), so Abraham travels the same length of time to the site (*Apoc. Abr.* 12.1). And, like Moses who fasted for forty days before receiving the ten commandments (cf. Exod. 34.28), Abraham is assumed to have fasted during that time because his food 'was to see the angel who was with me, and his discourse with me was my drink' (*Apoc. Abr.* 12.1–2).

Because Mt. Horeb and Mt. Sinai are names for the same mountain, Abraham receives his revelation from God in the same place that Moses received God's commandments (Exod. 19.9–20.21) and in the same location where Elijah received his divine communication (1 Kgs. 19.14). As the Lord 'was like a devouring fire on the top of the mountain' in the Exodus account (Exod. 24.17), so the fire on top of Mt. Horeb burns the sacrifices over which Abraham and the

12. E.R. Goodenough, *Jewish Symbols in the Greco-Roman Period* (13 vols.; New York: Pantheon Books for the Bollingen Foundation, 1958), vol. VIII, pp. 44, 121.

13. Christopher T. Begg, 'Rereadings of the "Animal Rite" of Genesis 15 in Early Jewish Narratives', *CBQ* 50 (1988), pp. 36–46 (44).

angel will eventually ascend to heaven, where the voice of God is found in the midst of the fire (*Apoc. Abr.* 17.1). In the *Apocalyse of Abraham*, Abraham is on the mountain known for the revelation of God to his people through chosen leaders. However, this time, the instrument God uses for revelation is Abraham.

In the *Apoc. Abr.* 13, the events of Gen. 15.11 are reinterpreted. Gen. 15.11 states, 'And when the birds of prey came down on the carcasses, Abraham drove them away'. However, the bird that comes upon the carcasses in this apocalypse is the demonic figure called Azazel. The demonic bird gives Abraham reasons for fleeing. Abraham turns to the angel who reveals the true character of the bird.

The words of Iaoel that follow assist us in understanding the position of the author. The dominions of Abraham and Azazel have been switched. Abraham's portion is now in heaven while Azazel's place is on earth (*Apoc. Abr.* 13.8, 14). It is because of Azazel that wrath falls upon the unrighteous (13.6–9). However, Azazel's power is limited; he cannot tempt the righteous. Iaoel states:

> For the Eternal, Mighty One did not allow the bodies of the righteous to be in your hand, so through them the righteous life is affirmed and the destruction of ungodliness… You have no permission to tempt all the righteous. Depart from this man! You cannot deceive him, because he is the enemy of you and of those who follow you and who love what you wish' (*Apoc. Abr.* 13.10–13).

In Iaoel's continuing address, he says that the 'Eternal One' has chosen Abraham. He orders Abraham to be bold, and to 'do through your authority whatever I order you against him who reviles justice [Azazel]' (*Apoc. Abr.* 14.3). Abraham has the ability to reject Azazel and does so according to what Iaoel tells him to say. Upon the order of the angel, Abraham then ceases to answer Azazel (*Apoc. Abr.* 14.9–14).

As the sun sets, the smoke from the sacrifice and the sacrificing angels ascend (*Apoc. Abr.* 15.1; Gen. 15.17). Abraham ascends with Iaoel, surveying Gehenna on his way (*Apoc. Abr.* 15.5–16.5). They hear the voice of God, and worship him. Abraham recites the song that the angel taught him.

The hymn that Abraham recites contains a number of significant elements. God is said to be Abraham's protector, he receives the petitions of those who honour him but turns away from the petitions of those who restrain him because of their provocations. God redeems those who live in an evil age in the midst of the wicked (*Apoc. Abr.* 17.14–17). Abraham further asks that his prayer be accepted, as well as the 'sacrifice which you yourself made to yourself through me as I searched for you' (*Apoc. Abr.* 17.20). Abraham prays for the revelation that has been promised to him.

As a result of the sacrifice, Abraham's search for the true God is over. He sees a vision of a throne and heavenly creatures (cf. Ezek. 1). The voice of God calls Abraham by name and he answers. God instructs Abraham to look at the expanse of the firmament under his position on the seventh firmament.

b. *God's Revelation to Abraham*
From his seventh firmament position Abraham is commanded to see 'that on no single expanse is there any other but the one whom you have searched for or who

has loved you' (*Apoc. Abr.* 19.3). Abraham looks at the firmaments above and below himself, and sees the creatures of God: angels and fiery living creatures. The fifth firmament contains 'hosts of stars' (*Apoc. Abr.* 19.9).

God again calls to Abraham, and asks him to tell him the number of the stars on the fifth firmament (*Apoc. Abr.* 20.1). Abraham protests that he is unable to do so because he is merely a human being (*Apoc. Abr.* 20.4). God then proclaims, 'As the number of stars and their power, so shall I place for your seed the nations and men, set apart for me in my lot with Azazel' (*Apoc. Abr.* 20.5).

The author has composed an apocalyptic rendition from verses found in the Genesis narrative. The first and most familiar verse is from Gen. 15.5, in which God brings Abraham 'outside and said, "Look toward heaven and count the stars, if you are able to count them"'. The author of the *Apocalypse of Abraham* places Abraham in the heavens using the same verse. The difference is that in Genesis, Abraham stands on earth and must look up at the stars, while in *Apoc. Abr.* 20.3 Abraham looks at the stars from his heavenly location.[14]

In a section that is full of textual corruptions, God is depicted as stating that Abraham's progeny and power will be like the stars and their power, 'set apart for me in my lot with Azazel' (20.5). Abraham questions how God could establish himself with Azazel, who has just insulted him (*Apoc. Abr.* 20.7). According to Rubinkiewicz, a corruption of the original text exists in the manuscript where God speaks of his 'lot with Azazel'.[15]

The reason for these corruptions that portray God as being in league with Azazel, the personification of evil, may have to do with a group known as the Bogomils. Rubinkiewicz states that the remarks in *Apoc. Abr.* 20.5, 7 in which God is associated with Azazel 'reveal that their author wanted to indicate that the God of Abraham is a God of evil'.[16] While this sort of depiction is usually associated with the gnostics, the type of text the author seems to have used in 20.5 shows that it only could be made in the Slavic world. Apparently, the only Slavs who claimed that the God of the Hebrew Bible was the God of evil were the Bogomils.[17]

God answers Abraham's question by showing him another vision. This vision is concerned with the history of the world. Abraham looks down upon the terrestrial world. It contains plants and animals and people. The people seem primarily to be impious, yet he also sees their justification. He then sees 'the abyss and its torments, and its lower depths and (the) perdition in it' (*Apoc. Abr.* 21.3). He sees the sea and Leviathan, who holds up the world and causes it destruction. Separated from this earth, he sees the Garden of Eden, where people perform justice (*Apoc. Abr.* 21.6). Abraham also sees a 'great crowd of men and women and children, half of them on the right side of the portrayal, and half of them on the left side of the portrayal' (*Apoc. Abr.* 21.7).

---

14. Rubinkiewicz, 'Translation', p. 699 n. 20a.
15. Rubinkiewicz, 'Translation', p. 699 n. 20e.
16. Rubinkiewicz, 'Translation', p. 684.
17. Rubinkiewicz, 'Translation', p. 684; cf. Obolensky, *The Bogomils: A Study in Balkan Neo-Manichaeism* (Cambridge: Cambridge University Press, 1948), p. 209.

Abraham asks God to explain this picture of creation. God makes it clear that he has predetermined and created everything that Abraham sees. Abraham asks about the people on the left and the right of the picture. God answers that those on the left of the picture are 'tribes who existed previously...and after you' (22.4). Presumably these are the Gentiles who existed before Abraham and who will continue to exist after him. Some of these Gentiles have been prepared for judgement and order, while others have been prepared for judgement that leads to condemnation (*Apoc. Abr.* 22.4).

God further explains that those 'on the right side of the picture are the people set apart for me of the people with Azazel; these are the ones I have prepared to be born of you and to be called my people' (*Apoc. Abr.* 22.5). According to Rubinkiewicz, the reading of the text in this verse that aligns people with Azazel gives evidence of another probable later Bogomil interpretation and gloss.[18] The Bogomils were cosmological dualists: to them, the Devil created the entire visible world.[19] People who live on earth, in the created, visible world, may have been considered as being with Azazel.

Abraham himself provides the point of reference between those on the left side of the picture and those on the right. Besides dividing the Gentile group into two parts according to their future judgement, God divides the Gentiles into groups who lived before and after Abraham (*Apoc. Abr.* 22.4–5). Rubinkiewicz assumes that this point of reference is God's covenant with Abraham.[20] However, the text does not actually state that the covenant with Abraham was the point of division. The question still remains concerning how the Gentiles would be judged and what Abraham had to do with that judgement. Furthermore, if the idea of covenant is less important than Rubinkiewicz has contended, what is it that defines the people of God? Through the remainder of the composition, the author of the *Apocalypse of Abraham* will reveal what characterizes the people of God.

In the continuing dialogue between God and Abraham, Abraham asks why he gave the evil one such dominion to ruin human beings (*Apoc. Abr.* 23.12). God replies that those who commit evil, whom he hates, were given to Azazel in order that he would have dominion over them. Unsatisfied with this answer, Abraham further asks God why he determined that some should desire evil, since God is only angered at what he himself chose (*Apoc. Abr.* 23.14). Fundamentally, Abraham is asking about evil and the validity of God's judgement. If God has created human beings with the desire to do evil, how is it that God can then judge them for that evil? In light of the recent destruction of the Temple attested in the *Apocalypse of Abraham* (27.1–12), this question about the validity of God's judgement of his chosen people for their evil is relevant. After all, if he created them with the propensity and desire for evil, how can God then judge his people? Abraham here is depicted as upbraiding God for his judgement of his people.

18. Rubinkiewicz, 'Translation', p. 684.

19. Obolensky, *Bogomils*, pp. 122–23.

20. R. Rubinkiewicz, 'La vision de l'histoire dans l'Apocalypse d'Abraham', *ANRW* 2.19.1 (Berlin: W. de Gruyter, 1979), p. 147.

More importantly, Abraham functions as a mouthpiece for the author to ask God what he and perhaps many others are asking: is God, who is our Creator, being fair in judging us so severely by the destruction of our Temple?

God does not solve the problem of evil for Abraham, but answers him with another vision in which he will show Abraham 'what will be, and everything that will be in the last days'. God shows Abraham 'the people of his tribe' and 'what is burdened on them' (*Apoc. Abr.* 24.1). The phrase 'what is burdened on them' can be understood to mean 'things which have been made grievous against' them.[21] Abraham looks again in the picture and sees those things which had come into being before his time: Adam and Eve, the 'crafty adversary', and Cain who had been led by this lawless adversary to murder Abel, whom he also sees. He sees fornication and those who desire it with the place of judgement for it; theft and the system of retribution; naked men who are in shame and the harm against their friends and their retribution; and desire herself who holds every kind of lawlessness in her hand and her destined destruction (*Apoc. Abr.* 24.5–9). This vision of universal lawlessness serves as the first part of the answer to Abraham's question. The evil of humanity is such that judgement is warranted.

As the vision continues, the evil of those who can only be understood as Abraham's descendants is described. Abraham sees the 'likeness of the idol of jealousy' that is like the carpenter's figure which his father made formerly (*Apoc. Abr.* 25.1). In front of this idol is a man who is worshipping it. Opposite the idol is an altar where boys are being slaughtered in the face of the idol. Abraham asks the identity of the idol and the other elements, and the 'hand-some temple...the art and beauty of your glory that lies beneath your throne' (*Apoc. Abr.* 25.3). God answers by saying that the Temple that he has seen and the works of art are his idea of 'the priesthood of the name of my glory, where every petition of man will enter and dwell; the ascent of kings, and prophets and whatever sacrifice I decree to be made for me among my coming people, even among your tribe' (*Apoc. Abr.* 25.4).

However, the priesthood and the Temple deviated from God's idea of what they should be. The priesthood angered God. The idol associated with the Temple was described as the 'idol of jealousy' (25.1). The description of the statue as 'God's anger' in 25.5 represents the image that provokes God's jealousy or anger.[22] The slaughter of boys on the altar is reminiscent of the offering of children to pagan gods.[23]

The association of the Temple priesthood with idolatry and consequential destruction is also found in the Hebrew Bible. For example, the actions of the priests in the Temple are similar to the actions of Manasseh described in 2 Chron. 33.1–9 and 2 Kgs 21.1–18. The writer of 2 Kings blames the fall of Jerusalem and Judah in 587–86 BCE on Manasseh's apostasy (2 Kgs 21.10–15). Manasseh not only restored the pagan altars that his laudable predecessor Hezekiah had torn down, but even built intrusive altars in Yahweh's Temple. The altars in the

---

21. Rubinkiewicz, 'Translation', p. 701 n. 24b.
22. Box, *Apocalypse*, p. 73 n. 3.
23. Box, *Apocalypse*, p. 73 n. 5.

Temple courts are said to have been built 'for all the host of heaven' (2 Chron. 33.5; 2 Kgs 21.5) referring to the practice of astrology and worship of the stars. He made burnt offerings of his sons to pagan gods in the Hinnom Valley, much like one of his most wayward predecessors, Ahaz (2 Chron. 28.3; 2 Kgs 16.3; 2 Chron. 33.4–7; *Ant.* 9.243). He resorted to every kind of sorcery, which was the sin of Saul (1 Chron. 10.13–14). At the peak of his apostasy, Manasseh set up the idol of Asherah in the very Temple itself (2 Kgs 21.7). Just as it was for Manasseh, idolatry is the culminating sin of the descendants of Abraham (*Apoc. Abr.* 25.5–6) in the first century CE.

The priests depicted in the Temple who arouse the anger of God are committing idolatry. It is noteworthy that the author of the *Apocalypse of Abraham* sees sin primarily in a cultic form. Box and Landsman point out that allusions to the cultus are rare in apocalyptic literature.[24] Nickelsburg contends that because cultic activity is important in the plot of the *Apocalypse of Abraham*, 'it is likely that the author believes the events of 70 CE were caused by some sort of wrong cultic activity, which he construes as idolatry'.[25]

In the *Biblical Antiquities* it was noted that assimilation with Gentile practices could be considered idolatry.[26] In his work which discusses the political struggles of the Jews in Palestine from 6–74 CE based upon the works of Flavius Josephus, Rhoads contends that the revolutionaries such as the sicarii saw their brigandage and assassination against the Jewish authorities as a 'repression of idolatrous contact with heathen masters, perhaps to "cleanse the land" of those who refused exclusive allegiance to God'.[27] According to the *Apoc. Abr.* 25.6, the man who is doing the sacrificing makes God angry. Those who performed the sacrifice in the Temple were the priests. In the years previous to the fall of Jerusalem especially pious Jews may have perceived certain practices to be idolatrous. Did the author of the *Apocalypse of Abraham* consider the two daily sacrifices offered in the Temple on behalf of the Roman emperor as idolatry (*War* 2. 197, 408–410)? Alternatively, was it the gifts and sacrifices brought to the Temple by Gentiles that represented idolatry (*War* 2.408–410)? Because the chief priests and many Pharisees did not want these sacrifices stopped, did the author of the *Apocalypse of Abraham* see them fundamentally as idolaters (*War* 2. 411–416)? The cessation of the practice of offering sacrifices on behalf of the emperor was tantamount to a declaration of war on Rome; the Jewish revolutionaries passionately pursued this course of action. According to Josephus, this action laid the foundation of the war with the Romans (*War* 2.409).

It is difficult to know to what the author of the text at hand is referring; what emerges from the text is that he seems to have considered some sort of errant cultic practice to be equal to idolatry. Just as the idolatrous practices of Manasseh

---

24. *Apocalypse*, p. 73 n. 2.

25. G.W.E. Nickelsburg, *Jewish Literature Between the Bible and the Mishnah* (Philadelphia: Fortress Press, 1981), p. 298.

26. See Chapter 4.

27. David M. Rhoads, *Israel in Revolution: 6–74 C.E.* (Philadelphia: Fortress Press, 1976), p. 180.

brought about the destruction of the Temple by the Babylonians, so the idolatry of the priests brought about the destruction of the Temple by the Romans.

Abraham further questions God, this time about why he established the history of his people in this way. God replies with his own question, 'why did your father Terah not obey your voice and abandon the demonic worship of idols until he perished, and all his house with him?' (*Apoc. Abr.* 26.3). Abraham replies that it was because Terah did not want to listen to Abraham that he perished, just as Abraham did not listen to his father Terah and lived. God replies, 'As the counsel of your father is in him, as your counsel is in you, so also the counsel of my will is ready' (26.5). Thus, it is by their respective judgements and choices that Terah perished and Abraham lived. Both Abraham and Terah were free either to follow idolatry or to turn from it to the true God. As Terah and Abraham were free to make their decisions, so God is free to permit sin and pronounce judgement reserved for the coming days.

Abraham again looks at the picture of history. From the left side of the picture come the heathen who capture men, women and children on the right. The Gentiles from the left kill some of Abraham's descendants, but keep others. The Gentiles burn the Temple and plunder the holy things within it. In reaction, Abraham cries out,

> Eternal One, the people you received from me are being robbed by the hordes of the heathen. They are killing some and holding others as aliens, and they burned the Temple with fire and they are stealing and destroying the beautiful things which are in it. Eternal Mighty One! If this is so, why now have you afflicted my heart and why will it be so? (*Apoc. Abr.* 27.4–6).

Just as Abraham poignantly cries out to God, so does the author and so do the readers. Why has God allowed the descendants of Abraham to be killed and imprisoned, and why has the Temple been destroyed? God answers, 'Listen, Abraham, all that you have seen will happen on account of your seed who will (continually) provoke me because of the body [statue] which you saw and the murder in what was depicted in the Temple of jealousy, and everything you saw will be so' (*Apoc. Abr.* 27.7).

Thus, the descendants of Abraham will be punished because of their idolatry and the murder depicted in the Temple. This burning of the Temple because of idolatry parallels the burning of Terah's house because of his idolatry in the narrative section (8.6).

Abraham asks how long his descendants will remain in the condition that God has shown him (*Apoc. Abr.* 28.1–2). God replies in symbolic terms, indicating that their situation will remain for hundreds of years to come (28.3–5). Abraham's concern is that of the Jews who live just after the destruction of the Temple. They want to know how long they will be without a Temple and how long they will have to bear Gentile reproach.

Once again, Abraham is told to 'look down at the picture' (*Apoc. Abr.* 29.4). A man comes out from the left, the heathen side. A great crowd from the left side follows and worships the man. Those from the right, the Jewish side, either insult, strike, or worship the same man. Azazel runs up, kisses and stands behind him.

Abraham asks for the identity of the man (*Apoc. Abr.* 29.4–7). The interpretation of the man in the vision is that he is the

> liberation from the heathen for the people who will be (born) from you. In the last days…I will set up this man from your tribe, the one whom you have seen from my people. All will imitate him…(you) consider him as one called by me…(they) are changed in their counsels. And those you saw coming out from the left side of the picture and worshiping him, this (means that) many of the heathen will trust in him. And those of your seed you saw on the right side…many of them shall be offended because of him (*Apoc. Abr.* 29.8–13).

Scholars of the *Apocalypse of Abraham* have usually understood 29.8–13 to be a Christian interpolation.[28] Robert G. Hall has noted that when the passage is viewed as a Christian interpolation, 'certain features of the interpretation conflict with the vision'.[29] Firstly, in the vision the man comes from the heathen side of the picture (29.3), while in the interpretation he comes from the right side, the side of the descendants of Abraham (29.9). Secondly, in the vision, the man is in league with Azazel. However, in the interpretation he is to be recognized as one called by God who brings deliverance (29.8), implying that he is a saviour figure.[30] Because the features that conform to Christian doctrine appear in the interpretation (he is insulted (29.12), he is a son of Abraham, he brings salvation), Hall contends that the vision is original (29.3–7) and the interpretation is the Christian interpolation (29.8–13).

The man spoken of serves to continue the theme of idolatry connected with Azazel.[31] It is this man whom the Gentiles worship and who separates the Jews who worship him from those who do not. The test of the mysterious man cuts short the age of impiety because the 'test purges the seed of Abraham by separating the idolatrous from the loyal Jews and turns God's wrath away from newly righteous Israel toward the newly united Jews and Gentiles under the sway of Azazel.'[32] Those who worship the man actually stumble into idolatry while those who insult him are faithful to God.

God foretells the judgement that will come upon the heathen by means of the ten plagues (*Apoc. Abr.* 29.14–16). From Abraham's seed 'will be left the righteous men in their number, protected by me, who strive in the glory of my name toward the place prepared beforehand for them…' (29.17). Furthermore, they will live 'affirmed by the sacrifices and the gifts of justice and truth in the age of justice. And they will rejoice forever in me, and they will destroy those who have destroyed them, they will rebuke those who have rebuked them through their mockery, and they will spit in their faces' (29.18–19). The new dwelling of Abraham's seed will function in the same way that the previous Temple functioned: as a place of worship and sacrifice to God.[33]

---

28. Rubinkiewicz, 'Translation', p. 694; Box *Apocalypse*, pp. 78–80.

29. Robert G. Hall, 'The "Christian Interpolation" in the *Apocalypse of Abraham*', *JBL* 107 (1988), pp. 107–110 (107).

30. Hall, 'Interpolation', p. 107.

31. Hall, 'Interpolation', p. 108.

32. Hall, 'Interpolation', p. 108.

33. Box, *Apocalypse*, p. 81 n. 6.

Abraham finds himself back on earth, although God is still speaking. God describes the ten plagues at Abraham's request (*Apoc. Abr.* 30.1–8). Finally, God describes the final vindication. He will sound the trumpet; his chosen one will summon God's people who have been humiliated by the heathen. Those who mocked and ruled over God's people are condemned to Gehenna, a place of punishment. Those who kept the commandments will rejoice at the downfall of those who 'followed after the idols and after their murders' (31.5). They are condemned because 'they glorified an alien (god). And they joined one to whom they had not been allotted, and they abandoned the Lord who gave them strength' (31.8).

God predicts that Abraham's descendants will go into an alien land where they will be enslaved; yet, God reassures Abraham that he is also their judge. The apocalypse concludes, "Have you heard, Abraham, what I told you, what your tribe will encounter in the last days?' Abraham, having heard, accepted the words of God in his heart' (32.5–6).

4. *Conclusion: The Function and Significance of Abraham in the* Apocalypse of Abraham

For the author of the *Apocalypse of Abraham*, Israel's culminating sin was idolatry. In the text, the reader is shown God's perspective on the destruction of the Temple, which was a recent event. This harsh judgement was because of the idolatry of Israel. God judged the idolatry of Israel with the same severity that he judged the idolatry of Terah found in the narrative section – both houses of idolatry were burned.

While Abraham is not explicitly associated with the Mosaic Law in the *Apocalypse of Abraham*, he does receive revelation from God on Mt. Horeb/Mt. Sinai. Whether or not this is significant is not clear. However, the author clearly reveals Abraham as rejecting idols and believing in the one, Creator God. Abraham provided a contrast both to the idolatry of Terah and of Israel. Unlike Terah, Abraham chose not to worship idols. Similarly, Abraham provides an example that was in opposition to that of the priests who were idolaters after the example of Manasseh, who provided the paradigm of idolatry that led to catastrophic destruction. In contrast to the priests, whom the author considered to be idolaters, and even in contrast to those who worshipped the man from 'among the heathen', because of his abhorrence of idolatry and his belief in the one God, Abraham was the example of the true person of God.

The author of the *Apocalypse of Abraham* was concerned with the crisis of the destruction of the Temple by the Romans. He wanted to show that ultimately the people of God would be vindicated over their hostile oppressors. The identity of the people of God and their hope for deliverance rested in their maintaining faithfulness to the one Creator God, after the example of their forefather Abraham.

Thus, Abraham again functions to identify who are the true people of God. As the author portrayed him, Abraham is the point of division between Gentiles and his descendants and also the point where God divides Gentiles into those who were before Abraham and those who came later. Presumably this is because of Abraham's rejection of idolatry and his association with monotheism: it is this which divides Gentiles from Abraham's descendants and which brings harsher judgement upon those Gentiles who do not believe in Abraham's God. And in the case of the mysterious 'man' about which the author speaks, those Jews and Gentiles who follow him are actually following an idol and are in league with Azazel. They will be cut off and destroyed.

Thus, the rejection of idolatry for monotheism after the example of Abraham is the ultimate and distinctive criterion for those who are faithful to God. It is noteworthy that in the midst of the pervasive idolatry that the author perceived around him, Abraham was chosen to represent those who rejected idolatry and remained faithful to God. Collins notes that although apocalypses were pseudonymous, the 'pseudonym had to be appropriate for the subject matter'.[34] Thus, the author and presumably his readers saw Abraham as the appropriate patriarch to address this problem. Perhaps the author saw the offering of sacrifices in the Temple on behalf of the Roman emperor or the gifts and sacrifices brought to the Temple by Gentiles as idolatry. Perhaps it was the association of the Temple officials with such practices that meant they too were idolaters in his mind. In any event, they are portrayed as idolaters in contrast to Abraham the true monotheist.

Thus, the identity of the true person of God is based upon the rejection of idolatry in whatever form and loyalty to the one God of Israel. Those who follow after the example of Abraham can expect great reward. However, those who do not follow Abraham's example, participating in idolatrous practices and forsaking the monotheistic foundation of Jewish religion, bring about their own destruction.

34. Collins, *Imagination*, p. 31.

Chapter 7

GALATIANS: WHO IS THE TRUE MONOTHEIST?

1. *Introduction: Moving from Early Judaism to Paul*

Although the authors wrote in different circumstances and political situations, the same traditions about Abraham continued to reappear in the early Jewish literature that we studied in previous chapters. These traditions were Abraham's discernment of the one God from the natural phenomena, his rejection of idolatry and his obedience to the law. The traditions about Abraham found in this literature span both Palestinian and Diaspora Jewish communities over a period of close to 300 years.

While I am aware that a definitively normative Judaism did not exist during the time of Paul, the texts do provide evidence of what being a child of Abraham meant for certain Jews. Because the portrayal of Abraham often reveals most clearly what an author is trying to say, Abraham as portrayed in Jewish literature serves as a cipher from which one is able to understand the discourse and expected behaviour of the ideal people of God. The authors used Abraham to support their own definitions of what it meant to be an ideal Jew, from the composers of *Jubilees* to Philo.

In his discussion of Jewish attitudes toward the Gentiles, T. Donaldson uses a kind of 'criterion of multiple attestation': 'if an approach to the Gentiles is documented in more than one sociological strand of Judaism, and in time periods both before and after that of Paul, I have taken it to be one of the live options in Paul's own situation'.[1] While the author of this study is primarily interested in how Jews understood themselves as children of Abraham, certainly multiple attestation exists before and after the time of Paul of the connection in Jewish discourse between Abraham, monotheism and the law. This connection also exists in a variety of strands of Judaism, from more nationalistic Judaism, as seen in *Jubilees*, to more assimilationist Judaism, as seen in the works of Josephus and Philo. Given these factors, I have taken these traditions about Abraham to be a live option in Paul's own situation.

As we approach the letters of Paul, we will ask the following questions: (1) How may Paul's opponents in Galatia and the 'weak' in Romans have used Abraham to define God's people? (2) Did Paul use or respond to the traditions of Abraham described above and if so, how? (3) How does Paul use Abraham to

---

1.   Terence L. Donaldson, *Paul and the Gentiles: Remapping the Apostle's Convictional World* (Minneapolis: Fortress Press, 1997), p. 51.

define the identity of the people of God in Christ? (4) How does knowledge of popular traditions about Abraham add to our understanding of the changes in identity that Paul perceives are necessary for the people of God in Christ?

2. *Paul's Opponents in Galatia*

a. *Parameters of the Debate*
From the letter itself one finds evidence of conflict in the community of believers in Galatia (1.6–7; 3.1; 5.7–8). The conflict apparently arose because of the confusion caused by those whom Paul perceives as his opponents (cf. Gal. 1.6–9, 10; 5.7–12). Who exactly Paul's opponents were has been a matter of much debate. Howard contends 'the opponents were Jewish Christian Judaizers supported by the apostles at Jerusalem…who believed that Paul, like them, taught the necessity of circumcision and the law for salvation and were totally unaware of his non-circumcision gospel'.[2] Lightfoot maintained that the opponents were Jewish Christian Judaizers, probably from Jerusalem, who were 'either abusing a commission actually received from the Apostles of the Circumcision, or assuming an authority which had never been conferred upon them'.[3] Others have believed that the opponents were succumbing to external pressure from the Zealots, that the opponents were actually two groups – Judaizers and libertines – that they were syncretists, that they were Gentile Judaizers who misunderstood Paul, that they were Jewish Christian Gnostics, or that they represented a Law-observant mission among Gentiles but not in reaction to Paul's gospel.[4]

Many scholars have noted that Abraham is central to Paul's argument in Galatians and must have been central to the arguments of Paul's opponents.[5] J.C.

2.   G. Howard, *Paul, Crisis in Galatia: A Study in Early Christian Theology* (SNTSMS, 35; New York: Cambridge University Press, 1979), p. 2.
3.   J.B. Lightfoot, *St. Paul's Epistle to the Galatians* (London: Macmillan and Co., 1884), p. 29.
4.   See, respectively, R. Jewett, 'The Agitators and the Galatian Congregation', *NTS* 17 (1971) 198–212 (205); H. Ropes, *The Singular Problem of the Epistle to the Galatians* (Cambridge, MA: Harvard University Press, 1929), p. 23; F.R. Crownfield, 'The Singular Problem of the Dual Galatians', *JBL* 64 (1945), pp. 491–500 (493); Munck, *Paul and the Salvation of Mankind* (trans. F. Clark; London: SCM Press, 1959), p. 89; W. Schmithals, 'Die Häretiker in Galatien', *ZNW* 47 (1956), pp. 25–66; see a brief review of the history of the interpretation of Paul's opponents in Robert Keith Rapa, *The Meaning of 'Works of the Law' in Galatians and Romans* (Studies in Biblical Literature, 31; New York: Peter Lang, 2001), pp. 84–89.
5.   J. Barclay, *Jews in the Mediterranean Diaspora: From Alexander to Trajan* (323 BCE–117 CE) (Edinburgh: T. & T. Clark, 1996), p. 387; C.T. Rhyne, *Faith Establishes the Law* (SBLDS, 55; Chico, CA: Scholars Press, 1981), pp. 193–235; R.B. Hays, *The Faith of Jesus Christ: An Investigation of the Narrative Substructure of Galatians 3:1–4:11* (SBLDS, 56; Chico, CA: Scholars Press, 1983), p. 56; on the centrality of Abraham in the arguments of Paul's opponents, see G. Walter Hansen, *Abraham in Galatians: Epistolary and Rhetorical Contexts* (JSNTSup, 29; Sheffield: Sheffield Academic Press, 1989), p. 172, cf. 262 n. 32; C.K. Barrett, 'The Allegory of Abraham, Sarah and Hagar in the Argument of Galatians', in J. Friedrich, W. Pöhlman and P. Stuhlmacher (eds.), *Rechtfertigung* (Festschrift E. Käsemann; Göttingen: Vandenhoeck & Ruprecht, 1976), pp. 1–16.

Beker believes that Paul's opponents were those who thought that the turning of the Gentiles to Christ was not enough. In order to be sure of God's blessing upon them and of their status as true children of Abraham, they had to observe the Torah fully. Abraham therefore played a central role in the theology of Paul's opponents.[6]

B.H. Brinsmead maintains that the opponents' argument revolved around the 'apologetic' Abraham.[7] What exactly Brinsmead means by the 'apologetic' Abraham is not altogether clear. He refers to the Hellenistic portrayal of Abraham as the 'philosopher-king, astronomer and father of all culture' and his enforced emigration from Chaldaea because of his beliefs in the Creator God.[8] Brinsmead also describes Abraham giving sciences to the Egyptians, and the link between Abraham and natural and cosmic law.[9] For Brinsmead, the opponents used the 'apologetic' Abraham because these traditions would have appealed to the Gentile Galatians.

John Barclay points out that it was highly probable that the opponents in Galatia 'argued from Scripture using, in particular, the Abraham narratives'.[10] He later states, 'Abraham represented both the beginning and the foundation of Judaism, and this made him a key figure in the representation of Judaism to outsiders'.[11] Having established the variety of views of Paul's Galatian opponents, we will now turn to the biblical text.

b. *Evidence of the Opponents: Gal. 1 and 4*
While we shall keep Barclay's warnings about faulty 'mirror-reading' from the Galatians text in mind, we must look to the letter in order to gain what information we can about the message of Paul's opponents in Galatia.[12] We find some information about Paul's opponents early in the letter. Because he believes that they have been preaching a 'different gospel' (1.8–9), it is most likely that these opponents were Christians. It is also likely that they were undermining Paul's credentials as an apostle and thus his gospel as evidenced by his vigorous defence of his call as being from God and not the apostles in Jerusalem (1.1, 11, 17–19) and his apostolic status being equal to those in Jerusalem (2.6–10; 11–14).

In other sections of the letter, we discover that the opponents particularly promoted circumcision, which they considered to be the 'condition *sine qua non* for salvation' (6.12–13, 15 cf. 5.2–6) along with calendrical requirements

---

6. J.C. Beker, *Paul the Apostle: The Triumph of God in Life and Thought* (Philadelphia: Fortress Press, 1980), pp. 42–44.

7. B.H. Brinsmead, *Galatians: Dialogical Response to Opponents* (SBLDS, 65; Chico, CA: Scholars Press, 1982), p. 114.

8. Brinsmead, *Response*, p. 112.

9. Brinsmead, *Response*, p. 112.

10. J. Barclay, 'Mirror-Reading a Polemical Letter: Galatians as a Test Case', *JSNT* 31 (1987), pp. 73–93 (88).

11. J. Barclay, *Obeying the Truth: A Study of Paul's Ethics in Galatians* (Edinburgh: T. & T. Clark, 1988), p. 54.

12. Barclay, 'Mirror-Reading', pp. 73–93.

(Gal. 4.8–11).[13] However, we also must ask if other clues exist in the letter that can tell us more about those who were 'preaching another gospel' particularly as that gospel related to Abraham.

Paul's final discourse on Abraham is found in his allegory of Sarah and Hagar in 4.21–5.1. We begin with this passage because Gal. 4.21–5.1 is the passage in which Paul faces most openly and explicitly the existence of those who are advocating the obedience of law for his Gentile converts.[14] Paul has just admitted his perplexity concerning the Galatians (4.20) and now he provides them with a pointed example upon which they must act. The rather wandering exegesis through which he finally reaches the point he wants to make indicates that this is not Paul's choice of text. He probably felt it necessary to use Hagar, Sarah and Isaac in his argument as he does because his opponents used a similar argument to their own advantage.[15]

Paul's central concern here is one of self-identification; he wants to define who Abraham's true children are.[16] Paul constructs his allegory around the literal sons of Abraham, Isaac and Ishmael. In contrast to the argument that the opponents were probably making which associated Sarah with the Mosaic Law, Hagar now represents the law. By showing how the believers in Galatia are actually sons of Abraham's 'free woman' (Sarah; 3.22–23) Paul is not only proving to the Galatians that they are true sons of Abraham through promise (4.23, 28) but he is concurrently proving to them that the opponents are not true sons. Anyone (even those at Jerusalem, 4.25b) who is in bondage to the law (4.24b) is actually enslaved and will not inherit with the true sons. The children of promise, who are born of Isaac (4.28), are members of the heavenly Jerusalem (4.26). Additionally, the children of promise are more numerous than those in bondage (4.27b).

Paul provides his conclusion to the allegory in 4.28–5.1. He identifies the Galatians as being like Isaac, the children of promise (4.28). At the present time, the persecution that they are experiencing is like the persecution that Isaac experienced at the hand of Ishmael (Gen. 21.9; Gal. 4.29). Although the tradition of Ishmael persecuting Isaac is not actually found in the Hebrew Bible, it is found in the Jewish *haggadah*, where Gen. 21.9 ('he jested, played, teased') was interpreted in a hostile way.[17]

Paul next uses Gen. 21.10 as instruction for the present time: the Galatians who are being persecuted for not being obedient to the law should 'cast out' those who are persecuting them (4.30).[18] They are children of the free woman;

13. Jewett, 'Agitators', p. 200.
14. See also J.L. Martyn, *Galatians: A New Translation with Introduction and Commentary* (AB, 33A; New York: Doubleday, 1997), pp. 455–56.
15. See also A.T. Lincoln, *Paradise Now and Not Yet: Studies in the Role of the Heavenly Dimension in Paul's Thought with Special Reference to his Eschatology* (repr., Grand Rapids, MI: Baker Book House, 1991), p. 12; Barclay, *Obeying*, p. 91; Barrett, 'Allegory', pp. 10, 15.
16. See also Richard N. Longenecker, *Galatians* (WBC, 41; Dallas, TX: Word Books, 1990), p. 219.
17. See H.D. Betz, *Galatians: A Commentary on Paul's Letter to the Churches in Galatia* (Hermeneia; Philadelphia: Fortress Press, 1979), pp. 249–50.
18. Lincoln, *Paradise*, pp. 27–29.

Christ has set them free from the law. They are commanded not to submit again to the law, the 'yoke of slavery' (5.1; see also 4.3, 9).

Paul not only does not associate Abraham with the law, but to be 'under the law' (4.21) disqualifies one from being a true son of Abraham; to be under the law is to be enslaved. Paul reasserts a point he made earlier in the text: the true sons of Abraham are children of the promise (3.8, 16–18, 26–29; 4.26–28) that has been fulfilled in Jesus Christ (3.16, 29; 5.1). The allegory illustrates Paul's strategy found elsewhere in the epistle where Paul attempts to show that the Galatians' attraction to circumcision and the law will achieve the very opposite of their intentions.[19] In 4.21–5.1, Paul shows his readers that by maintaining obedience to the law, they are not acting as sons of promise and they are actually no longer true sons of Abraham.

To Paul, those who are 'of the law' must have considered themselves to be the true sons of Abraham and were using this against the Galatian Gentile believers (4.29). It is most likely that they were Jewish Christians, or perhaps more correctly, Christian Jews.[20] Paul asserts, according to historical fact (cf. 3.15–18) and most likely to their angered surprise, that they are actually 'enslaved' (4.25) sons of Ishmael who will not 'inherit' (4.30) with the very believers they are persecuting. These opponents may even have been using the slogan 'Jerusalem is our mother' to support their agenda.[21] If this is the case, Paul's reinterpretation is even more pointedly radical. The present Jerusalem is earthly in contrast to the future Jerusalem that is 'above' (4.25–26). It is the present, earthly Jerusalem that is actually enslaved, and those who are her children are enslaved with her (4.26). The future, heavenly Jerusalem is the actual mother of the children of promise (4.22, 26–28). Here as elsewhere in the letter (as we shall see) Paul invokes an eschatological view of the crisis in Galatia as part of his case against those who would instruct his Gentile converts in Galatia to obey the Mosaic Law.

It is likely that Paul is responding to teaching on the part of the opponents in which Abraham and his progeny were shown to be obedient to the law.[22] In this case, the opponents would probably have said that since Abraham and his son Isaac were obedient to the law, the people of God are those who observe the law, particularly circumcision (cf. Gen. 17.9–14; 23–27; 21.4). As Jewett notes, 'In the light of the fact that Paul devoted a main portion of his argument to the question about the true sons of Abraham, it is likely that the agitators argued for circumcision on grounds that entrance into the elect spiritual community demanded prior admission into Abraham's covenant through circumcision'.[23] Given the strong traditions of Abraham discussed in earlier chapters as the proselyte who rejected idolatry for monotheistic faith and obedience to the law, it would not be

19. Barclay, *Obeying*, p. 91.
20. See also, for example, Robert Keith Rapa, *'Works of the Law'*, pp. 93–94.
21. Barclay, *Obeying*, p. 59; Lincoln, *Paradise*, p. 17; Jewett, 'Agitators', pp. 200–201.
22. See also Martyn, *Galatians*, p. 450.
23. Jewett, 'Agitators', p. 200.

surprising that Paul's opponents who were preaching to the Christian community in Galatia saw that Gentile obedience to law in addition to faith is crucial to their inclusion in the people of God.

c. *Paul's Opponents and the 'works of the law'*

While the purpose of this volume is not to discuss various approaches to Paul and the law, my argument depends in part upon the approach called the 'new perspective' on Paul. Based upon the work of E.P. Sanders, the concept of the law as understood within the framework of covenantal nomism has become popular among Pauline scholars in recent decades. In *Paul and Palestinian Judaism*, Sanders endeavoured to compare Judaism and Christianity holistically and to destroy the view of rabbinic Judaism that was prevalent in much of New Testament scholarship. After surveying Tannaitic, Pseudepigraphical and Apocalyptic literature as well the Dead Sea Scrolls, Sanders maintained that the view that post-biblical Judaism degenerated 'into the idea of petty legalism, according to which one had to earn the mercy of God by minute observance of irrelevant ordinances' was greatly mistaken.[24] Instead, Sanders proposed from the literature studied that '*obedience maintains one's position in the covenant, but it does not earn God's grace as such.* It simply keeps an individual in the group that is the recipient of God's grace'.[25] For him, the key phrase that described post-biblical Judaism was 'covenantal nomism'.[26]

James Dunn built upon Sander's theories, particularly in his ongoing work on the significance of Paul's use of the phrase 'works of the law'. For Dunn, these 'works of the law' 'marked out the distinction between the chosen nation and all others (= Gentiles). And by observing these laws, religious Jews maintained the boundary between Israel and the other nations'.[27] For the typical Jew of the first century, in order to participate in God's covenant and in God's covenant righteousness, one had to observe these 'works of the law'. Thus, Paul did not understand 'works of the law' as legalism that Christians could overcome through justification by faith, but as 'badges' like circumcision and food laws that marked out Jews as God's chosen people and its status as the nation of God.

Dunn based his argument in part on Gal. 2.15–16, where Paul states, 'We ourselves are Jews by birth and not Gentile sinners; yet we know that a person is justified not by the works of the law but through faith in Jesus Christ. And we have come to believe in Jesus Christ, so that we might be justified by faith in Christ, and not by doing the works of the law, because no one will be justified by

---

24. E.P. Sanders, *Paul and Palestinian Judaism* (repr., Philadelphia: Fortress Press, 1983), p. 419, see also p. 550.
25. Sanders, *Palestinian Judaism*, p. 420.
26. Sanders, *Palestinian Judaism*, p. 422.
27. James D.G. Dunn, 'Noch Einmal "Works of the Law": The Dialogue Continues', in Ismo Dunderberg, Christopher Tuckett and Kari Syreeni (eds.), *Fair Play: Diversity and Conflicts in Early Christianity* (Festschrift Heikki Räisänen; NovTSup, 103; Leiden/Boston/Cologne: E.J. Brill, 2002), pp. 273–90 (277).

works of the law'. What is striking about this text is that Paul is speaking from the standpoint of one who is Jewish: 'we ourselves are Jews by birth'. Paul contrasts his Jewish status with the Gentiles whom he labels as 'sinners'. From what we have seen previously in chapters on Abraham and the law, the Gentiles were perceived as 'sinners' primarily because of their idolatrous beliefs and their lack of adherence to the law. Thus the great divide: those who were Jewish saw themselves as within God's covenant, and the law maintained their status as the people of God. Gentiles, however, were outside of the people of God because of their lack of faith and lack of obedience to the law. Their lawless conduct marked them as separate from the Jews, outside the covenant and as destined for destruction (cf. *Jub.* 23.23–24).

Strikingly, Paul further states, 'we know that a person is justified not by the works of the law'. This is also spoken from one Christian Jew to another. It speaks of what they had already known; the law in and of itself did not justify them. Justification by faith is 'not a distinctively Christian teaching. Paul's appeal here is not to *Christians* who happen also to be Jews, but to *Jews* whose Christian faith is but an extension of their faith in a graciously electing and sustaining God'.[28] As Paul will explain later, in the fullness of time Jesus Christ came in order that by faith in Christ both Jews and Gentiles could be members of God's people by faith (3.23–29). However, Jews never earned justification by works of the law.

What then does Paul mean by 'works of the law', a phrase he uses three times in 2.15–16? If the Jews did not see themselves as justified by their obedience to the law, to what does Paul refer? Dunn suggests that the context of the passage speaks to what Paul has in mind. In the Antioch incident, Peter separated himself from eating with Gentiles when those from James arrived (2.12). Thus, the conflict at Antioch was over food laws. In his earlier discussion of conflict in Jerusalem (2.1–10), the problem arose over circumcision. Thus, it appears that, as Dunn suggests, Paul intends his readers to think of particular observances of law, such as circumcision and food laws.

From the viewpoint of Greco-Romans, observances such as food laws and circumcision were viewed as characteristically Jewish. For example, in the first century BCE, Horace spoke in such a way as to characterize the keeping of the Sabbath and circumcision as distinctively Jewish practices.[29] In the first century CE, Petronius characterized the Jews by their practising circumcision and avoiding pork.[30] In the late first century CE, Tacitus mentions Romans who become Jewish proselytes as those who adopt circumcision while alienating themselves from their families.[31]

---

28. J.D.G. Dunn, 'The New Perspective on Paul', in *BJRL* 65.2 (1983), pp. 95–122 (106).

29. *Sat.* 1.9.67–72.

30. *Satyricon* 102.14; *Satyricon* Fragment 371.

31. *Hist.* 5.5; see also multiple examples in Molly Whittaker, *Jews and Christians: Greco-Roman Views* (Cambridge Commentaries on Writings of the Jewish & Christian World 200 BC to AD 200, 6; Cambridge: Cambridge University Press, 1984), esp. pp. 63–130.

Thus, the Jews were seen in the Greco-Roman world as identified, at least in part, by these practices. As we have also seen in earlier chapters, the Jews identified themselves to a large degree by these practices as well. A Jew in Paul's time would have seen these practices as essential to participating in God's covenant righteousness. It is no wonder that Paul's opponents taught that in order to continue to participate in God's covenant righteousness, believers in Christ – even Gentiles – still needed to observe these practices.

'Works of the law', then, are rendered superfluous in the face of Paul's conviction that faith is now the primary identity marker of the people of God. Thus, membership in the covenant can no longer be seen in terms of what specifically defined Jews. Those who are the people of God are no longer defined in national or racial terms. Dunn believes that the covenant has been broadened, and that 'God's covenant purpose had reached its intended final stage in which the more fundamental identity marker (Abraham's faith) reasserts its primacy over against the too narrowly nationalistic identity markers of circumcision, food laws, and Sabbath'.[32]

In his book, *What Saint Paul Really Said: Was Paul of Tarsus the Real Founder of Christianity?*, N.T. Wright takes the paradigm of the new perspective a step further. He argues that the centre of Paul's gospel was not justification by faith, although it is implied, but Christ's death, resurrection and exaltation as Lord.[33] For Wright, Israel's destiny and vindication as foretold by the prophets had been achieved in Jesus the Messiah. 'The Age to Come had been inaugurated. Saul...was to declare to the pagan world that YHWH, the God of Israel, was the one true God of the whole world, and that in Jesus...he had overcome evil and was creating a new world in which justice and peace would reign supreme.'[34] Wright holds to a 'covenantal' reading of Paul through which he sees the gospel as 'the announcement of Jesus' lordship, which works with power to bring people into the family of Abraham, now redefined around Jesus Christ and characterised solely by faith in him. "Justification" is the doctrine which insists that all those who have this faith belong as full members of this family, on this basis and no other'.[35] For Wright, in its first-century context, Galatians has to do 'quite obviously with the question of how you *define the people of God*: are they to be defined by the badges of Jewish race, or in some other way?'[36]

For our purposes, what is noteworthy about Dunn's viewpoint is his emphasis on the 'works of the law' as practices which provided the Jews with much of their national identity in the Greco-Roman world, and that according to Paul, these should longer function as the identity markers of the people of God who follow Jesus as Messiah. Both Dunn and Wright also attest to the idea that Paul

---

32. Dunn, 'New Perspective', p. 115.
33. *What Saint Paul Really Said: Was Paul of Tarsus the Real Founder of Christianity?* (Grand Rapids, MI: Eerdmans, 1997), esp. p. 151.
34. Wright, *Founder*, p. 37.
35. Wright, *Founder*, p. 133.
36. Wright, *Founder*, p. 120.

puts forth a new definition of the people of God that has to do with one's relationship to Abraham, ultimately based upon following the example of Abraham's faith. Wright also puts Paul's monotheistic foundation in an eschatological framework; the present became the newly inaugurated age in which God's promise of the inclusion of all nations in the people of the one God have come to pass through Jesus Christ. Keeping these ideas in mind, we will now look at further selections from Gal. 3 and 4.

3. Galatians 3.1–14

In Gal. 3.1–5 Paul begins to define the members of Abraham's family, those who belong to the people of God now that Christ has come. Paul begins by calling the Galatians 'foolish' (3.1, 3), asking them who 'bewitched' (3.1) them into obeying the requirements of the law (3.2, cf. 3.3, 5). He reminds them that it was before their very eyes that he had 'placarded' Christ as crucified (3.1).[37] In subsequent questions, Paul sets up an antithesis between 'works of the law' (ἔργων νόμου) and 'hearing with faith' (ἀκοῆς πίστεως). Did the Galatians receive the Spirit by 'works of law' or by 'hearing with faith' (3.2, 5)? Did God work miracles among them by their doing 'works of the law' or by 'hearing with faith' (3.5)?

In Gal. 3.1–5, Paul alerts his readers to the contrast between hearing with faith and works of the law and thereby persuades them to consider the major error into which they have fallen. Rhetorically speaking, Paul is using the Galatians as eyewitnesses to provide the information inductively.[38] Of course, the anticipated answer is that both the Spirit and miracles were supplied because of hearing with faith rather than works of the law, particularly circumcision, which was accomplished 'in the flesh' (3.3).

Paul answers his own rhetorical questions by citing from Gen. 15.6: Καθὼς Ἀβραὰμ ἐπίστευσεν τῷ θεῷ, καὶ ἐλογίσθη αὐτῷ εἰς δικαιοσύνην ('just as Abraham believed God and it was reckoned to him as righteousness', 3.6). Byrne points out that the use of Καθὼς ('just as') implies that what follows corresponds to what has just been described.[39] Abraham becomes the one who believed in God, and by God's action, was reckoned righteous. This corresponds to the Spirit supplied by God because of the faith of the Galatian believers. The receiving of the Spirit by the Galatian believers is parallel to the righteousness that Abraham received (3.2, cf. Gal. 3.14). It is a sign that they are members of God's people.

Given Paul's statements about the law in passages such as 3.17–20 (see below), the opponents to whom Paul is replying in his passage were probably citing Abraham as the foundational example of faith plus obedience to the Mosaic Law before it was given. Paul does not try to refute their argument using Gen. 17, but

37. Lightfoot, *Galatians*, pp. 24, 133–34.
38. Betz, *Galatians*, p. 130.
39. Brendan Byrne, *Son of God – 'Seed of Abraham': A Study of the Idea of the Sonship of God of All Christians in Paul against the Jewish Background* (AnBib, 83; Rome: Biblical Institute Press, 1979), p. 148; *BDAG* 'καθὼς', pp. 493–96.

depends upon Gen. 15.6, capitalizing on the more foundational issue of faith. Rapa suggests 'Paul is reminding the Galatians that Abraham is the norm (in the sense of "pattern" or "standard') for all who are of faith and it is faith that replicates Abraham's faith that brings righteousness before God'.[40]

The larger and underlying issue is Abraham's faith. Paul uses πίστις or πιστεύω or their variations eight times in 3.6–14. One might be tempted to say that in Gal. 3.6 Paul refers to Abraham's faith in one God. While in some cases πιστεύω can mean the substance of faith rather than a personal commitment of trust, in Gal. 3.6 it is clear particularly from the literary context that ἐπίστευσεν τῷ θεῷ refers to Abraham's faith that God will accomplish what he has promised (cf. 3.16, 19).[41] Yet given the popularity of the Jewish tradition in which Abraham is portrayed as the first monotheist, one is left wondering if Abraham's monotheistic faith plays any part in Paul's argument.

As we have seen in earlier chapters, other Jewish authors of the time perceived Abraham's faith as monotheistic. Josephus and the authors of the *Apocalypse of Abraham* and the *Liber Antiquitatum Biblicarum* were obviously aware of this tradition.[42] Although he was interested in a more philosophical and intellectual faith than Paul, Philo interpreted Gen. 15:6 to mean that Abraham believed in the one Creator God in contrast to other gods or philosophies. In *On the Virtues*, Philo describes Abraham by saying, '…he is spoken of as the first person to believe in God (πιστεῦσαι λέγεται τῷ θεῷ πρῶτος), since he first grasped a firm and unswerving conception of the truth that there is one Cause above all and that it provides for the world and all that there is therein'.[43] Here again, as in Gal. 3.6, πιστεύω is used with the dative τῷ θεῷ. For Philo, Abraham is the first one to be spoken of as believing in God.

We find another indication that Abraham's monotheism is key to the opponents' argument when Paul later argues vociferously that Abraham could not have been obedient to the Mosaic Law (3.15–18) as if he were arguing against a tradition that his opponents were using. Here we must remember that in the view of Jews, in order to be obedient to the Mosaic Law, one needed to believe in the God of Israel in the first place. As the model of the first proselyte, Abraham would hardly have been perceived as obedient to law unless he was also a monotheist. As we have seen in much of the Jewish literature already discussed, monotheism necessitated obedience to the law, but the law would not have been necessary without monotheistic faith. N.T. Wright expresses this concept well when he states:[44]

40. Rapa, *Works of the Law*, p. 157.
41. See 4 Macc. 5.25; 7.18–19 and the discussion in Dennis R. Lindsay, *Josephus and Faith: Πίστις and Πιστεύειν as Faith Terminology in the Writings of Flavius Josephus and in the New Testament* (AGJU, 19; Leiden/New York: E.J. Brill, 1993), p. 184. See also *BDAG*, 'πιστεύω', pp. 816–18.
42. See *Ant.* 1.155–156; *Apoc. Abr.* 7.10; *LAB* 6.4, 23.5; See also the discussion on Philo's use of Gen. 15.6 in Lindsay, *Πίστις*, pp. 184–85.
43. *Virt.* 216.
44. *The New Testament and the People of God* (*Christian Origins and the Question of God*, I; Minneapolis: Fortress Press, 1992), p. 246; see also Hilda Hollis, 'The Phrase "God is One" in the

> Underneath the basic Jewish praxis there lies the belief that Israel is the people of the creator God. If this were not so, the *halakah* would lose its point, or at least radically change its character. If one said to an articulate first-century Jew, 'Why do you keep Torah?' the ultimate answer would be 'Because I am part of Israel, the chosen people of the creating and redeeming god'. For the question and answer to run the other way would be irreducibly odd: 'Why do you believe in the creating and redeeming god?' 'Because I keep Torah'. The fact of the creating and redeeming god is the greater whole, which gives meaning and purpose to the individual expression.

In using Abraham to discuss the contrast of faith versus works, Paul is using Abraham in a new way. Previously, Abraham's faith and his works have been seen together. For example, in *Jubilees*, Abraham is not only the first to separate from his family and worship the one Creator God (*Jub.* 11.16–17; 12.16–21), but he also observes stipulations of the Mosaic Law such as the Feast of Tabernacles (*Jub.* 16.20–31; cf. *Jub.* 22.1–2). In Philo's works, Abraham is portrayed as following the natural law. To Philo, the law of nature and the Law of Moses are identical. Only law that was revealed by God, the creator of nature, can really be in accordance with natural law. Abraham not only followed the natural law, but Philo states, 'For "he [Abraham] journeyed just as the Lord spake to him": the meaning of this is that as God speaks – and He speaks with consummate beauty and excellence – so the good man does everything, blamelessly keeping straight the path of life, so that the actions of the wise man are nothing else than the words of God. So in another place He says, "Abraham did all My law"' (*Migr. Abr.* 129–130; cf. Gen. 26.5; Sir. 44.19–20). Even in the works of Josephus, Abraham's faith in the one Creator God and his obedience to law are combined. For Josephus, following the law is conforming to the will of God. Abraham conforms to God's will laudably, particularly in his attempted sacrifice of his son, Isaac (*Ant.* 1. 225–236).

It may also be that Paul's opponents have anchored their arguments for obedience to the law in the traditions of Abraham's monotheistic faith. For the opponents, although faith was not enough, it was the foundational criterion for Abraham's status as father of their elect nation. Martyn points out that the opponents would have included the tradition of Abraham the monotheist in their preaching, saying, 'It all began with Abraham. Looking beyond the fascinating movement of the heavenly bodies, he was the first to discern that there is but one God. Because of that perception, he turned from the service of dumb idols to the worship of that true God. Therefore, God made him the father of our great nation Israel'.[45] However, the opponents included the law and as such excluded those Gentiles whose faith in Christ alone was not adequate in their eyes for membership in the family of Abraham. As Vincent Smiles puts it, 'In the opponents' thinking Gentiles as *Gentiles* are necessarily excluded from

New Testament: A Study of Romans 3:30, Galatians 3:20, and James 2:19' (Unpublished MA thesis, McGill University Faculty of Religious Studies, 1985), pp. 55, 57.

45. Martyn, *Galatians*, p. 303; see also Hollis, 'God is One', pp. 26, 84–95; David De Silva, 'Why did God Chose Abraham?', *BR* (June, 2000), pp. 17–21, 42–44.

God's elect'.[46] Thus for the opponents, the Gentiles who were not obedient to the law were not members of the people of God.

In Gal. 3.7, Paul commands the Galatian believers to recognize from his proof in 3.6 that 'it is the people of faith who are the sons of Abraham'. From the standpoint of the tradition of Abraham as the man of faith in the true God, Paul's scriptural proof (3.6–7) for the descendants of Abraham being those who have faith in the same God would ring true. However, as mentioned above, Paul is unique in that he is beginning to define this faith in contrast to works, and this is where the similarity between Paul and other Jewish traditions about Abraham ends.

Paul again uses Scripture to back up his claim that the sons of Abraham are those who have faith in God. In Gal. 3.8–9 he states, 'And the Scriptures, seeing that God would justify the Gentiles by faith, declared the gospel beforehand to Abraham saying "All the Gentiles will be blessed in you."' Paul understands the promise to Abraham that he would be a blessing to the nations (Gentiles; Gen. 12.3; 18.18) as the anticipatory preaching of the gospel to Abraham.[47] Because justification was by faith and Gentiles were then included in the people of God through justification by that faith alone without adherence to the 'badges' of Jewish nationalism, the announcement of the blessing of Gentiles through Abraham was in anticipation of the gospel of Jesus Christ. As Davis suggests, Abraham's 'promise is eschatological in nature; these blessings were yet to come.[48]

In the meantime Paul picks up the other thread of his argument, the 'works of the law' (Gal. 3.10). In Gal. 3.10–13, Paul argues that obedience to law does not bring righteousness; this is not the way that one becomes a member of God's people. In fact, according to Morland, the reader of Galatians who perhaps would have been shocked by Paul's use of *anathema* twice in 1.8–9 for those who preach contrary to his gospel would inevitably have connected it with the curse in 3.10: 'all who rely on the works of the law are under a curse'. The crimes are similar in both verses: 'To preach against the gospel (1.8–9) may be equated with a life based on the works of the law (3.10a)'.[49]

However, what is the reason for Paul's pronouncement that those who are under the law are under a curse? If we recall Paul's statement about Christ's delivering them from the 'present evil age' (1.4) he presupposes a paradigm from Jewish eschatological thought that saw world history as divided into two ages: the present age as characterized by sin and evil and the age to come as dominated by glory. Dunn points out, 'The formulation catches the ambiguity of the Chris-

46. Vincent Smiles, *The Gospel and the Law in Galatia: Paul's Response to Jewish Christian Separatism and the Threat of Galatian Apostasy* (Collegeville, MN: Michael Glazier/Liturgical Press, 1998), p. 67.

47. A.T. Hanson, 'Abraham the Justified Sinner', in *Studies in Paul's Technique and Theology* (Grand Rapids: Eerdmans, 1974), pp. 52–66 (64).

48. Stephan K. Davis, *The Antithesis of the Ages: Paul's Reconfiguration of Torah* (CBQMS, 33; Washington, DC: The Catholic Biblical Association of America, 2002), p. 157.

49. Morland, Kjell Arne. *The Rhetoric of Curse in Galatians: Paul Confronts Another Gospel* (Emory Studies in Early Christianity; Atlanta: Scholars Press, 1995), p. 168.

tian situation nicely: as a purposed rescue operation, begun but not yet completed; as still within the "present evil age", but no longer identified with it or ultimately dependent on it'.[50]

In 3.10–13 one hears echoes of Paul's treatment of the two Jerusalems in Gal. 4 as treated above: the present, earthly Jerusalem characterized by law which is enslaved and the future, heavenly Jerusalem which is the mother of the children of promise who are born according to the Spirit (4.24–26, 29; cf. Gal. 3.3). Paul also has eschatological purposes in his treatment of the law in Gal. 3.10–13. After showing how it is that those who are of faith are blessed with Abraham who had faith (v. 9), Paul castigates those who rely on the law. Verse 10a connects with the foregoing verses by means of its first γάρ (for): 'For all who rely on the law are under a curse'. Garlington points out that by virtue of this causative γάρ, Paul suggests that those who live by the works of the law are not blessed with Abraham but instead are cursed because 'they severed their connections with the patriarch by virtue of their preference for the Mosaic period'.[51] The second γάρ in 10b introduces Deut. 27.26, supporting the contention that those of the law are under a curse: ' "Cursed is everyone who does not observe and obey all the things written in the book of the law." ' The context of Deut. 27 is the curses which will fall upon Israel should they not be faithful to the covenant. Whether one is blessed or cursed depends upon this fidelity and obedience. Yet, according to Paul, those who are attempting to persuade the Galatians to obey the law are cursed themselves and, as such, are not among those who are blessed as Abraham is blessed.

By citing Hab. 2.4b in Gal. 3.11, Paul accentuates the other side of his argument; those who are righteous live by faith, not works. This faith characterizes the righteous, or those who are blessed with Abraham (3.6, 9). In Gal. 3.12, Paul uses Lev. 18.5 ('he who does them shall live by them') in order to contrast its description of a mode of life with that found in Hab. 2.4b ('the one who is righteous will live by faith'). The way of life described in Hab. 2.4 is by faith; that described in Lev. 18.5 is by law, and the two are on opposite ends of the spectrum. Garlington points out, 'To say that the law is "not of faith" is to affirm that the law and faith belong to distinctly different historical realms: the former does not occupy in the same turf in the salvation-historical continuum as the latter'.[52] As Longenecker suggests, it is possible that Paul is dealing with the very passages that his opponents used in their message in support of the law.[53] Assuming this is the case, Paul turns their appeal against them.[54]

Finally, using Deut. 21.23 in Gal. 3.13–14, ' "Cursed is everyone who hangs on a tree" – in order that in Christ Jesus the blessing of Abraham might come to the Gentiles', Paul shows that the era of faith has now come through Christ's

50. *The Epistle to the Galatians* (BNTC, 9; Peabody, MA: Hendrickson, 1993), p. 36; see also Longenecker, *Galatians*, pp. 8–9.
51. Don Garlington, 'Role Reversal and Paul's Use of Scripture', *JSNT* 65 (1997), pp. 85–121 (95).
52. Garlington 'Reversal', p. 101.
53. Longenecker, *Galatians*, pp. 116–21, 124.
54. Garlington, 'Reversal', p. 107.

becoming a curse and providing redemption from the curse of the law' (3.13).[55]
One should also remember that Deut. 21.23 occurs in a passage that describes a
son who is rebellious towards his parents and ultimately toward God. The son is
a 'glutton and a drunkard' (21.27) who is finally stoned to death. He represents
the evil that is purged from their midst and serves as an example to all Israel. In
this context it is said that the one who is hanged on a tree was likewise purged
from Israel's midst having been put under God's curse. Garlington points out
that this man was hanged as a 'curse' or 'repudiation' of God not because of an
infringement of an aspect of Torah but 'rather the repudiation of Yahweh
himself, along with his chosen people'.[56] In response, God repudiates the cursed
one, assigning him to a sphere outside of Israel where he is cursed. Thus in the
case of Jesus, Paul casts him as cursed and outside of the people of God.

Thus the background of the cursing, which Paul mentions, is based upon a
repudiation of God and his covenantal law. As the Judaizers encourage the Gentile believers to take on nationalistic aspects of Judaism they, in effect, encourage
the Galatians to remain in the era of the law rather than entering the era of faith
that was first inaugurated by the faith of Abraham and later fulfilled in the reali-
zation of the promises of God. Jesus, who was a cursed outsider, has now provided redemption for those like him who were once considered to be cursed and
outside of the people of God. As Garlington points out, the roles of the Judaizers
and the Gentiles have been reversed. Those who would have expected to be vindicated by works of the law 'as the appropriate arena and expression of their
faith, are now told that they are excluded from the community of salvation: they
are no longer the δίκαιοι who live ἐκ πίστεως; they cannot be justified while
they remain as they are; they are ὑπὸ κατάραν [under a curse] by definition.'[57]

By missing the eschatological cues that the Spirit now guides the people of
God and that the law was only a temporary measure (3.23–26), the Judaizers
have neglected to maintain their fidelity to God. Garlington believes that the
Judaizers have confused doing the law in the former age with doing the law in
the age in Christ. Now doing the law (believing in God and living in obedience
to God) is to have faith in Christ. 'It would be a fair assessment to say that for
Judaism generally God and the Torah were the twofold object of faith: to believe
in the one was *ipso facto* to believe in the other. But over against such a conviction, Paul makes God *in Christ* the focal point of faith(fulness) with no further
qualification.'[58]

Here we have the crux of the matter. It is *God* in Christ who is actually the
focal point. The Galatians are to emulate Abraham who is said to have 'believed
in God'. As we saw above, monotheism was foundational to obedience to the
law, not the other way around. Abraham's faith was in the promises of God that
eventually included the Gentiles. The Judaizers have lost their fidelity to God
because they have not really believed in the God of Abraham. In their zeal to

---

55. Byrne, *Seed*, p. 156.
56. Garlington, 'Reversal', p. 105.
57. Garlington, 'Reversal', p. 112.
58. Garlington, 'Reversal', p. 111.

inculcate the badges of Jewish nationalism, the Judaizers no longer show their faithfulness to the God through whom Gentiles were eventually included in the people of God through Christ. In this new eschatological age, the Judaizers have locked themselves into the old ways that deny true fidelity to the God of Abraham who fulfilled his promise through the inclusion of the Gentiles in the people of God as Gentiles.

What is especially noteworthy in the epistle thus far is that Paul refers to two aspects of Judaism which are also related to the major traditions about Abraham found in early Judaism: faith and law.[59] Paul has argued forcefully against the law; the Gentiles have received the blessing of Abraham, the Spirit, solely according to their faith. Because Paul is using Abraham to argue against observance of the law, it is reasonable to assume that his opponents are using Abraham in their arguments to convince the Gentiles that they must be obedient to the Mosaic Law, and that the opponents are aware of the tradition of Abraham's obedience to the law and probably also the tradition of Abraham's monotheistic faith and are making use of those traditions.[60]

4. *Galatians 3.15–18*

Paul begins the next section with an example from the everyday life of human beings and refers to a person's testament or will (διαθήκη) that is neither annulled nor added to once it has been ratified.[61] He uses this example to discuss Abraham again. Originally, the promises were made to Abraham and to his seed (3.16). Paul proceeds to prove that the offspring to whom the promises were made were not many (σπέρμασιν) but one (σπέρμα), which actually refers to Christ (Gen. 12.7; 22.17–18). Paul is referring to the generic singular in the Abraham promise that, according to Longenecker, was 'always understood within Judaism to refer to the posterity of Abraham as an entity'.[62] Paul plays upon the corporate and individual meaning of 'seed of Abraham'.[63] The one descendant, Christ, not only represents the fulfilment of the promises to Abraham (Gal. 3.8, 14) but also the solidarity of believers.[64]

This interpretation of Christ as the seed who represents the solidarity of believers refutes the exclusive Jewish concept of the seed of Abraham and prepares for the inclusion of the Gentiles in that seed 'in Christ' (3.22, 29). Now it is only 'in Christ' that the Abrahamic blessings are available.[65] According to

---

59. See also Friedrich E. Wieser, *Die Abrahamvorstellungen im Neuen Testament* (Europäische Hochschulschriften 23/317; Bern: Peter Lang, 1987), pp. 41–42.

60. See also Hansen, *Abraham*, p. 172.

61. Betz, *Galatians*, pp. 155.

62. *Galatians*, pp. 131.

63. E.E. Ellis, *The Old Testament in Early Christianity: Canon and Interpretation in the Light of Modern Research* (Tübingen: J.C.B. Mohr, 1991), p. 112.

64. E. DeWitt Burton, *A Critical and Exegetical Commentary on the Epistle to the Galatians* (ICC, 33; Edinburgh: T. & T. Clark, 1921), p. 181; Longenecker, *Galatians*, p. 132.

65. Barclay, *Obeying*, p. 90.

Brendan Byrne, the promise to Abraham and his seed, Christ, will paradoxically 'become a reality with an expansiveness that quite outstrips the purely Jewish perspective'.[66]

According to Paul in Gal. 3.17, the law actually came 430 years after the covenant that God ratified with Abraham. Not only did the law come later, but it also did not annul or change God's earlier, original promise to Abraham (3.16, 17–18). Paul is arguing that the promise made to Abraham is fundamental. Additionally, in 3.19a he states that the law was 'added': it was not eternal but it had a beginning in history after the promise.[67] Those who are children of Abraham 'in Christ' benefit from the promise and inheritance he received before the coming of the law.

If, as was pointed out above, the opponents of Paul in Galatia are using the popular tradition that Abraham obeyed the law, the opponents must have argued that Abraham was obedient to the law before it was given by Moses. They may even have argued that the law was eternal, as exemplified by the portrayal of Abraham's obedience to eternal law in *Jubilees*.[68] Alternatively, perhaps they argued that Abraham was obedient to the stipulations of the law based upon something equivalent to Philo's interpretation of the natural law. In that case, for the opponents and their message for the Galatian believers, Abraham functioned as an example of one who was obedient to the Mosaic Law before it was actually given to Moses. If this was the example of Abraham that the opponents were giving to the believers in Galatia, Paul has to argue forcefully that the Mosaic Law actually came after the promise made to Abraham. If the Mosaic Law actually came centuries after the promise to Abraham, then Abraham could not have been obedient to that law.

Paul has used the Genesis narrative to refute the Abraham traditions that the opponents are using. Not only did the law come centuries after the time of Abraham, but according to Gen. 12.3, an anticipatory gospel was also proclaimed to him. In the first century as in previous ages, the most ancient people and events were given the most importance and credibility. This new chronology establishes the priority of Paul's message of justification by faith over the opponents' insistence on obedience to the law.

5. *Galatians 3.19–22*

To a large degree, Paul's arguments in Galatians and Romans are based upon the concept of monotheism. Describing Paul's set of beliefs, N.T. Wright states, 'if we were to specify the content of this set of beliefs, it would be natural to begin with definitely Jewish categories, since Paul by his own admission continued to understand his work from the standpoint of one who had been a zealous Pharisaic Jew; and that would mean grouping them under the twin heads of Jewish theol-

---

66. Byrne, *Seed*, p. 160.

67. David J. Lull, '"The Law was our Pedagogue": A Study in Galatians 3:19–25', *JBL* 105 (1986), pp. 481–98 (483).

68. See Davis, *Antithesis*, pp. 161–62.

ogy, viz. monotheism and election'.[69] Terence Donaldson also sees monotheism as central to Paul's convictional background: 'monotheism was part not only of his [Paul's] debating strategy with Jews, but also of his basic message to Gentiles'.[70]

In Galatians, Paul expresses his monotheistic viewpoint most explicitly in his discussion of the law in Gal. 3.19–20, 'Why then the law? It was added because of transgressions, until the offspring should come to whom the promise had been made; and it was ordained through angels by a mediator. Now the intermediary is not one, but God is one'.

In this section, Paul logically turns to the question that he perceives to have been burning in his readers' minds. If the inheritance is through God's unchangeable, eternal covenant with Abraham, why was the law necessary (3.19a)? Paul contends that the law was added because of transgressions 'until the offspring should come to whom the promises had been made', meaning Christ (19b; see v. 16).

Paul further states that the law was 'ordained through angels by means of a mediator' (3.19d). The giving of the law by angels was a common Jewish tradition.[71] Paul deviates from the tradition here in that the activity of the angels is a point *against* the law. Although indirect communication of the law by God to the people of God could be understood to be in antithesis to the direct communication of the promise to Abraham, whether or not Paul has in mind the mode of God's communication of his promises to Abraham here is not clear.

Scholars have long discussed who this mediator might be and the significance of the mediation. Some have concentrated on the duality of parties involved, either between God and the Jewish people or the Jewish people and the angels.[72] For the sake of my argument, it is not necessary to establish precisely whom Paul had in mind. The most important concept to glean from Paul's statement is that somehow the law coming through angels via the agency of a mediator implies plurality that is in contrast to the one God who gave the promise to Abraham. Considering the general monotheistic tendency of much of Judaism of the day, this kind of statement that contrasts the oneness of God who gave the promise to Abraham with the plurality through which the law was given clearly demonstrates again the superiority of the promise to Abraham over the law.

At this point, one must ask to what argument of the opponents Paul may be reacting. It was noted in earlier chapters that popular traditions about Abraham in early Jewish literature were that he was the first monotheist and maintained obedience to the law before it was given. If the opponents were aware of the

---

69. N.T. Wright, *The Climax of the Covenant: Christ and the Law in Pauline Theology* (repr., Minneapolis: Fortress Press, 1992), p. 1; see also Barclay, *Diaspora*, pp. 389, 393.

70. Donaldson, *Gentiles*, pp. 87–88; see also E.P. Sanders' discussion in *Paul* (Past Masters; Oxford: Oxford University Press, 1991), p. 42.

71. Deut. 33.2 (LXX); *Jub.* 2.2; *1 Enoch* 60.1; cf. Acts 7.38, 53.

72. Supporting God and the Jewish people, Lightfoot, *Galatians*, pp. 146–47; R. Longenecker, *Galatians*, pp. 141–42; supporting the Jewish people and the angels, see A. Oepke, 'μεσίτης' *TDNT* vol. 4, pp. 598–624 (618–19). See also N.T. Wright's discussion in *Climax*, pp. 157–73.

popular traditions about Abraham, their appeal to the example of Abraham probably had something to do with his monotheism and obedience to law. As was discussed above, obedience to the Mosaic Law demanded a monotheistic foundation.

And if Dunn and Wright are correct, that by 'works of the law' Paul has in mind the nationalistic and racial 'badges' of Judaism such as calendrical laws and circumcision, then the opponents would in effect also be arguing along nationalistic lines. The monotheism which they would have espoused would have included the necessary obedience to Mosaic Law, including the 'badges' which had long identified the Jewish people. Their exclusive view of the identity of the children of Abraham – the people of God – would have excluded those who did not take on the law.

In Gal. 3.20, using the opponents' own contentions and the popular traditions which linked Abraham to monotheism and law, Paul demonstrates that the law actually is secondary when compared to God's promises to Abraham. Particularly if we keep Dunn's and Wright's contentions about the 'works of the law' as signifying Jewish nationalism, it appears that if one identifies the people of God in Christ as those who adhere to works of the law then one is creating the family of God around narrow, nationalistic symbols. To require Gentile believers to adhere to Mosaic Law is to require them to first become Jews before they can become members of the people of God in Christ. Consequently, if the promises are superior to the law, and if it is by faith that the promises to Abraham come to those united in Christ, the law becomes superfluous because it is no longer necessary to define God's people. Not only does being a descendant of Abraham no longer mean that one has to follow Jewish law, but obedience to the law which is based upon a plurality ('the mediator is more than one') is now a contradiction of the oneness of God.

6. *Galatians 3.23–29*

In this section, Paul uses the example of the παιδαγωγός to explain the function of the law. The use of a *paidagogos* was a prevalent custom in Paul's day; well-to-do Jews may have assimilated this custom.[73] The custom entailed placing one's child or children (primarily boys) in the care and oversight of a trusted slave until the child reached late adolescence.[74] The first task of a *paidagogos* was preventive and protective.[75] Some of the protection was in the area of morality, for example, protection from others such as undesirable lovers. The *paidagogos* was also associated with teaching his charge moral self-restraint, thus preventing the child from harming himself or others.[76] The *paidagogos* commonly accompanied the child to and from school, or would educate the

73. Norman H. Young, '*PAIDAGOGOS*: The Social Setting of a Pauline Metaphor', *NovT* 29 (1987), pp. 150–76 (168); *Leg. Gai.* 26–27.
74. Young, '*PAIDAGOGOS*', pp. 156, 168–69.
75. Young, '*PAIDAGOGOS*', p. 168; *Mut. Nom.* 217.
76. Lull, 'Pedagogue', p. 493.

child himself in matters such as etiquette.[77] The *paidagogos* could even administer physical punishment when necessary.

What characteristics of the *paidagogos* did Paul have in mind when he compared him to the law? Rather than viewing the *paidagogos* primarily in terms of his severity, as had previously been the case, in more recent years some scholars have concentrated upon positive aspects of the *paidagogos*. Young contends that Paul had the guardianship and temporariness of the *paidagogos* in mind.[78] To him, the law in Galatians refers to regulations that 'controlled Jewish social life and restricted association with the Gentiles'.[79] Lull believes that Paul had the temporary, protective view of the *paidagogos* in mind.[80] Gordon sees the guardian aspect of the παιδαγωγός as that which makes the most sense in the context of the epistle.[81]

Paul writes that before faith, he and the Jewish recipients of the letter were guarded (φρουρέω) and imprisoned (συγκλείω) by the law (3.23). Paul metaphorically replaces the law with the παιδαγωγός who functioned 'until Christ came, in order that we might be justified by faith' (3.24). Once faith came, the *paidagogos* was no longer necessary (3.25). In this case, Paul is stressing one aspect of the law that is like the *paidagogos*: both of them are temporary.[82]

One of the primary functions of the law as evidenced in early Jewish texts is that the law served to separate and protect Israel from her Gentile neighbours. The most prominent example of this function of the law was found in *Jubilees* where it kept the Jews from succumbing to the immorality and the idolatry of their Gentile neighbours. In fact in *Jubilees* Abraham was the proclaimer of separation from all things Gentile and obedience to the law.[83]

In the story of Abraham in Josephus's *Antiquities*, circumcision is a symbol of the Jews' separation from Gentiles. Circumcision was 'to the intent that his [Abraham's] posterity should be kept from mixing with others' (*Ant.* 1.192). Attridge contends that in Josephus circumcision 'becomes a distinguishing feature of the offspring of Abraham, to keep them separate from their neighbors'.[84] Additionally, in the account of the birth and circumcision of Isaac, Josephus makes Abraham and Sarah the model for subsequent generations (*Ant.* 1.214).

Aspects of the law such as circumcision also functioned to identify members of the people of God. As has been seen, when Philo mentions circumcision, he usually gives it an allegorical meaning, but this does not mean he perceives that the literal practice is unimportant. According to Philo in *Quaest. in Gen.* 3.49, the

---

77. Young, '*PAIDAGOGOS*', p. 164.
78. Young, '*PAIDAGOGOS*', p. 174.
79. Young, '*PAIDAGOGOS*', p. 173.
80. Lull, 'Pedagogue', pp. 496–97.
81. T. David Gordon, 'A Note on ΠΑΙΔΑΓΩΓΟΣ in Galatians 3:24–25', *NTS* 35 (1989), pp. 150–54 (153).
82. A.T. Hanson, 'The Origin of Paul's Use of ΠΑΙΔΑΓΩΓΟΣ for the Law', *JSNT* 34 (1988), pp. 71–76 (75).
83. *Jub.* 20.6–10; 21.21–24; 22.16–19.
84. H. Attridge, *The Interpretation of Biblical History in the Antiquitates Judaicae of Flavius Josephus* (HDR, 7; Missoula, MT: Scholars Press, 1976), p. 80.

nation which was 'given the command to circumcise (children) on the eighth (day) is called "Israel" in Chaldaean, and in [Greek] (this means) "seeing God."' Thus, circumcision is a sign of those who 'see God', meaning the nation of Israel. For Philo, Abraham was the first to discern or 'see' that God existed, and as such, he was the prototype of the nation known to 'see' God.[85]

In *Jubilees*, it is said that one who is not circumcised is annihilated because there is 'no sign upon him...that he might belong to the Lord because (he is destined) to be destroyed and annihilated from the earth and to be uprooted from the earth because he has broken the covenant of the Lord our God' (*Jub.* 15.26). In *Jubilees* circumcision is also seen as an identifying mark of the people of God.

In the context of Paul's epistle to the Galatians, he speaks primarily of those aspects of law that were especially known to identify the Jewish people. Circumcision, food laws, and the observance of festival days were the primary aspects of Jewish law that identified them and were known by Gentiles. More importantly, circumcision was identified with the figure of Abraham.

As mentioned above, one way that the law functioned as a *paidagogos* was to guard the Jewish people from the Gentiles and their idolatry and immorality.[86] The law as a protective device in a community where Jew and Gentile exist side by side is obsolete because they all have faith and belong to the community 'in Christ' (Gal. 3.26). Because of this, the separation by means of the law is now unnecessary. Additionally, now that both Jews and Gentiles were 'in Christ', these nationalistic identifying symbols are obsolete. The identifying symbols of the law had been abolished: all the believers in Galatia were now one in Christ Jesus (3.28).

The traditional exclusivity of being a descendant of Abraham is undermined. Because the believers in Galatia are one in Christ, they are Abraham's descendants and heirs of the promise made to him (3.29; cf. 3.8). The Spirit is the evidence of the efficacy of that promise made to Abraham since the Gentiles now also have that Spirit. The Spirit, whom the Galatian believers had already received (3.2–5), rather than the law, is now the identifying symbol of the people of God.

7. *Galatians 4.1–11*

In Gal. 4.1–2, Paul uses the imagery of an heir who, as a child, is under 'guardians and trustees' until the date set by his father. Paul is probably referring to practices in Roman law in which a father appointed guardians over a minor either in a will or a court of law. The father could also stipulate the age at which the child would no longer be under such guardians. By using the terms ἐπίτροπος and οἰκονόμος, Paul is referring to those who had 'effective control of the per-

85. See further in N.L. Calvert, 'Philo's Use of Jewish Traditions about Abraham' (*SBLSP* 33; Atlanta: GA, Scholars Press, 1994), pp. 463–76.
86. T. D. Gordon, 'The Problem at Galatia', *Int.* 41 (1987), pp. 32–43 (38).

son, property, and finances of a minor'.[87] The temporary nature of the law is again asserted; it is in effect until the date set by the father. According to this metaphor, the heir is not in control of his own affairs. The guardians control those affairs. In this sense, the heir is no better than a slave.

In 4.3, Paul begins his comparison of the slave/heir with the situation in which the believers presently find themselves. Considering Paul's recent discussion of the law as 'confining' (3.23), as a *paidagogos* (3.25), and its acting as a guardian/ trustee (4.1–2), it is best to understand Paul as meaning the Jews when he refers to the minor in 4.3.[88]

Additionally, it is the minors who were enslaved to the στοιχεῖα τοῦ κόσμου. Scholars have debated about the meaning of this phrase. A.J. Bandstra maintained that it may be derived from '*stoichos*' (στοῖχος), a military term that originally meant 'row'.[89] Bandstra understood the στοιχεῖα here, as joined with τοῦ κόσμου as the 'fundamental, inherent component forces of the cosmos'.[90] Earlier, Reicke identified them with the angels of Gal. 3.19.[91] While the precise meaning of the phrase στοιχεῖα τοῦ κόσμου is debatable (see also below), its function is sure: the στοιχεῖα τοῦ κόσμου enslaved those who turned to them.

In Gal. 4.4, Paul reasserts the concept that the previous age of slavery is over. The 'fullness of time' (4.4) has come which is parallel to the 'date set by the father' in Gal. 4.2. When the fullness of time had come, God sent his son who was 'born of a woman' and 'born under law'. In v. 5a we are told that the Son was sent in order that he might redeem those under the law, presumably meaning primarily Jews, but perhaps also including Gentiles who have been persuaded to obey aspects of Jewish law. In v. 5b it is most probable that Paul is speaking to the entire community, both Jews and Gentiles, given that the 'fullness of time has come', meaning that the promise to Abraham that God would justify the Gentiles by faith (3.8), and which is evidenced by the Spirit (3.14), has come to pass. Thus, the new eschatological era of the fulfilment of God's promises of the inclusion of Gentiles in the blessing of Abraham through Christ has arrived.[92]

Paul returns to an address of the whole community of believers, both Gentiles and Jews, in Gal. 4.6–7. In 3.1–5, his proof that the Galatian Christians are the people of God is the Spirit. In 4.6–7 the Spirit again is proof of their being sons of God. Because the believers at Galatia are sons (ἐστε υἱοί), God sent them the Spirit of his Son, through which they can experience an intimate relationship with God like that of a son to a father (4.6). If they are sons, they are no longer

87. Linda L. Belleville, ' "Under Law": Structural Analysis and the Pauline Concept of Law in Galatians 3:21–4:11', *JSNT* 26 (1986), pp. 53–78 (63).

88. See also Longenecker, *Galatians*, p. 165; T.L. Donaldson, 'The "Curse of the Law" and the Inclusion of the Gentiles: Galatians 3:14–24', *NTS* 32 (1986), pp. 94–112 (95, 108).

89. A. J. Bandstra, *The Law and the Elements of the World: An Exegetical Study in Aspects of Paul's Teaching* (Kampen: J.H. Kok, N.V., 1964), p. 31.

90. Bandstra, *Elements*, p. 57.

91. B. Reicke, 'The Law and this World according to Paul: Some Thoughts Concerning Gal. 4:1– 11', *JBL* 70 (1951), pp. 259–74 (262).

92. See further Richard Longenecker, 'Graphic Illustrations of a Believer's New Life in Christ: Galatians 4:21–31', *RevExp* 91 (1994), pp. 183–99 (188).

slaves but heirs (4.7). In 4.7, Paul again refers to the example of the child heir under guardians and stewards in vv. 1 and 2. The Galatians, presumably both Jews and Gentiles, are no longer slaves but true sons. The era of being enslaved to the στοιχεῖα τοῦ κόσμου which functioned as that which controlled the Jews and Gentiles in their experience before they were 'in Christ' is over. The era of sonship for both Jews and Gentiles evidenced by the Spirit and under the control of the Spirit has begun.

In his continued address to the Galatian believers (4.8), Paul concentrates upon the Gentiles among them. In the previous age, neither did they know God nor did God know them. Things that by nature were not gods enslaved them. This phrase (τοῖς μὴ οὖσιν θεοῖς) is a familiar one in Septuagint literature where it refers to idols.[93] The Gentiles were formerly idolaters. Paul is accusing them of returning to their idols 'again' (πάλιν: 4.9).[94] Morland points out that in his choice of the verb ἐπιστρέφω Paul uses missionary language: 'Instead of denoting conversion from paganism, Paul lets it denote apostasy back to it'.[95] What are the Galatian Gentile Christians actually doing which would cause Paul to make such an accusation?

As has been discussed, Paul is contending with persons who are being persuaded by certain 'agitators' to turn to a 'different gospel' (1.1–9). This different gospel is evidenced primarily by circumcision or the pressure to be circumcised (5.2–3; 6.12–13; 2.3–5) and may include other aspects of law, such as the calendrical observances noted in 4.10.[96] The believing Galatian Gentiles are being persuaded to obey Jewish law. Paul compares their obedience to law to idolatry (4.8) and to enslavement under the στοιχεῖα (4.9). Both obedience to law and idolatry are forms of enslavement under the στοιχεῖα τοῦ κόσμου (cf. 4.3–5a). Thus, obedience to law is not only a denial of the Galatians being true children of God, but from the perspective of being 'in Christ', obedience to law is tantamount to worshipping idols.

Paul's use of Abraham is usually attributed only to Gal. 3.6–29 and 4.21–5.1. More often than not, it is also maintained that Paul's opponents used Abraham in their own argumentation. If the traditions about Abraham we have discussed were popular, it may have been that these opponents were persuading the Gentile believers in Galatia that now that they had rejected idolatry and were believers in Christ, in order to be true children of Abraham they also had to obey the Jewish law.

But another of the Jewish traditions about Abraham previously discussed may come into play in Paul's discussion in Gal. 4.1–11. The tradition that Abraham was an idolater previous to his monotheistic belief has already been discussed. Most often, this idolatry was shown to have manifested itself in his former belief in astrology, that the stars and planets were in control of the events on earth and

93. 2 Chron. 13:9b–10; Isa. 37:18–19; Jer. 2:11–28.

94. Donaldson, 'Inclusion', p. 96.

95. Morland, *Curse*, p. 146; see also *BDAG*, 'ἐπιστρέφω', p. 382.

96. For example, see J.D.G. Dunn, 'Intra-Jewish Polemic in Galatians', *JBL* 112 (1993), pp. 459–75 (470–72).

that they were gods in and of themselves. Abraham's connection to astrology is found, for example, in *Jub.* 12.16–20, *Ant.* 1.154–165, *Abr.* 70, 81–84, *Virt.* 212–213 and *Apoc. Abr.* 7.9.

R. Longenecker points out that the term στοιχεῖα τοῦ κόσμου could have several meanings: the basic elements of which the cosmos is composed, especially the four elements of earth, water, air, and fire; the fundamental principles or rudimentary teachings of subjects; the stars and other heavenly bodies; the stellar spirits, gods, demons, and angels.[97]

Longenecker rules out the last two options, based upon their appearance after the time of Paul. He takes the view that the second option, principles or teachings, is what Paul has in mind. In Gal. 4.3, the term refers to the Jews' 'basic principles' of religion. He further takes κόσμου in an ethical sense meaning 'worldly' as opposed to 'spiritual'.[98] The term τὰ ἀσθενῆ καὶ πτωξὰ στοιξεῖα ('the weak and poor elements') in Gal. 4.9 refers to the basic principles of religion found in paganism, such as its cultic rituals and nature worship. For Longenecker, while Paul may mean the basic principles in both passages, the exact meaning varies in each passage in terms of its specific context.[99] However, if Paul means only the basic principles of the law and the basic principles of paganism, one has to wonder why he did not say so more simply. Fundamentally, the Jews and the Gentiles are turning back to different things: for the Jews, the rudimentary teachings are of the Mosaic Law; for the Gentiles, the rudimentary teachings are of paganism. Is there a way to understand more fully how they can both be equal to enslavement?

G.B. Caird believed that the στοιχεῖα τοῦ κόσμου referred to the demonic forces of legalism, both Jewish and Gentile, which are made weak and beggarly in comparison with the glory of Christ.[100] But even he admitted that τὰ στοιχεῖα referred to the heavenly bodies and that

> under the influence of their regular motions the whole of human life was controlled by bonds of inexorable necessity… With the advent of astrology the anthropomorphic gods had begun to give place to the 'army of unalterable law'. The iron rule of an impersonal fate robbed life both of meaning and of hope, and no small part of the appeal of Paul's preaching must have been that it offered release from servitude to the elemental spirits.[101]

Even though Reicke identified the στοιχεῖα with angels, he also noted that the talk of days and months in Gal. 4.10 in the context of slaves and sonship 'makes us think of the astrological fatalism of antiquity'.[102]

More recently, Clinton Arnold has asserted that in the context of magic and astrology 'the term *stoicheia* was indeed used of personalized spiritual forces that

---

97. *Galatians*, p. 165.
98. Longenecker, *Galatians*, p. 165.
99. Longenecker, *Galatians*, p. 166.
100. *Principalities and Powers* (Oxford: Oxford University Press, 1956), pp. 51, 86.
101. Caird, *Principalities*, pp. 50–51.
102. 'The Law and this World According to Paul: Some Thoughts Concerning Gal. 4:1–11', *JBL* 70 (1951), pp. 259–74 (264).

have significant influence over the affairs of day-to-day existence'.[103] While he summons a vast collection of material in order to make his point, one remains somewhat sceptical because the texts which are central to his argument are dated later than the first century CE. To say that *stoicheia* meant spiritual powers or angels associated with astrology based upon examples of texts from the second century CE and later strikes one as rather tenuous.

Martyn has suggested that the best meaning of *stoicheia* during Paul's time is 'elemental substances', referring to the traditional four elements, 'earth, water, air, fire'. These are the basic elements of which everything was considered to be composed in the Greco-Roman world.[104] Jews commonly held that when Gentiles worshipped idols, they were only worshipping the elements. Martyn further notes how in the Wisdom of Solomon 13.2 (c. late 1st century BCE), the author describes those who were 'ignorant of God' as supposing that fire, swift air, the circle of the stars, turbulent waters, or the luminaries of heaven were the gods that ruled the world and from this concludes that Paul could have been referring to the stars and astrological practices by his phrase 'elements of the world'.[105]

In Wis. 19.18–19, *stoicheia* is used to refer to the four basic elements: 'For the elements changed places with one another...fire retained its normal power and water forgot its fire-quenching nature'. In Wis. 7, we find that *stoicheia* is used in connection with the stars, 'For it is he [God] who gave me unerring knowledge of what exists, to know the structure of the world and the activity of the elements ...the alterations of the solstices and the changes of the seasons, the cycles of the years and the constellations of the stars...' (Wis. 7.17–19). Thus *stoicheia* is used in connection with both the traditional elements like fire and water, but also with the heavenly bodies.

While scholars believe that the *Testament of Solomon* was written in the early third century CE or perhaps earlier, there is general agreement that much of the testament reflects first-century Judaism in Palestine.[106] In ch. 18 we find the author uses *stoicheia* to refer to 'heavenly bodies [*stoicheia*], the world rulers of the darkness of this age' (*Test. Sol.* 18.2) that are later related to the zodiac (*Test. Sol.* 18.5). In ch. 8, where heavenly beings are also spoken of, seven spirits commanded by Solomon appear to identify themselves as 'heavenly bodies [*stoicheia*], rulers of the world of darkness' (*Test. Sol.* 8.2).

The sense of the στοιχεῖα τοῦ κόσμου as stars generally began to develop in the second century CE.[107] However, as we have seen, the term *stoicheia* had referred to the basic four elements (air, water, earth, fire) of the universe for centuries. Generally speaking, because the heavenly phenomena were thought

103. Clinton E. Arnold, *The Colossian Syncretism: The Interface between Christianity and Folk Belief* (Grand Rapids: Baker Book House, 1996), p. 173; see also Arnold, 'Returning to the Domain of the Powers: *Stoicheia* as Evil Spirits in Galatians 4:3,9', *NovT* 38 (1996), pp. 55–76 (60).

104. Martyn, *Galatians*, pp. 394–95.

105. *Galatians* pp. 397–400.

106. From D.C. Duling, 'Testament of Solomon', *OTP*, vol. 1, pp. 935–87 (940–43, 969 n. 8a, 977, n. a and d; 978, n. f); see also 15.5. See also Arnold, *Syncretism*, p. 171.

107. G. Dellling, 'στοιχεῖον', *TDNT*, vol. 7, p. 684.

to be composed of these elements, they could be included in a description of the elements of the universe. In the Sybilline Oracles, we find statements such as, 'And then all the elements of the world will be bereft – air, land, sea, light, vault of heaven, days, nights' (2.206). Or in 8.337, 'Then in time all the elements of the world will be bereft, air, land, sea, light of blazing fire, and heavenly dome and night and all days…For all the stars of luminaries will fall from heaven'. And in 3.80:

> then all the elements of the universe will be bereft (τότε δὴ στοιχεῖα πρόπαντα χηρεύσει κόσμου), when God who dwells in the sky rolls up the heaven as a scroll is rolled, and the whole variegated vault of heaven falls on the wondrous earth and ocean…raging fire will flow, and burn earth, burn sea, and melt the heavenly vault and days and creation itself into one and separate them into clear air.[108]

Book eight is thought to be a Christian rendition, from the second to third centuries while book two is thought to be after the fall of Jerusalem but before 150 CE.[109] The only place in Jewish literature before the time of Paul where we find the words στοιχεῖα and its modifying genitive κόσμου alluding to the heavenly bodies is in the *Sybilline Oracles* 3.80, which is thought to have been written soon after the battle of Actium (31 BCE).[110] Nevertheless, is Paul referring to the stars when he speaks of the *stoicheia tou kosmou*?

Paul does seem to be referring literally to the Jewish observance of the Mosaic Law and the Gentile observance of pagan idols and ritual in Gal. 4.1–10. According to Paul, the observance of Mosaic Law and idolatrous practices enslaved the Gentiles formerly. However, Paul may have had the heavenly phenomena in mind because they were believed to have been composed of the universal elements and as he uses *stoicheia*, they, like the stars, control those who look to them. In the context of the passage, the *stoicheia tou kosmou* function like the ἐπίτροπος and οἰκονόμος that figuratively controlled the Jews in centuries previous to the coming of Christ. In using the term, Paul implies that the law and paganism had the same kind of enslaving control over the Jews and Gentiles in Galatia as astrology does over those who believe in it. In the Abraham traditions, these controlling elements have idolatrous associations.

As has been noted above, the tradition of Abraham leaving behind the idolatry of Chaldaea to follow the one God was widespread. Abraham was known to be a Chaldaean, and Chaldaeans were known for the practice of astrology. The practice of astrology was equated with idolatry in much early Jewish literature. It also controlled the lives of those who held to it, enslaving them to the fatalistic workings of the stars and planets just as the lives of Jewish and Gentile believers were once enslaved to their former practices. Just as Abraham left behind the

---

108. English text from J.J. Collins, 'Sibylline Oracles: A New Translation and Introduction', *OTP*, vol. 1, pp. 354–80. For the Greek text, see V. Nikiprowetzky, *La Troisième Sibylle* (Études Juives, IX; Paris: Mouton, 1970), p. 296.

109. John R. Bartlett, *Jews in the Hellenistic World: Josephus, Aristeas, the Sibylline Oracles, Eupolemus* (Cambridge Commentaries on Writings of the Jewish and Christian World 200 BC to AD 200 I.1; Cambridge: Cambridge University Press, 1985), p. 41; Collins, 'Oracles', vol. 1, p. 332.

110. Collins, 'Oracles', vol. 1, p. 360.

practice of astrology for faith in the one God, now that the believers in Galatia are in Christ, they are to leave behind their former practices.

J. Louis Martyn suggests that the opponents actually made use of the tradition about Abraham and astrology in which Abraham 'made the journey to the knowledge of God by an astrological contemplation of the elements, being the first to observe the holy feasts at the correct times (e.g. *Jubilees* 16)'.[111] Interpreting the phrase to mean an observance of astrology makes sense of Paul's next concern, that they observe days, seasons, months and years (4:10), because these segments of time are based upon the movement of the heavenly phenomena. Most traditions about Abraham and astrology suggest that while Abraham was first enamoured by such belief, he gave up his devotion to astrology for his monotheistic faith. Whether or not the opponents were actually using the tradition about Abraham and astrology, it is probable that they were using traditions about Abraham's monotheism and law. Paul's *stoicheia tou kosmou* are those things that controlled the Jews and the pagans – the law and idolatry – previous to their being 'in Christ' just as the stars and planets were thought by some to control people's lives.

In the epistle, Paul has consistently argued against the Galatians being obedient to the law. The law is a curse (3.13); it produces transgressions and was mediated by angels rather than the one God (3.19). The law is unable to impart salvation (3.21): it functioned like a temporary *paidagogos* (3.23–25) and like guardians and trustees (4.1–2) and it is a form of enslavement (4.3–5) to the στοιχεῖα τοῦ κόσμου. Finally, Paul equates the law with idolatry (4.3, 8–10) which also was a form of enslavement under the στοιχεῖα τοῦ κόσμου. Both Jews and Gentiles are now true sons of Abraham (3.29; 4.6–7) meaning they are no longer slaves, but true sons and heirs. They are no longer to be under the control of the στοιχεῖα τοῦ κόσμου, which formerly, for Gentiles, functioned as paganism, but now functions as law which is how it also functioned formerly for the Jews. Instead, they are to live by the Spirit, which is evidence of their inclusion in the people of God, the children of Abraham (3.2, 5, 8–9, 14; 5.16). If they turn to the Mosaic Law, they return to the former era from which Christ has redeemed them, which is as good as paganism. In equating observance of law with idolatry, Paul makes the law the ultimate taboo for a child of Abraham. The outlined Jewish traditions about Abraham who rejected astrological idolatry for monotheism illuminate Gal. 4.1–11 because according to them, the true children of Abraham are to avoid idolatry. However, in his letter to the Galatians, Paul has used the Abraham traditions for his own ends. Now that these children of Abraham have a new identity 'in Christ', the idolatry to be avoided is obedience to the law.

8. *Galatians 5.1–12*

Several passages in Galatians imply that law-abiding believers are relegated to the sphere outside of the people of God. Earlier we looked at the Sarah and Hagar

111. Martyn, *Galatians*, p. 400.

allegory (4.21–5.1) in which those who are in bondage to the law (4.24b) are actually enslaved and will not inherit with the true sons (4.25, 30). Those who belong to the future, eschatological Jerusalem are free (4.26) while the opponents who belong to the present, earthly Jerusalem are actually enslaved (4.25). The Galatians who are being persecuted for not being obedient to the law are to 'cast out' those who are persecuting them (4.30). However, the most explicit statements of exclusion in the epistle occur in Gal. 5.1–12.

If Matera, Dunn and Sumney are correct, Gal. 5.1–12 comprises a polemical and climactic section that concludes Paul's argument that begins in 3.1 concerning reasons not to accept the law.[112] In this section, we find some of the strongest statements condemning those who believe that aspects of law must be maintained for one to be a member of the people of God.

Perhaps the most explicit verse, Gal. 5.4, speaks of those who adhere to law as outside of the realm of salvation: 'You who want to be justified by the law have cut yourselves off from Christ; you have fallen away from grace.' J. Louis Martyn translates it in such a way as to underline their separation from Christ: 'You have nothing more to do with Christ; you have fallen out of the realm of grace.'[113]

Because the beginning and the end of Greek sentences were reserved for items to be emphasized, the emphasis here is on the aorist verbs and their genitive constructions 'you are cut off from Christ' (κατηργήθητε ἀπὸ Χριστοῦ) and 'you have fallen away from grace' (τῆς χάριτος ἐξεπέσατε) at the beginning and the end of the sentence.[114] The grammatical emphasis of the sentence shows that this is Paul's focus: those maintaining the law have apostatized.[115]

Using very direct and quasi-political language, Paul speaks of those who would persuade them to be circumcised in 5.8 and 10: 'Such persuasion does not come from the one who calls you...whoever it is that is confusing you will pay the penalty'. Paul echoes his previous statements about their 'deserting him [God] who called you' (1:6) and 'those who trouble them' (1.7) with these verses.

The phrase that describes those persuading the Galatians as not following 'the one who called' them (5.8), echoes 1.6 where he charges the Galatians with deserting 'the one who called them'. It is clear given the context that it is not simply that they were abandoning Paul or his message. It is because they have taken on aspects of Jewish law as necessary for the people of God in Christ that Paul now considers them as unfaithful to God.

Τὸ κρίμα in v. 10 probably refers to the eschatological judgement since it is used in its articular form. As Longenecker states, 'Paul is likely thinking of the

---

112. Frank J. Matera, 'The Culmination of Paul's Argument to the Galatians: Gal. 5,1–6,17', *JSNT* 32 (1988), pp. 79–91 (83); see also Dunn, *Epistle*, p. 21; J.L. Sumney, *'Servants of Satan', 'False Brothers' and Other Opponents of Paul* (JSNTSup, 188; Sheffield: Sheffield Academic Press, 1999), p. 141.

113. Martyn, *Galatians*, p. 467.

114. Longenecker, *Galatians*, p. 228.

115. Morland, *Curse*, p. 147.

Judaizers as coming under God's judicial condemnation at the end of time'.[116] This term is reminiscent of the curse Paul pronounces on those who preach a contrary gospel in 1.8, 'let them be anathema!' In either case, it is God's eschatological judgement that is in view.[117] Those who adhere to a doctrine of law-maintenance for the people of God are now actually no longer within the sphere of salvation.

Paul finishes his thoughts with one of his severest recorded statements, 'I wish those who unsettle you would castrate themselves!'(5.12). Although some have understood ἀποκόπτω (to 'cut off' or to 'cut away) as referring to withdrawal from the church, today most modern commentators recognize Paul as referring to castration here.[118] Paul's passion for his gospel is so great that violence becomes explicit in his rhetorical wish that his opponents perform castration, a caricature of circumcision. Martyn sees Paul's parallel between castration as practised in the Cybele cult in the first century and circumcision as expressing that both 'are signs of a trust in the redemptive power of religion' over faith in the God of the crucified Christ.[119]

Nevertheless, something else seems to be suggested here. Males who were castrated were not allowed admittance into the assembly of the Lord (Deut. 23.1; cf. Lev. 21.20). Paul's caricature of circumcision works here because in his argument in Galatians those who imposed circumcision as essential upon Galatian believers are excluded from God's people just as those who were castrated were excluded from the assembly of the people of God. The rules that the opponents foisted upon the Galatian Gentile believers that they must be circumcised in order to be included in God's people are now twisted.[120] Those who would be castrated would be excluded from God's people by an action similar to circumcision. They ultimately would end up in the same predicament if they were castrated as they end up by their view that the law remains essential for God's people – they 'cut themselves off' from God's people in Christ.[121]

9. Conclusion: Paul, Monotheism and the People of God in Galatians

The previous discussions of the traditions of Abraham in early Jewish literature informed the interpretation of Galatians. The popular tradition in which Abraham was obedient to the Mosaic Law and its use by the opponents explained why Paul argued so forcefully that the law was a curse (3.10), did not bring righteousness (3.11) and did not rest on faith (3.12). The law was a temporary guardian (3.23–26) until the coming of faith. Paul showed how chronologically, the promise to Abraham came before the coming of the law: the law was *added* to the promise to Abraham 430 years *after* the promise was given (3.17, 19). Those who have

---

116. *Galatians*, p. 232.
117. Behm, 'ἀνάθεμα', *TDNT* vol. I, pp. 354–55.
118. *Galatians*, p. 234; see also *BDAG*, 'ἀποκόπτω', p. 113.
119. Martyn, *Galatians*, p. 478.
120. See also Dunn, *Epistle*, pp. 282–84.
121. See also Morland, *Curse*, p. 171.

the Spirit of God by virtue of their having been justified by faith possess membership 'in Christ' and are now identified as the children of Abraham (3.6–9, 14, 22, 29) as opposed to those who live as if they are members of the previous era in which the law was necessary for this identification.

The tradition of Abraham the first anti-idolater and monotheist further informed the interpretation of the text. The promise was superior to the law because the one God gave the promise, while the law was given by more than one (3.18–20). Obedience to the law was consequently a denial of the oneness of God. Ultimately, obedience to this law was tantamount to idolatry (4.1–11). Through his allusion to the elements of the world that formerly controlled the lives of Jews and Gentiles, Paul shows that at one time Jews and Gentiles were enslaved by their former beliefs in the law and in idols. Rather then submitting to the control of the Spirit, which was the new sign of the people of God, the elements of the world controlled people in a way similar to astrological practices. All those who were true children of Abraham should shun the law, just as Abraham was known to have shunned idolatry, particularly in the form of astrology, which was believed to control the lives and actions of human beings.

In the context of the allegory of Sarah and Hagar, Paul again turns the traditions about Abraham on their head (4.21–5.1). Instead of the law-abiding opponents being the children of Sarah, they become the children of Hagar. These enslaved children of Hagar are to be cast out (4.30). Those who are free of the law, who are the promised children of Sarah by virtue of their faith in Christ (3.26), are true children of Abraham (4.28).

What changes in behaviour does Paul expect from the believers in Galatia? First, and most importantly, they are to give up obedience to the Mosaic Law as a prerequisite for membership in the people of God. The law which once identified the people of God, especially the practice of circumcision, is no longer valid. It served its purpose of protection and identification, but now it has become obsolete (3.24–26). Secondly, the believers in Galatia are to cast out the opponents who have so confused them by preaching another gospel (4.30). Thirdly, the people of God are no longer to be identified by the Mosaic Law, but by the Spirit and the fruits that come from this Spirit (5.22–23). They are the new creation of God and his people (6.15–16).

Paul has radically revised what it meant to be a descendant of Abraham. Rather than Abraham exemplifying the ideal Jew who believed in the one God and obeyed the law, particularly circumcision, the descendant of Abraham who is now 'in Christ' is justified by his faith in Christ and identified by the Spirit and the fruits thereof. Obedience to the law is now actually a form of idolatry that God's people are to reject for faith in the one God.[122] Paul uses the Abraham traditions for his own ends, providing a new definition of the people of God who are guided not by law, but by the Spirit, and whose faith rests in the one God

---

122. See also N.L. Calvert, 'Abraham and Idolatry: Paul's Comparison of Obedience to the Law to Idolatry in Galatians 4:1–10', in J. Sanders and C. Evans (eds.), *Paul and the Scriptures of Israel* (JSNTSup, 83; SSEJC, 1; Sheffield: Sheffield Academic Press, 1993), pp. 222–37.

through whom the promise of Abraham that he would be a blessing to all the nations is brought to fruition in Jesus Christ. The foundational boundary marker for the people of God in Christ is monotheistic faith and the true monotheists are those who reject the law as necessary for membership in God's people just as Abraham rejected idolatry.

Chapter 8

ROMANS: THE STRONG AS TRUE MONOTHEISTS

1. Introduction

Paul probably wrote his epistle to the Romans from Corinth during the middle to late 50s CE. He identifies himself in the greeting of the letter as an apostle (1.1) who is called to preach the gospel among the Gentiles (1.5, 13). The recipients of the epistle were a Christian community composed of both Jews (2.17) and Gentiles (1.13), designated by Paul as 'God's beloved in Rome' (1.7).

Paul writes, among other reasons, in order to address specific problems that exist amidst the believing community in Rome.[1] In order to understand what those specific problems may have been and subsequently the function of Abraham in Paul's epistle to the Romans, it is necessary to consider the historical and cultural background of the believing community in Rome.

a. The Jewish Community in Rome

An understanding of the Christian community in Rome begins with an understanding of the Diaspora Jews who had settled there. In the last few decades, several scholars have noted the importance that the Jewish community in Rome played in the inception of Christianity.[2] It has usually been assumed that a dispute about Christ in the synagogues in Rome led to the expulsion of the Jews under Caesar Claudius in 49 CE based upon Suetonius's statement that 'Chrestus' was the reason for the disturbance in *The Deified Claudius* 25.4.[3] However, that the riot occurred over Christ has been questioned in recent years.[4]

---

1. Some scholars have also seen Romans as a theological treatise based upon his past work, while others have seen it as preparation for his future travels. See the discussion in K. Donfried (ed.), *The Romans Debate* (Minneapolis, MN: Augsburg, rev. edn, 1991), pp. 16–28.

2. Mark D. Nanos, *The Mystery of Romans: The Jewish Context of Paul's Letter* (Minneapolis, MN: Fortress Press, 1996), pp. 13–14, 68–75; J.D.G. Dunn, *Romans* (WBC 38A/B, Dallas, TX: Word Books, 1988), vol. I, pp. xlvi, xlvii; F.F. Bruce, *The Letter of Paul to the Romans* (TNTC, 6; Leicester: InterVarsity Press; Grand Rapids, MI: Eerdmans, rev. edn, 1987), pp. 15–17; P. Lampe, *Die stadtrömischen Christen in den ersten beiden Jahrhunderten: Untersuchungen zur Sozialgeschichte* (Tübingen: J.C.B. Mohr, 2nd edn, 1989), pp. 3, 108; J. Ziesler, *Paul's Letter to the Romans* (London: SCM Press, 1989), pp. 6, 12.

3. 'Iudaeos impulsore Chresto assidue tumultuantis Roma expulit' which is translated as 'Since the Jews constantly made disturbances at the instigation of Chrestus, he expelled them from Rome'. *The Deified Claudius* 25.4. Those who have supported the view that Suetonius meant 'Christ' include: A. Momigliano, *Claudius: The Emperor and his Achievement* (repr. New York: Barnes & Noble,

Dixon Slingerland produced what is perhaps the best summary of reasons that 'Chrestus' could refer to a person of that name rather than 'Christ'.[5] He maintains that Chrestus was a quite common Greco-Roman name during the time that Suetonius wrote and that in *Nero* 16.2, Suetonius correctly spelled 'Christian'.[6] Thus, Suetonius did not misspell 'Christ' but had someone named Chrestus in mind as the cause of the conflict within the synagogues in Rome during Claudius' reign.

Joseph Fitzmyer counters arguments like these by stating that precisely because Chrestos and Chrestus were common Greek and Latin names, Suetonius did not understand the name Christos, 'Christ' or 'anointed' and 'confused it with the commonly used Greek name *Chrēstos* which would have been pronounced at that time as *Christos*'.[7] Presumably, Suetonius could have understood the name that he reported in *The Deified Claudius* incorrectly and even though he may have known how to spell 'Christian', he may not have believed Christos was the cause of the conflict in the synagogues. Fitzmyer also questions the idea that someone whose common name was Chrestos or Chrestus could have so incited the Jews of Rome to have them banished.[8] Whatever happened that caused him to expel the Jews from Rome, law and order must have been seriously disturbed for Claudius to order an expulsion.[9] It seems best to assume that it was actually a dispute over Christ that caused Claudius to expel Jews from Rome. Thus the expulsion of Claudius as reported by Suetonius offers us evidence for the serious disturbance between Jewish communities which differed in their view of and allegiance to Jesus Christ in Rome in the first century CE.

The expelled Jews did not make a substantial return to Rome until the reign of Nero (54–68 CE). W. Wiefel maintains that Claudius' decree in which the Jews no longer had the right to assemble occurred after their expulsion from Rome in 49 CE rather than in 41 CE as reported by Cassius Dio.[10] He bases his conclusion

Inc., 1961), p. 33; R.E. Brown and J.P. Meier, *Antioch and Rome* (London: Chapman, 1983), pp. 100–102; Wiefel, 'The Jewish Community in Ancient Rome and the Origins of Roman Christianity', in Karl P. Donfried (ed.), *The Romans Debate* (Minneapolis, MN: Augsburg, rev. edn, 1991), pp. 85–101 (110).

4.   See Mark Nanos, 'Some Problems with Reading Romans through the Lens of the Edict of Claudius', *Mystery*, pp. 372–87.

5.   Dixon Slingerland, 'Chrestus: Christus?', in Alan J. Avery-Peck *et al.* (eds.), *The Literature of Early Rabbinic Judaism: Issues in Talmudic Redaction and Interpretation* (Vol. 4 of *New Perspectives on Ancient Judaism*; Studies in Judaism; Lanham: University Press of America, 1989), pp. 135–38.

6.   In *Nero* 16.2 Suetonius states, 'Punishment was inflicted on the Christians [christiani], a class of men given to a new and mischievous superstition'. Suetonius, *Suetonius in Two Volumes* (trans. J.C. Rolfe; LCL; London: William Heinemann, 1920); Slingerland, 'Chrestus', pp. 136–37; see similar argumentation in Stephen Benko, 'The Edict of Claudius of A.D. 49 and the Instigator Chrestus', *TZ* 25 (1969), pp. 406–18.

7.   Joseph Fitzmyer, *Romans: A New Translation with Introduction and Commentary* (AB, 33; New York: Doubleday, 1993), p. 31.

8.   Fitzmyer, *Romans*, p. 31.

9.   Leonard Victor Rutgers, 'Roman Policy towards the Jews: Expulsions from the City of Rome during the First Century C.E.', *Classical Antiquity* 13 (1994), pp. 56–74 (64, 69); E.M. Smallwood, *The Jews Under Roman Rule* (SJLA, 20; Leiden: E.J. Brill, 1976), p. 212.

10.   Wiefel, 'Jewish Community', pp. 93–94; Cass. Dio, *Hist.* 60.6.6.

on Claudius' reported favourable attitude toward the Jews early during his reign (c. 41 CE) and upon the fact that Cassius Dio does not report the expulsion of the Jews from Rome, but does include Claudius' decree that they could not assemble. He concludes that we 'come to a more fruitful conclusion if we see the denial of free assembly as a first step in moderating the eviction edict'.[11] Thus, synagogue assemblies were prohibited for those Jews who remained in or returned early to Rome, and 'Christians could only assemble in Rome if they, as a group, had broken ties with the synagogue.'[12] For Wiefel, when the Jews finally returned to Rome under Nero, they were concerned to re-establish their disbanded synagogues, and those who were Jewish Christians who had been members of the synagogues found Christians who had developed a form of organization independent of the synagogue form.[13]

However, before jumping on to Wiefel's bandwagon, a few items must be considered. In his *Historia Romana* 60.6, Dio states that since the Jews in Rome by that time again 'had…become so numerous that they could not all be expelled without causing a great commotion, Claudius instead deprived them of their right of assembly'.[14] Instead of this report being Dio's version of what happened just after 49 CE in contrast to Suetonius' report of Claudius's expulsion of the Jews, Dio may be explaining why in 41 CE Claudius does not repeat the earlier action of Tiberius (19 CE), when Tiberius expelled the Jews.[15]

Secondly, we must consider Wiefel's contention that in 41 CE Claudius' relation with the Jews was too good (primarily in the person of Agrippa) for him to have curtailed their assembly. His curtailment of Jewish privilege was limited to those Jews in Rome. Thus, as Smallwood points out, 'there was no fundamental contradiction between Claudius' confirmation of the Jews' right of religious liberty in general and his almost simultaneous removal of one right from the community in one particular locality because its abuse had in some way constituted a threat to public security.'[16] In addition, Roman emperors are hardly known to have been consistent in their proclamations and the primary concern of Rome was maintaining authority and public order. Thus, the evidence seems to show that the Jews were expelled in or around 49 CE, but that the right of assembly was not taken away at that time. Those Jews who remained could freely gather in their synagogues and, upon their return, the exiles would have been free to again join their synagogues or re-establish their own communities.

---

11. Wiefel, 'Jewish Community', p. 94.

12. Wiefel, 'Jewish Community', p. 94.

13. Wiefel, 'Jewish Community', p. 94.

14. Smallwood's translation, *Rule*, p. 210.

15. F. Watson, *Paul, Judaism, and the Gentiles: A Sociological Approach* (SNTSMS, 56; Cambridge: Cambridge University Press, 1986), p. 92. For accounts of the expulsion of the Jews by Tiberius, see Cassius Dio *Hist.* 57.18.5; Josephus's *Ant.* 18.81–84.

16. Smallwood, *Rule*, p. 215; cf. E.M. Smallwood, 'Some Notes on the Jews under Tiberius', *Latomus* 15 (1956), pp. 314–29; See also Dixon Slingerland, 'Suetonius *Claudius* 25.4 and the Account in Cassius Dio', *JQR* 79 (1989), pp. 305–322 who also argues that the date of the account of the curtailment of the right of assembly in Dio is most likely 41 CE and is not the same event as that reported by Suetonius.

Further evidence exists of the Jewish beginnings of the Christian community in Rome through the fourth century writings of Ambrosiaster. In his commentary on Romans he states,[17]

> It is established that there were Jews living in Rome in the time of the apostles and that those Jews who had believed [in Christ] passed on to the Romans the tradition that they ought to profess Christ but keep the law… One ought not to condemn the Romans, but to praise their faith; because without seeing any signs or miracles and without seeing any of the apostles, they nevertheless accepted faith in Christ, although according to Jewish rite.

Scholars have differed concerning the validity and significance of Ambrosiaster's statement.[18] However, if we recognize that Ambrosiaster is probably correct that early Christianity in Rome would have had a Jewish cast (as in much of the rest of the Empire) he may not be far wrong when he suggests that Jewish rite formed a part of this early faith.

Thus, the Christian community to which Paul is writing probably does have some association with the synagogue within which tensions existed in 49 CE that were severe enough to cause a Jewish/Jewish Christian expulsion from Rome. And if members of the synagogues had not been kept from meeting together, as others have contended, then there would have been opportunity for Jews, Gentile proselytes to Judaism, Jewish Christians and Gentile Christians to meet in those synagogues although given the expulsion of the Jews the proportion of Gentiles may have been greater.[19]

A variety of scholars have also contended that the Jewish community in Rome was highly influenced by the Jewish community in Jerusalem.[20] For example, one of the earliest reported connections between the two communities is initiation of Jewish contact by Maccabaean/Hasmonaean high priests 140 years before Christ.[21] Pompey also brought Jewish captives to Rome after his conquest of Palestine in 61 BCE. Leon states that 'a considerable portion of the Jewish immigrants to Rome came from the area of the eastern Mediterranean and especially from Palestine and Syria.'[22] If this is true, as Brown states, it is also possible that the '*dominant Christianity at Rome had been shaped by the Jerusalem Christianity associated with James and Peter, and hence was a Christianity appreciative of Judaism and loyal to its customs*'.[23]

17. Translation by K.P. Donfried, 'A Short Note on Romans 16', in Donfried, *Debate*, p. 47.
18. See C.E.B. Cranfield, *A Critical and Exegetical Commentary on the Epistle to the Romans* (ICC; 2 vols.; repr.; Edinburgh: T. & T. Clark, 1985), vol. I, p. 20; F. Watson, *Paul*, p. 94; John Knox, 'Romans', in George A. Buttrick (ed.), *The Interpreter's Bible* (12 vols.; New York: Abingdon Press, 1954), vol. IX, pp. 355–72 (362–63); D. Moo, *The Epistle to the Romans* (NICNT; Grand Rapids, MI: Eerdmans, 1996), pp. 4–5.
19. See also Moo, *Romans*, p. 5.
20. Brown, Meier, *Antioch*, pp. 95–97; H.J. Leon, *The Jews of Ancient Rome* (Philadelphia: The Jewish Publication Society of America, 1960), p. 240, cf. Acts 2.10; S. Safrai, 'Relations Between the Diaspora and the Land of Israel', *Jewish People in the first Century* (CRINT, 1.1, Assen: Van Gorcum, 1974), pp. 184–215; E. Mary Smallwood, *Rule*, pp. 129–30.
21. Brown, Meier, *Antioch and Rome*, p. 93.
22. Leon, *Rome*, p. 240.
23. Brown, Meier, *Antioch*, p. 110.

From Rom. 16 we discover that the Roman Christians to whom Paul is writing are meeting in house churches. For example, Priscilla and Aquila are hosts to a house church (16.5). Wedderburn suggests, 'if they [Priscilla and Aquila] were... associated with Paul in his Corinthian ministry, then it is more likely that they at least were, like Paul, also representatives of a form of Christianity which held that non-Jews could become part of God's people without submitting to the Jewish Law'.[24] Given the Judaistic beginnings of the Christian communities in Rome and that to some degree the community might still be influenced by law-abiding Jews and Jewish Christians from the synagogue and the return of Jewish Christians who were of the law-free persuasion, at least one of the issues to which Paul is presently responding in his letter to the Romans may indeed be whether the law was necessary for the members of the emerging people of God.

In previous chapters, I not only investigated the function of Abraham in Early Jewish literature, but also used Abraham as a kind of 'cipher' in order to understand who was the ideal Jew. It was shown that Abraham was believed to have been not only the premier anti-idolater and first monotheist, but also that he was obedient to the law before it was given in written form.[25] He was portrayed not only as a purveyor of important aspects of Hellenistic culture,[26] but also as the figurehead for those members of the nation of Israel who were faithful to their God in contrast to the surrounding nations.[27] The Christian communities in Rome may have been influenced to a large degree by Jewish Christians, particularly those from Palestine who, in addition to faith in Christ, still found their religious identity in their monotheistic faith and its necessary obedience to the law after the example of Abraham. Jewish Christians would have a difficult time accepting as members of the people of God those Gentile believers in Christ who did not practise the law and, as mentioned above, would be in contention with other Jewish Christians who believed in a law-free gospel.

b. *Gentile Proselytes to Judaism in Rome*

From the description of the house churches in Rom. 16 and Paul's frequent mention of Gentiles (Rom. 1.5–6, 1–15; 11.13, 17–18, 24, 28, 30–31; 15.15–16, 18), it is obvious that many of those in Rome to whom Paul is writing are Gentiles.[28] How do we reconcile this with the described Jewish beginnings of the church and its continuing Judaistic practices? A part of the answer may be found in the success of Jewish proselytization in Rome before the advent of Christianity.

The Jews had a considerable presence in Rome before the first century CE. Concerning the Jews, in the first century BCE Cicero stated 'you know how large

---

24. A.J.M. Wedderburn, *The Reasons for Romans* (Minneapolis, MN: Fortress Press, 1991), p. 56.

25. See *Jub.* 16.20–31; cf. *Jub.* 22.1–2; *Migr. Abr.* 129–130; cf. Gen. 26.5, Sir. 44.19–20; *2 Apoc. Bar.* 57.

26. For example, see *Ant.* 1.166–168; *Abr.* 107–114.

27. For example, see *Jub.* 22.10–23.

28. That the list is predominantly Gentile, see J.D.G. Dunn, *Romans*, vol. I, p. lv, vol. II, pp. 896, 900; P. Lampe, 'The Roman Christians of Romans 16', in Karl P. Donfried (ed.), *The Romans Debate* (Minneapolis, MN: Augsburg, rev. edn, 1991), pp. 216–30 (225).

a group they [the Jews] are, how unanimously they stick together, how influential they are in politics'.[29] While Jewish proselytization may not have been as enthusiastic as that of later Christians, from literary evidence of the time it seems that the Jewish community in Rome did participate to some extent in proselytizing Gentiles. For example, Horace, who lived in Rome during the late first century BCE, derided the Jews 'whose tenacious efforts to proselytize are difficult to avoid'.[30] The expulsion of the Jews from Rome under Tiberius in 19 CE may have been because the Jews were converting many of the native Romans to Judaism and these converts were numerous enough to be conspicuous.[31] Tacitus speaks from Rome of proselytes of the late first century CE with derision. They not only renounce their ancestral traditions but also adopt circumcision and are taught 'to despise the gods, to disown their country, and to regard their parents, children, and brothers of little account'.[32] The Jews were often successful proselytizers who were known by the Gentiles for their exclusivity and supposed hatred of humanity. Because of Jewish success, Romans sometimes believed that their own religion, country and even families were threatened.[33]

Many Gentiles in Rome were either sympathetic towards Judaism or became full proselytes of Judaism. For example, Augustine quoted Varro, a second-century Roman scholar, who lauded the Jewish people for their imageless worship of God.[34] The boundary that the Jews set up between themselves – the purer, chosen nation – and the Gentiles 'was always crossable and not always clearly marked. A Gentile might associate with Jews and observe Jewish practices, or might "convert" to Judaism and become a proselyte'.[35] The major reasons why Gentiles turned to Judaism were basically the same reasons that they also ridiculed the Jews: their belief in the one Creator God and their law that provided a code of moral conduct.[36] A further reason that the Gentiles turned to Judaism was the antiquity of their religion.[37] Jewish communities in different geographical regions had somewhat different requirements for Gentiles to become full proselytes.[38] Members of the Jewish community in Rome needed to maintain devotion to God, practise the Sabbath and festivals, adhere scrupulously to dietary laws and circumcision and maintain devotion to the family and

---

29. *Flac.* 28.66–67.

30. *Sat.* 1.14.129.

31. E.M. Smallwood, 'Notes', pp. 319, 320.

32. *Hist.* 5.5.

33. See Juv., *Sat.* 14.102–104; Tac., *Hist.* 5.5; Jerry L. Daniel, 'Anti-Semitism in the Hellenistic-Roman Period', *JBL* 98 (1979), pp. 45–65 (61, 63); see also A.N. Sherwin-White, *Racial Prejudice in Imperial Rome* (Cambridge: Cambridge University Press, 1970), pp. 86–101; J. Gager, *The Origins of Anti-Semitism* (New York/Oxford: Oxford University Press, 1983), p. 41.

34. *Civ.* 4.31.2. See also Strabo, *Geogr.* 16.2.37.

35. Shaye J.D. Cohen, 'Crossing the Boundary and Becoming a Jew', *HTR* 82 (1989), pp. 13–33 (13).

36. Smallwood, *Rule*, p. 205.

37. Gager, *Anti-Semitism*, p. 66.

38. Ross S. Kraemer, 'On the Meaning of the Term "Jew" in Greco-Roman Inscriptions', *HTR* 82 (1989), pp. 35–53 (35).

Jewish community.[39] These requirements were presumably also demanded of proselytes.[40]

According to Smallwood the number of proselytes – those who accepted circumcision, or in the case of women a ritual bath, or the full rigors of the law – were relatively few. Most Gentile proselytes were women.[41] The majority of Gentiles adhered to Judaism loosely, 'clinging to its fringes by the adoption of monotheism, Sabbath-observance, dietary laws, and the major requirements of the moral code, but shrinking from the decisive commitment of stamping themselves as Jews'.[42]

Socially the conversion of Gentiles to Judaism was a major step. Philo noted the social aspects of Gentiles who converted to Judaism when he said proselytes should be accorded every favour and consideration and equal rank with the native born because 'they have left their country, their kinsfolk and their friends for the sake of virtue and religion. Let them not be denied another citizenship or other ties of family and friendship'.[43] Because Abraham was the first to leave his home and family in order to search for the true God, Abraham became the example for proselytes.[44] Although the separation of Gentiles from their backgrounds was due to circumcision, Sabbath observance and food laws, it was ultimately due to monotheism:[45]

> Jewish monotheism might win the respect of the philosophically sophisticated, but proselytes who abandoned the worship of pagan gods would thereby be cut off from many civic and social activities… Even Jews who minimized their observance of strange customs would still be set apart socially if they refused to worship the pagan gods… Practical monotheism, with its social consequences, was a more significant dividing line between Jew and Gentile than an individual ritual such as circumcision. Conversion to Judaism involved joining a new community and being accepted as a member of a synagogue.

If many of those to whom Paul is writing are Gentiles, it may be that they were first attracted to Judaism to a large degree first because of its monotheistic beliefs and secondly the law that accompanied this belief. Assuming, then, that the synagogue provided the foundation for the inception of Christianity, these Gentile proselytes who became believers in Christ may not have wanted to take on the entire law, particularly circumcision, but they may have wanted primarily to maintain monotheistic faith and their connection to a synagogue community.

---

39. H.J. Leon, 'The Jews of Rome in the First Centuries of Christianity', in E.J. Vardanam and J.L. Garrett, Jr (eds.), *The Teacher's Yoke: Studies in Memory of Henry Trantham* (Waco, TX: Baylor University Press, 1964), pp. 154–63 (161).

40. Leon, *Rome*, p. 256.

41. Smallwood, *Rule*, p. 541; Leon, *Rome*, pp. 253–56.

42. Smallwood, *Rule*, p. 206. See also John J. Collins, 'A Symbol of Otherness', in J. Neusner and E.S. Frerichs (eds.), *To See Ourselves as Others See Us: Christians, Jews, and Others in Late Antiquity* (Chico. CA: Scholars Press, 1985), pp. 163–86.

43. *Spec. Leg.* 1.52; Collins, 'Symbol', p. 175.

44. *Virt.* 214.

45. Collins, 'Symbol', pp. 175–76.

c. *Romans 14–15.6: The Weak and the Strong*

The text itself provides us with additional clues concerning the problems in Rome. In Rom. 14.1–15.6 Paul discusses two groups of people whom he calls the 'weak' and the 'strong' in faith. The weak in faith are those who eat only vegetables (14.2, 6, 21), observe holy days (14.5) and drink no wine (14.21). The strong in faith are those who do not have to observe these rules because 'nothing is unclean in itself' (14.14). The strong are commanded not to injure their fellow Christians by what they eat or drink, since by doing so they are no longer walking in love (14.15).

The weak in faith were probably ethnic, law-abiding Jewish Christians but could have included Gentile proselytes to Judaism who were now Christians. The strong in faith would be those who adhered to a law-free gospel, probably primarily Gentiles but also Jews, perhaps after the example of Prisca and Aquila (see above; cf. 16.5) and after the example of Paul who includes himself among the strong (15.1).[46]

While Jews were known for their lifestyle that, besides circumcision, was distinctive in their diet and observance of holy days, they would eat meat as long as it had been slaughtered correctly. Similarly, wine was not forbidden for them. Why, then, are vegetarianism and avoidance of wine being practised by the weak?

Wedderburn discusses the examples of Daniel, who ate only vegetables and abstained from wine (Dan. 1.12,16) and the Therapeutae, a group of pietistic Jews who lived near Alexandria who also seem to have avoided meat and wine (*Vit. Cont.* 73–74).[47] Watson similarly provides examples of Jewish heroes who, while in a Gentile environment, and 'cut off from their community in which ceremonially pure meat and wine might be obtained' abstained from the food and wine offered by their hosts or captors (Jdt 12.1–4).[48] Lampe cites an example from Josephus of Jewish priests who went on a trip to Rome in the time of Nero who ate only figs and nuts 'um nicht mit Götzenopferfleisch in Berührung zu kommen'.[49] Lampe includes both Jewish Christians and God-fearers within the realm of the weak who avoided wine for reasons similar to those for avoiding meat, 'Nie konnte der "Schwache" sicher sein, nicht doch von einem Weinhändler zu kaufen, der aus seinen Amphoren auch greulichen Libationswein schöpfte'.[50]

Paul's also indicates that he is speaking to Judaistic believers when he states that certain food is κοινός or ceremonially impure (14.14). In Acts, this word refers to food that is 'unclean' according to Jewish law (Acts 10.14, 28; 11.8).[51] All of the occurrences of κοινός in Acts are in the story of Peter who is given the vision of food that is considered by Jews to be unclean. Of course, the point of the vision is that these foods are now to be considered clean.

---

46. Watson, *Paul*, p. 95.
47. Wedderburn, *Reasons*, pp. 33–34.
48. Watson, *Paul*, p. 95.
49. '...so as not to come into contact with meat offered to idols'. Lampe, *Christen*, p. 57.
50. 'The weak could never be sure whether or not he was buying from a wine-merchant, who also ladled abominable libation wine from his amphorae.' Lampe, *Christen*, p. 57.
51. See also Mk 7.2, 5; 1 Macc. 1.47; *Ant.* 3.181.

Judaistic Christians who observed the law completely or partially may have held condemnatory attitudes towards the law-free Christians who did not believe it necessary to adhere to the law. In turn, the law-free Christians would probably resent the judgements by their Judaistic brothers and sisters while judging them for their maintenance of the Jewish law. If the strong were primarily Gentiles, they may also have seen themselves as superior to their law-abiding and primarily Jewish brothers and sisters, as Paul's argument suggests in Rom. 9–11. Perhaps this is why Paul repeats his command that the Judaistic and law-free Christians welcome one another (14.1; 15.7) and that they not pass judgment on one another (14.3–4, 10, 13).

The observance or non-observance of days (Rom. 14.5–6) probably refers to the Jewish practice of observing the Sabbath and feast days.[52] As was stated above, the Jews were particularly known for their Sabbath practice. The Sabbath was central to Jewish identity; it was believed to have been established when God created the world.[53] According to J.D.G. Dunn, 'Acceptance of the sabbath was to be a mark of proselytes and of their participation in the covenant'.[54]

If the synagogues in Rome had not had the right to assemble curtailed after many Jews and Jewish believers left Rome in 49 CE, it may be that the synagogue community still maintained some hold on Jewish and former proselyte believers in Christ. In contrast, those who are strong are probably primarily Gentiles, most of whom did not obey the entire law even before the first preaching of the gospel in Rome. These strong believers hold that obedience to law is no longer necessary for the emerging people of God.

This also explains why Paul spends so much time arguing over obedience to the law in a letter that appears to address a majority of Gentile believers. Rather than argue that Paul's letter to the Romans is written primarily with its focus to move Gentile Christians to an attitude of consideration for their Jewish brothers, as does Elliott, or that the weak are actually Jews rather than Jewish Christians as Nanos contends, in light of previous discussion it seems best to assume that Paul is writing to both Jewish and Gentile Christians who have had and still have some attachment to the synagogue and who are struggling over the place of the law for the people of God in Christ.[55]

2. *Abraham and the Gentile Sinners*

Many scholars have noted that when Paul declares that Abraham gave glory to God in 4.20 he recalls his earlier statement in Romans 1 about the Gentiles refusing to glorify God (v. 18).[56] Edward Adams has noted that a more extensive tex-

---

52. Lampe, *Christen*, 57.
53. *Jub.* 2.17–20; cf. Gal. 4.10; Gen. 2.2–3; Exod. 20.8–11.
54. Dunn, *Romans*, vol. II, p. 805.
55. Neil Elliott, *The Rhetoric of Romans: Argumentative Constraint and Strategy and Paul's Dialogue with Judaism* (JSNTSup, 45; Sheffield: Sheffield Academic Press, 1990), pp. 96, 290–92; Nanos, *Mystery*, pp. 21–40.
56. Dunn, *Romans*, vol. I, pp. 220–21, 238; Cranfield, *Romans*, I, p. 249; Brendan Byrne, *Reckon-*

tual linkage exists between Romans 1 and 4 which illustrates the contrast between Abraham's faith and Gentile disobedience and that the contrast builds upon Abraham traditions roughly contemporary with Paul.[57] Building upon the observations of Adams and others before him, we will investigate the characterization of the Gentiles in Rom. 1 and the contrasting figure of Abraham in Rom. 4 to better understand Paul's use of Abraham and relevant traditions in his letter to the Romans.

Within his discussion of the plight of Jews and Gentiles who stand before God needing justification in chs. 1-3, Paul discusses the plight of the Gentiles in particular in 1.18–32. Rom. 1.18–32 is normally considered by scholars to be an invective against Gentiles to a large degree because it characterizes Gentiles as idolatrous and sexually immoral, characteristics that many Jews attributed to them. Many scholars see the passage as referring solely to Gentiles while others believe he is addressing Jews as well.[58] Many have noted Paul's allusion to Ps. 105.20 (LXX) in which the Jews are condemned for their worship of the golden calf (Exod. 32) in Rom. 1.23, and have concluded that while Paul may have been explicitly condemning Gentiles for their idolatry that he implicates the Jews as well.[59]

Paul sets up a major theme of the epistle when he states, 'For I am not ashamed of the gospel, for it is the power of God for salvation to all who believe, to the Jew first and also to the Greek' (1.16). In 1.17, Paul states that this is true because (γάρ) the righteousness of God is revealed 'through faith for faith'. Moreover, in 1.18, this is true because (γάρ) it is the wrath of God that is revealed against all 'ungodliness and unrighteousness'. Both verses use ἀποκαλύπτω, (to reveal) signifying a revelation from God with the emphasis in 1.18 particularly on the universal perspective of God as Creator which becomes clear later in the text.[60]

Immediately Paul sets up a contrast between those to whom the righteousness of God and the wrath of God are revealed. Paul first describes those who are recipients of God's revelation of wrath in Rom. 1.18, where he speaks of the ἀσέβεια (ungodliness) and ἀδικία (wickedness) of the Gentiles. He actually uses ἀδικία twice, once to describe his subjects as wicked (ἀδικία) and secondly to describe their obstruction of the truth by this ἀδικία. As Adams points out, the

---

ing with Romans: A Contemporary Reading of Paul's Gospel (Good News Studies, 18; Wilmington, DE: Michael Glazier, 1986), p. 101; Fitzmyer, *Romans*, p. 388; Moo, *Romans*, p. 286; C.K. Barrett, *The Epistle to the Romans* (BNTC; repr. London: A. & C. Black, 1984), p. 98.

57. Edward Adams, 'Abraham's Faith and Gentile Disobedience: Textual Links Between Romans 1 and 4', *JSNT* 65 (1997), pp. 47–66; much of his work is based upon my earlier research, such as 'Abraham and Idolatry: Paul's Comparison of Obedience to the Law to Idolatry in Galatians 4:1–10', in J. Sanders and C. Evans (eds.), *Paul and the Scriptures of Israel* (JSNTSup, 83; SSEJC, 1; Sheffield: Sheffield Academic Press, 1993), pp. 222–37.

58. Those who believe Paul is addressing Gentiles include J. Fitzmyer, *Romans*, p. 269; Moo, *Romans*, pp. 96–98; those who believe he is addressing both Gentiles and Jews include Cranfield, *Romans*, pp. 105–106; Dunn, *Romans*, vol. I, pp. 105–106.

59. R. Hays, *Echoes of Scripture in the Letters of Paul* (New Haven: Yale University Press, 1989), pp. 93–94; Dunn, *Romans*, vol. I, pp. 72–73.

60. Dunn, *Romans*, vol. I, p. 54.

use of ἀσέβεια and ἀδικία in 1.18 is strikingly similar to the collocation of δικαιόω (to justify) and ἀσεβής (ungodly) in 4.5 where Paul speaks of God's justifying the ungodly who trusts in him.[61] While δικαιόω and ἀδικία are common in Pauline texts, ἀσεβής and ἀσέβεια are not, occurring only at Rom. 5.6 and 11.26 in the undisputed Pauline epistles, and without the addition of a dik- or adik- word in either case.[62] As Adams further notes, 'In the LXX, ἀσέβεια denotes sinful and transgressive conduct. Such behaviour is characteristic of the nations' (Deut. 9.5).[63]

However if we investigate further, we find that ἀσεβής means 'sinful' or 'godless', particularly in the sense that it implies disregard for God. For example, in Deut. 9.5, the wickedness (ἀσέβεια) of the nations who follow other gods is the reason that God dispossesses them before Israel (Deut. 8.19; 9.4–5). In Prov. 1.7 it is the fear of the Lord that is the beginning of wisdom; those who do not have the fear of the Lord are sinners (ἀσεβεῖς). When Paul speaks of the ἀσέβεια and ἀδικία of the Gentiles, he is using language packed with implicit meaning. The Gentiles are identified as those who disregard God even before they are literally said to be idolaters later in the chapter. Their behaviour and attitudes correspond to the behaviour and attitudes of nations other than Israel who are outside of the sphere of those who would acknowledge and obey God.

In Rom. 4.5, in contrast to the revelation of the wrath of God found in 1.18–32, Paul shows us how God's righteousness is revealed. Paul tells us that Abraham believes 'in the one who justifies the ungodly' (πιστεύοντι δὲ ἐπὶ τὸν δικαιοῦντα τὸν ἀσεβῆ) and he is reckoned as righteous. Abraham symbolizes the Gentile in his or her sinful state (ungodly) portrayed in 1.18–32. As Cranfield states concerning v. 5, 'To say that Abraham was one who had no claim on God on the ground of works (τῷ...μὴ ἐργαζομένῳ)is tantamount to saying that he was ungodly..., a sinner'.[64]

In v. 6, previous to quoting from Ps. 32.1–2, Paul states 'So also David pronounces a blessing on the one whom God reckons righteous apart from works.' Being apart from 'works' signifies being apart from the works of the law that were the necessary correlation to faith in the one God. While Abraham symbolizes the Gentile sinner, he is reckoned righteous because of his faith. God fully accepted Abraham solely on the grounds of that faith.

In Rom. 4.7–8, Paul incorporates Ps. 32.1–2 ('blessed are those whose iniquities are forgiven, and whose sins are covered; blessed is the one against whom the Lord will not reckon sin) through the rabbinic practice of *gezera shawa*, which is a rabbinic method of interpretation in which the interpreter uses the

---

61. Adams, 'Gentile', p. 51.

62. As Adams also notes, outside the undisputed epistles ἀσεβής occurs in 1 Tim. 1.9 and ἀσέβεια in 2 Tim. 2.16; Tit. 2.12.

63. Adams, 'Gentile', p. 51.

64. Cranfield, *Romans*, I, p. 232; see also A.T. Hanson, 'Abraham the Justified Sinner', in *Studies in Paul's Technique and Theology* (London: SPCK, 1974), pp. 52–66; U. Wilckens, 'Die Rechtfertigung Abrahams nach Römer 4', *Studien zur Theologie der alttestamentlichen Überlieferungen* (Festschrift G. von Rad; Neukirchen–Vluyn: Neukirchener Verlag, 1961), pp. 33–49.

same words or cognates in two passages of Scripture to call attention to their mutual relationship. In this way, Paul associates Ps. 32.1–2 with Gen. 15.6 based upon the key verb 'to reckon'. Many scholars such as Douglas Moo, in commenting on Ps. 32.1–2, speak almost solely of Paul's concern 'to portray justification as a free act of God that has no basis in a person's works'.[65] While this may be a theological tenet that can be drawn from the text, if we understand that Paul has been speaking about Abraham the ungodly (4.5), lawless (4.3) Gentile, we see that by citing Ps. 32.1–2 he is still referring primarily to Abraham who was reckoned righteous 'apart from works', whose sins were covered and not reckoned to him.[66] Paul represents Abraham as a justified Gentile sinner.

It is noteworthy here that Paul apparently sees no reason to provide any explanation as to why Abraham could be called 'ungodly'. As Adams notes,[67]

> An awareness of the tradition of Abraham turning from idolatry to the one true God on the part of both Paul and at least some of his Jewish readers does seem to be presupposed in 4.5. The characterization of Abraham as an ungodly Gentile is most readily understood against the background of this tradition… It is noteworthy that Paul asserts rather than argues for Abraham's prior ungodliness. Paul evidently does not expect this point to be either an alien or a particularly controversial one for his readers, but appears to assume their familiarity with the notion.

If we return to ch. 1, we find that in order to establish his theme of God the Creator which he began in 1.18, Paul declares that God has made himself evident in his creation (1.19) and that he is Creator in contrast to the created things which the Gentiles worship (1.25). Paul alludes to God's creation of the world in 1.20: 'Ever since the creation of the world his invisible attributes (τὰ…ἀόρατα αὐτοῦ) have been perceived intellectually (νοούμενα καθορᾶται) by the things he has made, that is his eternal power and deity, so that they are without excuse'. Richard Bell suggests that νοούμενα καθορᾶται should be translated as 'seeing with understanding'.[68] The translators of the NEB state it well when they refer to God's invisible qualities as being 'visible to the eye of reason'.

Adams focuses on the textual link of God as creator in these verses when he compares 1.20 and 25 with 4.17b.[69] Even though the Gentiles in ch. 1 'knew' God (1.21) from the manifestation of God in creation (1.19–20) they chose to serve the creature rather than the Creator (1.25). Instead, Abraham is said to believe in the God 'who gives life to the dead and calls the things that do not exist into existence' (4.17b). While in the immediate context Paul is alluding to the deadness of Abraham's body and Sarah's womb (4.19) and God's power to resurrect Jesus from the dead (4.25), Paul also uses the language of creation when he speaks of Abraham's faith. The verb ζῳοποιέω (to make alive; give life) used broadly in

---

65. Moo, *Romans*, p. 266.
66. See also Hanson, 'Sinner', p. 53.
67. Adams, 'Gentile', pp. 59–60.
68. Bell, *No One Seeks for God: An Exegetical and Theological Study of Romans 1:18–3:20* (Tübingen: Mohr Siebeck, 1998).
69. Adams, 'Gentile', p. 52.

4.17b, denotes God's creative, sustaining, or renewing power. The same power that brought creation later is said to bring resurrection.[70]

Abraham is also said to believe in the God 'who calls things that have no existence into existence' (τὰ μὴ ὄντα ὡς ὄντα; 4.17b). Creation here is a 'calling out of nothing'. Paul is again drawing on Hellenistic Jewish language. This 'calling out of nothing' as an attribute of God was a particular feature of Philo's theology for whom God is τὸ ὄν who brings non-being into being.[71] In the Old Testament the verb 'call' also refers to God's creative work (cf. Isa. 41.4; 48.13), and 'later Jewish authors perpetuate this usage, sometimes adding the idea that this creative "calling" involves a bringing into being things that were not'.[72] As the Gentiles in ch. 1 had been, Abraham is confronted with the creator. As Adams states, 'unlike the Gentiles of Romans 1, Abraham acknowledges and places his faith in the life-giving God. Abraham's simple and unreserved trust in God the creator contrasts with their "sophisticated"...rejection of the revelation of the creator in favour of idol-worship'.[73] If we consider the traditions about Abraham as the first to reject idolatry for monotheistic faith, he provides a clear contrast to those Gentiles who have rejected faith in the Creator God for idolatry.

If we look more carefully at 1.20, we find that although God as Creator is implied, it is God's invisible attributes, specifically his power and deity that are central. Dunn points out that the language here is not characteristic of earliest Christian thought and that it bears resemblance to Stoic thought and particularly to language found in the work of Philo of Alexandria.[74]

What is significant for this study is that in Philo's works, Abraham begins his life glorifying the visible world as a Chaldean who practises idolatry particularly in the form of astrology. For example, in *De Abrahamo*, Philo says about the Chaldeans, 'Thus they glorified the visible (ὁρατός) existence, leaving out of consideration the intelligible (νοητός) and invisible (ἀόρατος)...they concluded that the world itself was God, thus profanely likening the created to the Creator' (*Abr.* 68–69; cf. *Virt.* 212–213).

Of the deluded Chaldeans, Abraham alone is able to see the 'charioteer and pilot presiding over the world and directing in safety his own work...' (*Abr.* 70). For Philo, this 'charioteer and pilot' represents the Logos that permeates and holds together the entire cosmos.[75] Philo gleaned the image from the myth of Zeus who drives a winged chariot in the heavens. Further, in the context of discussing Abraham's migration from Chaldaea, Philo refers to his version of God repeatedly as the invisible mind (*Abr.* 73; ἀόρατος) and the invisible God (*Abr.* 75; ἀειδής). In the Stoic thought which Philo often incorporated into his texts, it was this invisible mind that governed the world just as the minds of human beings are

70. Dunn, *Romans*, vol. I, p. 217.

71. Dunn, *Romans*, vol. I, p. 218; for example, see *Migr. Abr.* 183.

72. Moo, *Romans*, p. 281; see also Heb. 11.3.

73. Adams, 'Gentile', pp. 52–53.

74. Dunn, *Romans*, vol. I, p. 57.

75. David Runia, *Philo Judaeus and the Timaeus of Plato* (Philosophia antiqua, 44; Leiden: E.J. Brill, 1986), p. 214.

to govern their own bodies. It is Abraham who is said to receive the vision of the one who so long lay hidden and invisible (ἀειδής; *Abr.* 79). And for Philo, God manifested himself to Abraham, because it was 'impossible that anyone should by himself apprehend the truly Existent, did not He reveal and manifest himself' (*Abr.* 80).

A summary of how Abraham perceived the invisible God is found in *Abr.* 84–88. Here we find that Abraham 'sees' (ὁράω) the 'master and pilot' with 'more discerning eyes'. The sense that ὁράω has here is of mental or spiritual perception.[76] At the end of the section Philo states that Abraham did not 'remain for ever deceived nor stand rooted in the realm of sense, nor suppose that the visible (ὁρατός) world, was the Almighty and Primal God, but using its reason sped upwards and turned its gaze upon the intelligible order which is superior to the visible and upon Him who is maker and ruler of both alike' (*Abr.* 88).

Both Philo and Paul give evidence for Hellenistic Jewish traditions about the invisibility of God and his manifestation in creation and that God was evident through intellectual perception. In fact, Paul and Philo are not alone in putting forth these concepts; they are also found in the Wisdom of Solomon, where all people who are 'ignorant of God' are said to be foolish and that 'they were unable from the good things that are seen to know the one who exists' because they do not 'recognize the artisan' (Wis. 13.1).[77]

In Romans 1 and 4, Paul is speaking of those for whom God could be known through creation. For example, in 1.21 he states that they did not glorify God even though they 'knew (γινώσκω) him'. Also that since the creation of the world, they have 'perceived intellectually (νοούμενα καθορᾶται) the things that have been made' (1.20). Yet, they did not see fit 'to acknowledge (ἐπίγνωσις) God (1.28) and God gave them up to an 'unfit mind (νοῦς)'. In contrast to those who knew God and settled for idolatry, Abraham believed in God (4.3) and had faith in his creative powers (4.17).

It is probably not the case that Paul actually used Philo when he wrote Romans 1.1. However, as we have seen, the tradition that Abraham discerned the invisible God from his observations of creation was present in the works of Philo, Josephus, *Jubilees*, and the *Apocalypse of Abraham*. It might have been the case that the tradition of Abraham 'seeing' God was widely known enough for Paul and his readers in Rome to have been aware of it and to have understood the implicit contrast between Abraham who discerned the invisible God from creation and the Gentiles who did not.

While many are cautious about reading Paul as espousing ancient natural theology, it is fairly evident that here Paul believes that human beings can in some sense know God from creation.[78] Paul contends in 1.20–21 that although Gentiles knew God they did not glorify (δοξάζω) God and that this is why the Gentiles are without excuse. As was mentioned above, many scholars have noticed the use of

---

76. BDAG, 'ὁράω', pp. 719–20.

77. See also 13.5 and W. Sanday and A.C. Headlam, *The Epistle to the Romans* (ICC; New York: Charles Scribner's Sons, 1911), pp. 51–52.

78. See Dunn, *Romans*, vol. I, p. 56; Fitzmyer, *Romans*, p. 273.

δοξάζω in this verse and the noun δόξα (glory) in Rom. 4.20, where Abraham is said not to have doubted God's earlier promise (4.18) that he should have descendants even with the visible evidence of the deadness of both his body and Sarah's womb (4.19), but gave glory (δόξα) to God. For the Gentiles, this refusal to honour God leads eventually to death (1.32) while Abraham's demeanour leads to life from the dead (4.17, 19, 24). Thus, Abraham again provides a positive foil to the Gentiles described in ch. 1. While the Gentiles do not acknowledge God through their refusal to give him glory, Abraham acknowledges God through his glorifying God.

Thus, in contrast to the Gentiles in ch. 1, Abraham acknowledges and gives glory to God. If the Gentiles are faulted for having known God and yet falling into idolatry, traditions about Abraham the former idolater who forsook his idolatry for belief in the one, true God provide the necessary contrast. Yet, what of the scholarship in which Adam has been thought to be the idolater in ch. 1?

It has often been argued that the Genesis narrative of the creation and the fall (Gen. 1–3) has formed the background to Paul's thinking in Rom. 1, and particularly so in 1.23, where Paul speaks of the Gentiles who adopted idolatry: 'and exchanged the glory of the immortal God for the likeness of the image of mortal humans or birds or four-legged creatures or reptiles'. In this passage Paul echoes Ps. 105.20 (LXX), 'They exchanged their glory for the image of a grass-eating bullock', which alludes to the golden calf at Sinai (cf. Exod. 32.1–34) and probably also is influenced by discussions of idolatry in Jer. 2.11 and Deut. 4.14–18.

Considerable scholarship has been written to discuss the contention that in his quotation Paul takes his language for the order of the figures mentioned from the creation account because birds, four-legged creatures and reptiles comprise the threefold division of the animal kingdom (Gen. 1.20–5).[79] In her often quoted article from an early volume of *New Testament Studies*, Morna Hooker contended that in writing Rom. 1.18–32 'Paul had the figure of Adam in mind, and that in these verses he deliberately described man's predicament in terms of the biblical narrative of Adam's fall. Not only does the language of this section echo that of Gen. i.20–6, but the sequence of events is reminiscent of the story of Adam in Gen. i–iii'.[80]

While disagreement exists over how much the narratives of the Creation and Fall influenced Paul in Rom. 1.18–32, most commentators see Paul as having been influenced to some degree by the narrative.[81] As Wedderburn states, 'it is hardly surprising if, when he comes to consider how God's judgment has come to rest upon man or how sin has taken a grip on man, Paul finds his thoughts naturally turning to the account of Adam's fall in Gen. 3'.[82]

79. M.D. Hooker, 'Adam in Romans 1', *NTS* 6 (1959–60), pp. 297–306 (300); see also 'A Further Note on Romans 1', *NTS* 13 (1966–67), pp. 181–83.

80. Hooker, 'Note', p. 181.

81. For example, see Moo, *Romans*, pp. 109–10; Ziesler, *Romans*, p. 75, cf. p. 79; Dunn, *Romans*, vol. I, pp. 60–61, 69, 72, 93.

82. A.J.M. Wedderburn, 'Adam in Paul's Letter to the Romans', in E.A. Livingstone (ed.), *Papers on Paul and Other New Testament Authors* (Studia Biblica 3; JSNTSup, 3; Sheffield: Sheffield Academic Press, 1980), pp. 413–30 (414).

While most scholars see an allusion to Genesis 1–3 in Paul's description of the sinfulness of the Gentiles in Rom. 1.18–32, in order to explain how Adam could be associated with idolatry, most have to resort to rather dubious explanations. For example, Hooker admits that one might object that 'there is nothing in the narrative in Genesis to suggest that Adam ever offered worship to idols' yet offers her explanation that Adam can be seen as 'accused of serving the creature rather than the Creator, and it is from this confusion between God and the things which he has made that idolatry springs… In listening to the voice of the serpent, Adam has not only failed to exercise his rightful dominion over creation, but, by placing himself in subservience to a creature, has opened up the way to idolatry.'[83]

While it does seem possible that Paul had the Creation and Fall account in mind when he categorized idols (Rom 1.23) and speaks of God's decree against sinfulness which leads to death (Rom 1.32), it does seem to be a bit of a stretch to say that by virtue of Adam's having been given dominion over the animals, his subservience to a creature is tantamount to worshipping an idol. Wedderburn has rightly questioned whether Paul would have seen Adam's sin as idolatry because he saw Adam as turning away from God after his sin while humanity turns from God and then only does he fall into idolatry.[84] Wedderburn comes to the conclusion that although the passage describes 'Israel's fall into idolatry and later experiences of idolatry…it is not to be pinned down to any particular point in the Old Testament story; the essence of Israel's history and man's history as a history of turning ever further away from God is summed up vividly in this account.'[85]

However, as we have said, the recipients of the wrath of God in Rom. 1.18–32 are primarily Gentiles. If one needed a contrast for the Gentiles who, knowing God, followed after idolatry, it would be the Gentile Abraham, who rejected idolatry for monotheistic faith. Near the end of his article, Adams surmises that the echoes of Rom. 1 in Rom. 4 'set up a structural contrast between Abraham's faith and Gentile disobedience, a contrast likely to have been intended by Paul. It is probable that underlying this reversal pattern is the tradition of Abraham's rejection of idolatry and discovery of the creator'.[86]

3. *Abraham in Romans 3.27–4.25*

We shall next consider how Paul uses Abraham in Rom. 3.27–4.25 in order to speak to the situation at hand. Previous to the shift in Pauline studies beginning in the 1970s that has been described as the 'new perspective', this passage, among others, was seen to support the notion that Christianity with its creed of justification by faith was superior to Jewish legalism. For example, in the conclusion of

83. Hooker, 'Adam', p. 301.
84. Wedderburn, 'Adam', pp. 415, 419; cf. Moo, *Romans*, p. 109 n. 85.
85. Wedderburn, 'Adam', p. 419.
86. Adams, 'Gentile', p. 65.

his article, 'Abraham the Justified Sinner', A.T. Hanson states, 'The notion of two contrasted ways of life stands out clearly: the way of faith began with Abraham, was supremely demonstrated in Jesus, and is continued in Christians in contemporary life. The way of the law was promulgated through Moses, has been continuously but unsuccessfully attempted by most Jews ever since, and is now the great obstacle to contemporary Jews becoming Christians'.[87]

As was noted earlier in this volume, Abraham was used as a primary example for the ideal Jew or person of God because of his rejection of idolatry for monotheistic faith and obedience to the Mosaic Law. Previously, many scholars have also noted the importance of the Abraham traditions for early Judaism and the study of Paul, particularly in Rom. 4. As Stuhlmacher states, '[Romans four] becomes transparent in terms of its content only when one keeps in mind the biblical narrative of Abraham from Genesis 12 and recognises that Paul makes use of the Old Testament and early Jewish tradition concerning Abraham in an entirely new manner.'[88]

However, while Stuhlmacher attests to the importance of Early Jewish tradition concerning Abraham, he provides only a superficial treatment, devoid of consideration of Pseudepigraphical material.[89] Often New Testament scholars who have looked at the Abraham traditions since the advent of the new perspective have looked at the Abraham traditions primarily in order to find connections between Abraham and the law. For example, in his treatment of Abraham Glen N. Davies capitalizes upon Abraham's obedience to law and his faithfulness, but does not address the traditions in which Abraham is described as firmly rejecting idolatry for monotheism.[90]

If we move to the text itself, we find that Rom. 3.27–31 functions both as a clarification of what Paul has already discussed in the letter and as an introduction to the example of faith provided by Abraham in ch. 4. Stanley Stowers focused on the dialogical style of a Cynic-Stoic Diatribe in his dissertation on Romans. He identified the style in several passages in Romans, the most important for our purposes being Rom. 3.27–4.25. Stowers argues that 3.27–4.2 is a dialogical exchange in the mode of indictment, with 4.3–25 as the *exemplum* which provides a positive model for life.[91] In a dialogical exchange, 'the teacher is in control and guides the discussion to a resolution'.[92] In this case, the rhetorical questions that Paul includes may be those he expects from the community of believers in Rome.

---

87. Hanson, 'Sinner', p. 65.

88. Peter Stuhlmacher, *Paul's Letter to the Romans: A Commentary* (Louisville, KY: Westminster/John Knox Press, 1994), p. 69.

89. Stuhlmacher, *Romans*, pp. 70–71.

90. Glenn N. Davies, *Faith and Obedience in Romans: A Study in Romans 1–4* (JSNTSup, 39; Sheffield; JSOT Press, 1990), pp. 143–72.

91. S.K. Stowers, *The Diatribe and Paul's Letter to the Romans* (SBLDS, 57; Chico, CA: Scholars Press, 1981), p. 155.

92. Stowers, *Diatribe*, p. 164.

Stowers' work is helpful for us here, because he enables us to conceptualize how Paul may have understood those who had objections to the law-free gospel in Rome. He constructs Rom 3.27–28 as follows:[93]

A.   Interlocutor: What then becomes of boasting?
B.   Paul: It is excluded
C.   Interlocutor: By what sort of law? Of works?
D.   Paul: No, but through the law of faith. For we consider a man to be justified by faith apart from works of the law...

Paul begins with his statement that shows that the privileged boasting of the Jews in the law is now excluded (3.27). This statement has an important connection to Rom. 2.17 in which Paul outlines the major components of Jewish boasting, 'But if you call yourself a Jew and rely on the law and boast of your relation to God...'[94] These components of relationship to God and works of the law characterized membership in the covenant. In response to the question of the interlocutor about whether boasting is now excluded, Paul says that the works of the law are no longer a source of boasting based upon the law of faith.

His statement about justification by faith in v. 28 that people are justified by faith apart from works of the law echoes what is found in Gal. 2.16. If we assume that Galatians was written many years before Romans, it is a fundamental statement of what he has long believed and preached.[95] In Gal. 2.15–16 Paul states, 'We ourselves are Jews by birth and not Gentile sinners; yet we know that a person is justified not by the works of the law but through faith in Jesus Christ'. When Paul states, 'we know that a person is justified not by the works of the law...' it is spoken from one Christian Jew to another. It speaks of what they had already known; the law in and of itself did not justify them. It is also clear that just as he used ἄνθρωπος (human being) in Rom. 1.18 to express the people, both Jews and Gentiles, against whom the wrath of God is revealed, in Rom. 3.28 he uses ἄνθρωπος to describe all people, both Jews and Gentiles, who are made righteous by faith.

In 3.27–30, Paul is fundamentally interested in establishing that the boasting of the Jews in the law or in their relationship to God is no longer tenable and by virtue of this, Gentiles are included in the people of God. This is contrary to those who assume that Paul is primarily interested in proving justification by faith here.[96] It seems rather that Paul is using justification by faith to prove that boasting mentioned in 3.27 is excluded. First, Paul uses the word γάρ (for, because) indicating that justification by faith is the reason that boasting mentioned in v. 27 is excluded.[97] Secondly, Paul uses the first-person plural, λογιζόμεθα (to believe,

93.   Stowers, *Diatribe*, p. 164.
94.   J.D.G. Dunn, 'Works of the Law and the Curse of the Law: (Gal. 3.10–14)', in *Jesus, Paul and the Law: Studies in Mark and Galatians* (Louisville, KY: Westminster/John Knox Press, 1990), p. 221.
95.   Dunn, *Romans*, vol. I, p. 187.
96.   For example, see Cranfield, *Romans*, I, p. 219; Moo, *Romans*, pp. 243–45.
97.   Most exegetes believe this is the preferred reading of the text. Bruce M. Metzger, *A Textual Commentary on the Greek New Testament* (Stuttgart: Deutsche Bibelgesellschaft, 1994), p. 450. See

think, hold the opinion of) indicating that this is something they had believed all along. Thus, as justification by faith is not the *conclusion* to which Paul wishes to lead his readers at this moment, it is the *premise* on which he bases his conclusion that boasting is excluded.[98]

In 3.29 Paul asks a rhetorical question based upon the conclusion one must draw if boasting is not excluded and justification by faith for all people is not the primary criterion: 'or (ἤ) is God the God of the Jews only? Is he not (οὐχί) the God of Gentiles also?' His question about God as the God of the Gentiles as introduced by οὐχί points to his expectation that the answer will be in the affirmative, which it is: 'Yes (ναί), of Gentiles also' or more colloquially, 'Of course of the Gentiles!' His affirmative answer as begun with ναί emphasizes his stress on God being the God of the Gentiles.[99]

In 3.30, Paul gives the basic, theological reason for the law of faith as foundational for Jews and Gentiles being justified in the same way: 'since, after all (εἴ περ), God is one. Ἐἴπερ, which can mean 'if indeed', 'if after all', 'provided that' or 'since' introduces Paul's necessary condition for the affirmation just made.[100] Thus, the necessary condition for God to be 'of the Gentiles' is that God is one. Although the statement of monotheism in 3.30 (εἴπερ εἷς ὁ θεός) serves to show why it is that God is also God of the Gentiles, its corollary follows: God 'will make the circumcised righteous by faith and the uncircumcised righteous through faith' (3.30).

Jan Lambrecht has pointed out that the relative clause in 3.30 which describes God as '[the God] who will justify circumcision from faith and uncircumcision from faith' is not to be taken as a causal relative clause but as 'solely descriptive' as it 'qualifies Paul's vision of God'.[101] Lambrecht writes in response to scholars such as James Dunn who believes that here faith in Jesus is 'described simply as "faith" since it is the basic trust-reliance of creature on the only Creator which is in view' and sees Paul as arguing against Jewish pride in election and a kind of particularistic monotheism.[102] Lambrecht does not see 3.30 as a two-step argument, that God is God of the Gentiles because he is one *and* that Jews and Gentiles are both justified by faith in this one, Creator God. For Lambrecht, '[h]is "one and the same God" is christologically active. God is qualified as the God who justifies through faith in Christ. That faith is the sole condition, equally for Jew and Gentile.'[103] Thus, while God justifies both Jews and Gentiles in the same way because he is one, the faith that justifies is not faith in the Creator but faith in Christ. Therefore in 3.30 Paul is describing primarily how God functions

---

also Richard W. Thompson, 'The Inclusion of Gentiles in Rom 3,27–30', *Bib* 69 (1988), pp. 543–46; see also his 'Paul's Double Critique of Jewish Boasting: A Study of Rom 3,27 in Its Context', *Bib* 67 (1986), pp. 520–31.

   98. See also Richard W. Thompson, 'Inclusion', p. 544.
   99. BDF §441.
  100. BDAG 'εἰ', pp. 277–79; see also Rom. 8.9,17.
  101. 'Paul's Logic in Romans 3:29–30', *JBL* 119 (2000), pp. 526–28 (527).
  102. Dunn, *Romans*, vol. I, pp. 189 and 193, respectively.
  103. 'Logic', p. 528.

concerning justification by faith rather than describing the content of the faith itself. However, given the context of the passage in reference to Paul's proving how both Jews and Gentiles are made righteous by faith which is after the example of Abraham the first monotheist and that Paul then redefines the faith of Abraham in Rom. 4.24–25, as we shall see, it would seem that Paul had this corollary of faith in the Creator in mind.

If we return to what we argued earlier, that Abraham is depicted in Rom. 4.5 as the ungodly Gentile, then Abraham becomes the example (Stower's *exemplum*) of the Gentile who is included in the people of God by virtue of God being 'one'. We also saw how it was that in Rom. 4.6–8, Paul integrated Ps. 32 about the blessing pronounced upon the 'lawless one' or the 'sinner', both of which are similar in meaning to ἀσεβής (ungodly). Instead of assuming that Paul has immediately switched in vv. 6-8 to a discussion of God generally making individuals righteous by faith, it is probably the case that Paul still has Abraham in mind. If we further consider the example of Abraham, we must conclude that because he was previously a sinner who did not follow after God (see the discussion of, ἀσεβής above) then the faith by which he is justified by God has to be monotheistic faith. The traditions of Abraham, who as the first proselyte rejected idolatry for faith in the one God, assists us in establishing the larger content of the faith that is alluded to in 3.30 although the specific content of his faith is outlined in Rom. 4.18–21.

One also cannot help but notice the paucity of references to Christ in 3.27–4.25 in contrast to the references in chs. 1-3. Paul mentions Christ numerous times in chs. 1 through 3 (e. g. Rom. 1.1, 4, 6, 7; 2.16; 3.22, 24) and Jesus as well (1.1, 4, 6, 7, 8; 2.16, 3.22, 24, 26) and makes it clear that justifying faith is faith in Jesus Christ (esp. 3.22–26). Yet in 3.27–4.25 no references are made to Christ, although Jesus is mentioned in 4.24. On the other hand, God is mentioned (3.29, 30; 4.2, 3, 6, 17, 20 (2×) or referred to (4.5, 8, 21, 24) thirteen times. Why does Paul change from a Christocentric focus in 1–3 to a Theocentric focus in Rom. 4?

If we consider again Stower's contention that Paul is responding to perceived interlocutors as mentioned above, Paul may assume that his interlocutor at this point would bring up the example of Abraham: 'What should we say that Abraham our forefather "according to the flesh" has found?' (4.1)[104] It seems most likely here that Paul is using κατὰ σάρκα (according to the flesh) in a way similar to his usage in Rom. 1.3 and 9.3, with the sense of natural physical generation which is also narrowly restrictive.[105] It would not be surprising for a Jew to look to the example of Abraham for guidance, since he was one of the primary figures of the time that served as an example for the Jewish people.

The interlocutor's statement, 'for if Abraham was justified by works' (4.2) belies the common assumption of Abraham's obedience to the law. As we saw in earlier chapters, one of the major early Jewish traditions about Abraham was that

104. Contra the translation in Richard Hays, ' "Have We Found Abraham to be Our Forefather According to the Flesh?" A Reconsideration of Rom. 4:1', *NovT* 27 (1985), pp. 76–98.
105. Cranfield, *Romans*, vol. I, p. 227 n. 3.

he was obedient to the law even before it was given.[106] He provided an example of covenant faithfulness: faith in God that necessitated the practice of the commandments. Surely, if anyone would have reason to boast, Abraham would. Many commentators have noticed this tradition of Abraham's obedience to the law.[107] As Dunn states, 'There was evidently an already well established and influential view of Abraham as pattern for the faithful Jew which ran almost directly counter to Paul's gospel'.[108]

My argument would be incomplete here without a consideration of Rom. 4.4, 'Now to the one who works his wages are not reckoned as a gift but as his due.' My suspicion here is that Dunn and Wright are correct in their contention that Paul is using a technical term in commercial dealings, which 'obviously suggested an analogy from the business world, as also the talk of "works" '.[109] Thus, Paul is not arguing that the Jewish law was practised in order that righteousness might be attained as what was due. Even Douglas Moo who is not a fan of the new perspective believes Paul is referring to a 'general principle about the "reckoning" or "accounting" of "wages" to a worker…the employer "owes" the worker a certain wage and is not giving it "freely" or "without compulsion" '.[110]

One might argue that there is an implicit theological argument here that since Abraham was often connected with the law in the literature of the time that Paul here reveals that his righteousness was earned as a result of his obedience to the law. However, in the literature that we investigated in earlier chapters it was primarily the case that Abraham's obedience to the law was as a result of his faith in the one God and as an expression of that faith. It was because of his monotheistic faith in this literature that Abraham was the first member of the people of God. The obedience to law was an outworking of his faith not that by which he earned his place in the people of God. What Paul does here that is different from the Jewish literature we studied is that he divides faith from law.

However, as Hanson has noted, Paul is more concerned to speak about Abraham's faith than he is to speak about his being made righteous 'apart from works'.[111] Abraham's faith (πίστις) is mentioned 8 times in Rom. 4 (4.5, 9, 11, 12, 13, 16, 19, 20), and his believing (πιστεύω) is mentioned 4 times (4.3, 5,17, 18,). 'Works' is mentioned two times (4.2, 6) with the second mention in the context of David's speaking blessing upon those who are righteous apart from works, and the law is mentioned four times (4.13–16).

This brings us back to our interlocutor and Paul in Rom. 4.2. The interlocutor believes that if works justified Abraham, he had something to boast about. Paul replies, 'but not before God. For what does the Scripture say?' Paul argues that

---

106. For example, see *Jub.* 16.20–3, 22.1–2; *Migr. Abr.* 129–130; Sir 44.19–20; *Ant.* 1.154–156.

107. Cranfield, *Romans*, vol. I, p. 227.

108. Dunn, *Romans*, vol. I, p. 226.

109. Dunn, *Romans*, vol. I, p. 203; N.T. Wright, 'The Letter to the Romans', in Leander Keck *et al.* (eds.), *The New Interpreter's Bible: A Commentary in Twelve Volumes* (Nashville: Abingdon Press, 2002), vol. X, pp. 393–770 (491–92).

110. Moo, *Romans*, p. 263.

111. Hanson, 'Sinner', pp. 65–66.

righteousness is bestowed upon Abraham based upon his faith (4.3–4) which, in turn, is the same way that everyone is justified because God is one (3.29–30). However, Paul turns the relatively narrow conception of 'Abraham our forefather according to the flesh' into a more universalistic idea. Abraham, the 'ungodly' (4.5) and upon whom Ps. 32.1–2 pronounces a blessing, becomes the representative of the Gentile sinner, one from another nation which meant that he was obedient to other gods. Yet, by faith, this Gentile (he is not circumcised, 4.9–10) has been made righteous.

One reason that Abraham apparently cannot boast before God is because by virtue of his Gentile status, as Paul interprets it, Abraham originally had no works to boast about. Paul sees Gen. 15.6 without the later interpretations afforded by Gen. 17 (circumcision) that those in Rome probably used. In essence, Abraham cannot boast because he is a Gentile and he has been made righteous by virtue of the fact that God is one and he justifies people in the same way – by faith. Abraham can provide the example of righteousness by faith for the Jewish interlocutor because contrary to the interlocutor who believes in a covenantal and particularistic monotheism, Abraham is a Gentile who is made righteous by believing in the one, Creator God (4.17; see earlier discussion). Chapter 4 contains its theocentric emphasis because Paul, knowing the tradition of Abraham the first monotheist, explains how it is that the monotheistic faith of Abraham which brought him righteousness has, now that Christ has come, found its fulfilment and ultimate definition in faith in 'him that raised from the dead Jesus our Lord' (4.25).

Moreover, as Abraham turned from idols to faith in the one God, Paul's gospel becomes that which is for both Gentile and Jew by faith in the same God without works of the law that would separate them by nationalistic boundaries. N.T. Wright sees monotheism as central to Paul's gospel: 'The "gospel" of Paul the apostle was also a message about God, the one God of Israel, the creator of the world. It…was a summons to reject pagan idolatry and to turn to the true God, the source of life and all good things… The "gospel" is for Paul, at its very heart, an *announcement about the true God as opposed to the false gods*'.[112] If this is the crux of the gospel, Abraham serves as the foundational example of one who rejected idolatry for faith in the one God.

4. *Abraham, the 'Weak' and the 'Strong'*

Most tend to see Paul's description of Abraham in Rom. 4 from a solely theological perspective. Not many have worked out what implications Paul's comments about Abraham may have for the Romans themselves.[113] Working from the pre-

---

112. N.T. Wright, *What Saint Paul Really Said: Was Paul of Tarsus the Real Founder of Christianity?* (Grand Rapids, MI: Eerdmans, 1997), pp. 58–59.

113. A.T. Lincoln, 'Abraham Goes to Rome: Paul's Treatment of Abraham in Romans 4', in Michael J. Wilkins and Terance Paige (eds.), *Worship, Theology and Ministry in the Early Church* (JSOTSup, 87; Sheffield: Sheffield Academic Press, 1992), p. 169.

supposition that while writing Romans Paul also has in mind the situation and needs of believers in Rome (see above), we will now consider how Paul's description of Abraham in Rom. 4 instructs his readers in Rome.

As was mentioned above, the groups that existed in Rome were characterized as the 'weak' and the 'strong'. The 'weak' were probably primarily Jewish Christians, although some could have been former Gentile proselytes to Judaism who still maintained adherence to the law. The strong were probably primarily Gentile Christians but included perhaps some Jewish Christians who did not maintain adherence to the Mosaic Law.

Significant verbal similarities exist between ch. 4 and the latter two chapters of the epistle; this may suggest that Paul used the figure of Abraham in order to provide instructions for the situation at hand. For example, it is probably not an accident that when Paul describes Abraham's faith in 4.19–20 he does so in terms similar to those being used for believers in Rome: μὴ ἀσθενήσας τῇ πίστει …ἀλλ ἐνεδυναμώθη τῇ πίστει (he did not weaken in his faith…but he was strengthened in faith). In contrast, in 14.1, Paul speaks of the one who is weak in faith: Τὸν δὲ ἀσθενοῦντα τῇ πίστει. Paul uses the aorist participle of ἀσθενέω (weaken) in 4.19 with the dative of πίστις (faith) which compares to the present participle of the same verb used in 14.1 as a substantive again with the dative of πίστις. On the other hand, those who are strong in faith, including Paul, are described in 15.1 as οἱ δυνατοὶ (the strong) which is 'a cognate adjective of the verb [ἐνδυναμόω; to become strong] in 4.20 being used as a substantive'.[114] Paul further speaks of the weak in 15.1 as the ἀδυνάτων, literally, those who are 'not strong'.

The qualities of the faith that Paul ascribes to Abraham are required for the faith of those in Rome. For example, in Rom. 4.20–21, Abraham does not doubt, but is fully convinced and gives glory to God. As Lincoln points out, 'the terminology employed in 4.20 is οὐ διεκρίθη [he did not doubt] and significantly the only other place in Paul's writings where the middle or passive διακρίνεσθαι, "to doubt" is found is in Rom. 14.23, where doubt is one of the symptoms displayed by the weak in faith.'[115] Those who doubt are condemned, because they are not acting according to their own conviction but according to the conviction of others.

In 4.20, Abraham is also said to have the kind of faith that gave glory to God (δοὺς δόξαν τῷ θεῷ) just as he commands all the Romans, both weak and strong, to live in harmony in order that they may glorify (δοξάζω) God with one voice (15.5–6) and welcome each other for God's glory (δόξα; 15.7). The Gentiles among them are told to glorify (δοξάζω) God because of his mercy (15.9).

Thus, Paul is concerned that the believers in Rome have faith as Abraham did. They are not to doubt but to be convinced in their own minds and give glory to God. Paul above all wants their faith to result in unity in belief and action towards one another. Although he gives concessions to the weak and instructs the strong to act sensitively to them (14.20–21; 15.1–3), as Lincoln states, 'Paul

114. Lincoln, 'Abraham', p. 172.
115. Lincoln, 'Abraham', p. 174.

signals clearly ahead of time where he stands theologically in the debate in Rome. Abraham does not merely exemplify the Pauline gospel as one who is righteous by faith, but he also joins the debate in Rome on the side of the strong in faith'.[116]

In this case, Paul is siding with those who are probably primarily Gentiles of the law-free persuasion. Fellow Jews who realize the thrust of Paul's argument, that obedience to laws concerning the Sabbath and idolatry (the reason for the avoidance of buying meat and wine in the market, cf. Rom. 14.2, 21), are contrary to the oneness of God would probably be scandalized. As he did in ch. 4, Abraham once again represents the Gentile Christian in Rome in chs 14–15. Those law-abiding Jews hearing the message may then be persuaded that Gentiles do not need to adhere to laws about wine and meat and holy days if Abraham was justified by faith alone. After all, adherence to the law as an identity marker was what divided Jews and Gentiles from one another. Implicit in Paul's argumentation, adherence to the law meant that there were two ways of justification: one by law and one without the law. Paul showed earlier that because God is one, then both Jews and Gentiles are justified by faith in the same way. Thus, obedience to the law is actually a denial of the oneness of God. The obedience to law that was actualized by avoiding wine and meat (see 14.2, 21) sold in the marketplace and thus avoiding possible idolatry is now portrayed as a denial of God's oneness. Ironically, their obedience to the law becomes a kind of idolatry in and of itself.[117]

5. *Conclusion: Paul's Redefinition of the People of God*

By virtue of his reworking of the biblical material and traditions about Abraham, Paul has redefined the people of God. As Adams has said, '[t]he phrase "τὸν δικαιοῦντα τὸν ἀσεβῆ" [the one who justifies the ungodly] from an Old Testament point of view is a definition of gross injustice.'[118] While some Old Testament passages do support God's mercy towards the ungodly (e.g. Ezek. 18.23), many point out that the wicked are not to be acquitted (Isa. 5.23; Exod. 23.7). Stuhlmacher also notes the import of Paul's statement here when he says that Paul 'coins a new description of God that is highly paradoxical and of great rhetorical power: God already demonstrated himself toward Abraham to be the God who justifies the ungodly (the wicked) through Christ'.[119]

As we have seen in much of the early Jewish literature from previous chapters, for the people of God faith was to be coupled with obedience to the law. Given Paul's response to his Jewish interlocutor in 4.2 about Abraham's justification by works, one can surmise that those in Rome who were among the weak were argu-

---

116. Lincoln, 'Abraham', p. 172.

117. See also Don Garlington who believes that Israel's attachment to the law is idolatrous particularly as presented in Rom. 1.18–32 and 2.2 in *Faith, Obedience and Perseverance: Aspects of Paul's Letter to the Romans* (WUNT, 79, Tübingen: J.C.B. Mohr [Paul Siebeck], 1994), pp. 38–39.

118. Adams,'Gentile', p. 52 n. 16.

119. Stuhlmacher, *Romans*, p. 72.

ing that Abraham was obedient to law, probably primarily circumcision (4.9–12) and that the new people of God in Christ should follow that example.

However, Paul takes the biblical narrative and popular traditions about Abraham and twists them to make his own point. He bases his point on his commitment to Jewish monotheism, using the association of Abraham and monotheism to show how it is that faith in Christ for both Jew and Gentile, now that Christ has come, is really a continuation of Abraham's monotheistic faith. Now that Christ has come, to maintain obedience to the law is to hold on to divisive symbols of nationalism. The strong are those, like Abraham, who have no need to rely on the law, but who convinced of the power of the God in whom they have faith, give glory to Him.

The early Christian attachment to the synagogue, and especially to Palestinian Judaism, may have meant that the weak based their position on the law from traditions of Abraham in which he was not only separate from Gentiles, but also obedient to the law. Those who did not meet these requirements were traditionally excluded from God's people.

However, those who are now inside God's people are those who have faith in the God who raised Jesus Christ from the dead. The obedience to the law is now something that divides Jew from Gentile. Paul seems to use Abraham to say that the strong, indeed, are of the correct mindset. Those who are righteous by faith alone – without the nationalistic symbols of the law – will eventually win the day. Thus those Gentiles who may have been proselytes to Judaism before the introduction of Christianity in Rome who were attracted to Judaism to a large degree because of its monotheistic basis and who suffered estrangement from their Gentile communities are now included in the community for which Paul contends by virtue of their faith.

However, Paul does not exclude those who maintain aspects of the law based upon their own conscience without insisting that others do the same. Who he does exclude are those whose view of God's people are so particularistic as to believe that those who do not practise the law – particularly circumcision – are not members of God's people. Ironically, those who were once primary candidates for membership in God's people are now cast outside.

Ironically, it is these weak who maintain the law that bring division and which ultimately denies the oneness of God (3.29–30). One can only wonder at the irony involved when those who see themselves as Abraham's children continue to adhere to the very thing that compromises monotheistic faith, contrary to the example of Abraham the first monotheist.

Chapter 9

CONCLUSION

1. *Abraham, Monotheism and Jewish Literature*

In the variety of early Jewish texts we considered, Abraham appeared as the ideal person of God who forsook idolatry for faith in God and, in many cases, lived out that faith through his obedience to the Mosaic Law. Although each text was written against different historical and political backgrounds, the same traditions about Abraham continued to emerge and they provided a prototype for the identity of the ideal Jew.

In *Jubilees,* Abraham was a central transmitter of the covenant who sees beyond astrological reasoning and is known for his vehement anti-idolatrous stance and obedience to law particularly as these characteristics separated him from the Gentiles that surrounded him and his descendants. He likewise represents the true Jew who has maintained faithfulness to God in the midst of other Jews who compromise their monotheistic faith and forsake the law. In the political circumstances in which *Jubilees* was probably written, either just before or immediately after the beginning of the Hasmonean era, the author encourages his readers to face persecution and even death in order to remain faithful to their God.

For the author of *Jubilees,* those who are within the boundaries of God's people reject idolatry and obey covenantal stipulations. Those who are outside of the boundary of God's people are the Gentiles who are idolaters and sinners and the Jews who assimilate to their ways. Monotheistic faith excludes anyone who would venture into this sphere of assimilation and Abraham represents the legitimisation of this monotheistic boundary and the prototype for those who would heed *Jubilees'* warning.

In the works of Philo, Abraham appears as the prototype of the proselyte who is the first to believe in the one God and forsake idolatry in the form of astrological determinism. Abraham also follows the Mosaic Law before it was actually given because, according to Philo, he followed the natural law that was later codified in the Law of Moses. For Philo, Abraham was actually a living law.

In the context of increasing conflict between ethnic groups in Alexandria and the desire for Jews to acquire status and full civil rights, Abraham functions as one who ultimately puts his faith in the one God. Philo encourages his readers not to put too much faith in the accoutrements of status acquired in the Hellenistic world but in the one God who alone is worthy of that faith.

In accord with his goal to provide an apologetic for Judaism for Gentile readers, Abraham is shown to be one who discerns God according to respected philosophical practices of the day. The law that Abraham obeys is in accordance with the natural law and later forms the basis for the Mosaic Law. Both provide reasons for Gentiles to believe in the one, true God and to obey the Jewish law that is the revealed, natural law of God. At the same time, Jews in Alexandria can find reason to maintain faithfulness to God and his law or to return to their faith from which they may have apostatized.

In the works of Philo, Abraham stands for those things which make the Jews distinctive from their Gentile neighbours in Alexandria: monotheistic faith and obedience to the Mosaic Law. However, the essence of what characterized those who were members of the people of God was primarily monotheism. Abraham was the prototypical monotheist whose example functioned to define the true Jew and thereby include or exclude persons from the people of God.

For the author of the *Biblical Antiquities* Abraham's stance against idolatry and his trust in the one God are his most notable functions. Because of these characteristics, God bestows upon him a covenant and many blessings, not only for himself but also for his descendants forever.

As the first to spurn idolatry in the form of his refusal to participate in the building of the tower of Babel and to maintain allegiance to the one God, Abraham set the pattern for the leaders who would come after him. Later good leaders in the *Biblical Antiquities* are those who maintained devotion to the one God. The bad leaders were most often known for practising idolatry and often this idolatry was a result of assimilation to the beliefs of Gentile neighbours.

What emerges from much of the *Biblical Antiquities* is that idolatry is the root of sin. It symbolizes abandonment of God and his claim on his people. Thus, Abraham's rejection of idolatry for faith in the one God provides the ultimate prototype for the identity of the people of God. Even before God's commandments comes allegiance to him.

Abraham functions as a prototype against idolatry in the *Biblical Antiquities* particularly in that he refused to participate in the activities of those who intended to glorify and make a name for themselves. Abraham would not assimilate to the self-aggrandizing intentions of these people because he saw this assimilation as idolatry. Because Jews often perceived the Romans as idolatrous people in first-century Palestine, the author of the *Biblical Antiquities* may be telling his readers that assimilation with the self-aggrandizing plans of the Romans is idolatry. If the *Biblical Antiquities* was written during the increasing conflict between the Romans and the Jews in Jerusalem previous to the destruction of the Temple in 70 CE, the author uses Abraham to call his compatriots to single-minded devotion to God. To be like their forefather Abraham, the Jewish people had to maintain non-assimilation with idolatrous practices. To be like Abraham meant that devotion to the one God was so paramount that they should be willing to face death rather than practise idolatry.

Abraham is part of Josephus' apologetic agenda as he portrays him as the Hellenistic philosopher that would have spoken best to his Hellenistic, non-Jewish readers. For Josephus, Abraham was the first to proclaim monotheism using a popular philosophic proof of God. Abraham is able to refute empty arguments and persuade his audience convincingly on any topic he chooses.

According to Josephus, those who hold to the doctrines given by the lawgiver participate in the virtue of God. Abraham was shown to obey a few specific Jewish laws, but the major indication of Abraham's living in accordance with God's will before it was given is his virtue, which for Josephus is the essence of Jewish law.

The most distinctive element of Josephus' portrayal of Abraham is his mono-theism. As portrayed by Josephus, this belief is based upon sound, reasonable philosophical principles. In contrast to the polytheistic milieu of the day, this made the Jews themselves distinctive. Abraham the first monotheist provides the foundation for this distinctive faith.

However, because Josephus shies away from describing the covenant or the election of the Jews, he never says explicitly that those who do not adhere to monotheism are not members of the people of God. Yet if in his apologetic to an audience that is primarily Gentile he is trying to prove the attractiveness of the essential elements of Judaism, it would follow that in order to be of the community of the Jews one would need to identify oneself at least in these ways. Circumcision and monotheism appear as the key elements of Judaism that are associated with Abraham. They then become ways to identify who are among the community of Jews and, insofar as one is interested, in taking on Jewish identity.

For the author of the *Apocalypse of Abraham,* Abraham provides an example of one who sees beyond the natural phenomenon including the stars and who refuses to participate in the idolatry of his father, Terah. Abraham is rewarded with an apocalyptic revelation of God. It is not clear what, if any, association Abraham has with the law in the *Apocalypse of Abraham*. However, he does provide an example of one whose rejection of idolatry for faith in God becomes the antithesis to the unfaithfulness and idolatry of members of ethnic Israel, par-ticularly the priests who, as portrayed by the author, participate in idolatry.

Given that the apocalypse was written not long after the destruction of the Temple by the Romans in 70 CE, one of the author's major concerns is to show that ultimately the people of God would be vindicated over their hostile oppres-sors. Once punished for their idolatrous ways, the identity of the people of God and their hope for deliverance now rest in their maintaining faithfulness to the one Creator God after the example of their forefather Abraham.

Thus the rejection of idolatry for monotheism after the example of Abraham is the ultimate and distinctive criterion for those who are faithful to God. Those who follow after the example of Abraham can expect great reward. However, those who do not follow his example can expect eventual annihilation.

Thus what we have found in these examples of the portrayal of Abraham in Jewish literature is that Abraham functions as the prototype of one who rejects idolatry for faith in the one God and, in many cases, expresses that faith in obedi-ence to the law. Even in the differing historical and political circumstances in which each of the texts was written, Abraham functioned to identify primary characteristics of the people of God.

Those who leave behind idolatry for monotheistic faith and in many cases actualize that faith through obedience to the law are exalted. Those who do not practise monotheism and in many cases the law cannot be identified as God's people. Thus, the traditions about Abraham function to define whom the members of God's people are and, in contrast, who are excluded from the people of God.

2. *Abraham and the Identity of God's People in Galatians and Romans*

When we come to the letters of Paul, we found that he also uses Abraham to identify who are members of God's people. In Galatians, he most probably responds to opponents who use the example of Abraham's obedience to the law that is based upon his monotheistic faith in order to persuade Gentile believers in Christ that in order to become true members of God's people they must take on obedience to the law in addition to their faith.

We found that Paul counters his opponents' arguments by fashioning his own definition of Abraham's faith that is a recreation of Abraham's monotheism. For Paul, Abraham's trust in God's promises that Gentiles would eventually be included in the people of God was central to his faith. These promises, of course, were realized in the coming of Christ through whom Gentiles could now be included in God's people as Gentiles without first taking on the law. To modify Abraham's faith by requiring Gentiles to take on the Jewish law, particularly that which identified the Jewish people like circumcision and festival days was not in accordance with the monotheistic faith of Abraham. By requiring them to take on the law meant that they in essence became Jews first and negated God's promise to Abraham that Gentiles would become members of God's people as Gentiles.

Eschatologically, Paul suggests that those who maintain obedience to the law are really still acting as if they are members of the former era of law that is not in accord with Abraham's faith and consequently they are cursed. While they believe that their continued obedience to the law means they are true members of God's people, Paul shows instead that they are the ones who have not remained true to God. By their actions they are succumbing to forces that function like astrological principles that once controlled the pagan Gentiles and those who were under the law (4.8–11). Paul wants them to break free from their idolatry in order that they might have true faith like that of Abraham who rejected idolatry for faith in the one God and through whose faith the Spirit eventually came upon Gentiles when that faith was fulfilled in Jesus Christ.

Yet Paul's monotheistic influence does not stop there. Paul also suggests that the giving of the law through a mediator also implies plurality that is in contrast to the one God who gave the promise to Abraham (3.19–20). In essence, to maintain obedience to the law becomes a contradiction of the oneness of God. Because his opponents are not acting in accordance with their monotheistic faith that has been brought to completion in Jesus Christ, Paul consigns them to a sphere outside of the people of God (e.g. 5.4, 8, 10).

Thus in Galatians as well as in early Jewish texts, Abraham's anti-idolatrous and monotheistic faith functions to identify who are members of the people of God and thereby includes some but excludes others. However, the major difference between Paul's Abraham and the Abraham of popular discourse is that Abraham is no longer considered to have been obedient to the law. To the contrary, Paul refashions Abraham so that he represents just the opposite: the patriarch who is considered to be righteous apart from the Mosaic Law.

In Romans, the tradition of Abraham's discernment that one God exists beyond the natural phenomena and thus rejects idolatry for monotheistic faith provides the necessary contrast to the idolatry of the Gentiles who, although God has revealed himself through Creation, succumb to idolatry and its temptations. The 'weak' among the Romans who probably still maintain a connection with the synagogues in Rome and are probably influenced to some degree by the Jewish Christians in Jerusalem may very well look to Abraham as the example of faith and obedience to the law as described in popular discourse. Instead Paul makes it clear that because God is one there is only one way to be made righteous and thus members of God's people: through faith. For Paul the addition of the law means that there is more than one way to be a member of God's people, which is in contradiction of the oneness of God (3.29–30). Now that Christ has come this monotheistic faith has been redefined as faith in the God 'that raised from the dead Jesus our Lord' (3.29–30; 4.24).

The weak, then, who attempt to avoid idolatry through not eating meat or drinking wine and who maintain adherence to Jewish Sabbaths and festivals in effect wind up doing the very thing that they attempt to avoid. For by practising such things and assuming that their practices are necessary for God's people, they actually set up another way in which God's people are to be made righteous in addition to faith. In this sense they support a kind of idolatry that is contrary to the fulfilled monotheistic faith revealed by Paul as the single criterion for membership in God's people. In this way the weak act contrary to the faith of Abraham in which he rejected idolatry for monotheistic faith.

Thus as in Galatians and the early Jewish literature as discussed above, monotheistic faith like that of Abraham becomes the litmus test for membership in God's people. Except that as in Galatians, in Romans the major difference is that Paul turns the law, which was formerly a characteristic of God's people, into the idolatry that God's people are now to avoid.

BIBLIOGRAPHY

Aageson, James W., 'Scripture and Structure in the Development of the Argument in Romans 9–11', *CBQ* 48 (1986), pp. 265–89.

—'Typology, Correspondence, and the Application of Scripture in Romans 9–11', *JSNT* 31 (1987), pp. 51–72.

Abegg, M., Jr, '4QMMT C 27,31 and "Works Righteousness"', *Dead Sea Discoveries* 6.2 (1999), pp. 139–47.

Adams, Edward, 'Abraham's Faith and Gentile Disobedience: Textual Links Between Romans 1 and 4', *JSNT* 65 (1997), pp. 47–66.

Alexander, Philip S., 'Rabbinic Judaism and the New Testament', *ZNW* 74 (1983), pp. 237–46.

—'Retelling the Old Testament', in D.A. Carson and H.G.M. Williamson (eds.), *It is Written: Scripture Citing Scripture* (Cambridge: Cambridge University Press, 1988), pp. 99–121.

Amaru, Betsy Halpern, 'Land Theology in Josephus' *Jewish Antiquities*', *JQR* 71 (1980–81), pp. 201–229.

Ambrosiaster. *Ambrosiastri qui dicitur Commentarius in Epistulas Paulinas* (CSEL, 81.1; Vienna: Hoelder-Pichler-Tempsky, 1966).

Applebaum, S., 'The Legal Status of the Jewish Communities in the Diaspora', *Jewish People in the First Century* (CRINT, 1.1; Assen: Van Gorcum, 1974), pp. 420–503.

Aristotle, *The Metaphysics, Books I–IX* (trans. Hugh Tredennick; LCL; London: Heinemann, 1933).

Arnold, Clinton E., 'Returning to the Domain of the Powers: *Stoicheia* as Evil Spirits in Galatians 4:3,9', *NovT* 38 (1996), pp. 55–76.

—*The Colossian Syncretism: The Interface between Christianity and Folk Belief* (Grand Rapids: Baker Book House, 1996).

Arnold, E.V., *Roman Stoicism* (repr., New York: The Humanities Press, 1958).

Attridge, H.W., *The Interpretation of Biblical History in the Antiquitates Judaicae of Flavius Josephus* (HDR, 7; Missoula, MT: Scholars Press, 1976).

—'Historiography', *Jewish Writings of the Second Temple Period* (CRINT, 2.2; Assen: Van Gorcum, 1984), pp. 157–84.

—'Josephus and His Works', *Jewish Writings of the Second Temple Period* (CRINT, 2.2; Assen: Van Gorcum, 1984), pp. 185–232.

—'Jewish Historiography', *Early Judaism and its Modern Interpreters* (SBLBMI, 2; Atlanta, GA: Scholars Press, 1986), pp. 311–43.

Augustine, *The City of God Against the Pagans* (trans. William M. Green, Philip Levine and George E. McCracken; LCL; London: Heinemann, 1963).

Aune, D.E., *The New Testament in Its Literary Environment* (Library of Early Christianity, 8; Philadelphia: Westminster Press, 1987).

Baird, William, 'Abraham in the New Testament: Tradition and the New Identity', *Int.* 42.4 (1988), pp. 367–79.

Baltzer, Klaus, *The Covenant Formulary* (Philadelphia: Fortress Press, 1971).

Bammel, E., 'Gottes DIAΘHKH (Gal. III.15–17) und das jüdische Rechtsdenken', *NTS* 6 (1959–60), pp. 313–19.

Bandstra, A.J., *The Law and the Elements of the World: An Exegetical Study in Aspects of Paul's Teaching* (Kampen: J.H. Kok, N.V., 1964).

Barclay, J.M.G., 'Mirror-Reading a Polemical Letter: Galatians as a Test Case', *JSNT* 31 (1987), pp. 73–93.

—*Obeying the Truth: A Study of Paul's Ethics in Galatians* (Edinburgh: T. & T. Clark, 1988).

—*Jews in the Mediterranean Diaspora: From Alexander to Trajan* (323 BCE–117 CE) (Edinburgh: T. & T. Clark, 1996).

Barrett, C.K., *From First Adam to Last* (New York: Charles Scribner's Sons, 1962).

—'The Allegory of Abraham, Sarah, and Hagar in the Argument of Galatians', in J. Friedrich, W. Pöhlman and P. Stuhlmacher (eds.), *Rechtfertigung* (Festschrift E. Käsemann; Göttingen: Vandenhoeck & Ruprecht, 1976), pp. 1–16.

—*The Epistle to the Romans* (BNTC; repr., London: A. & C. Black, 1984).

Bartlett, John R., *Jews in the Hellenistic World: Josephus, Aristeas, the Sibylline Oracles, Eupolemus* (Cambridge Commentaries on Writings of the Jewish and Christian World 200 BC to AD 200, I.1; Cambridge: Cambridge University Press, 1985).

Bassler, Jouette, *Divine Impartiality: Paul and a Theological Axiom* (SBLDS , 59; Chico, CA: Scholars Press, 1982).

Bauckham, Richard, 'The Liber Antiquitatum Biblicarum of Pseudo-Philo and the Gospels as "Midrash"', in R.T. France and David Wenham (eds.), *Gospel Perspectives: Studies in Midrash and Historiography* (Sheffield: JSOT Press, 1983), vol. III, pp. 33–76.

—'Early Jewish Visions of Hell', *JTS* 41 (1990), pp. 355–85.

—*God Crucified: Monotheism and Christology in the New Testament* (Grand Rapids, MI: Eerdmans, 1998).

Bauernfeind, O., 'αρετή', *TDNT*, vol. I, pp. 457–61.

Becker, Jurgen, and Ulrich Luz, *Die Briefe an die Galater, Epheser und Kolosser* (Das Neue Testament Deutsch 8/1; Göttingen: Vandenhoeck & Ruprecht, 1998).

Beer, B., *Leben Abrahams nach Auffassung der jüdischen Sage* (Leipzig: Oskar Leiner, 1859).

Begg, Christopher T., 'Rereadings of the "Animal Rite" of Genesis 15 in Early Jewish Narratives', *CBQ* 50 (1988), pp. 36–46.

Behm, J., 'ανάθεμα', *TDNT*, vol. I, pp. 354–55.

Beker, J.C., 'The Faithfulness of God and the Priority of Israel in Paul's Letter to the Romans', *HTR* 79 (1986), pp. 10–16.

—*Paul the Apostle: The Triumph of God in Life and Thought* (Philadelphia: Fortress Press, 1980).

Bell, Richard H., *No One Seeks for God: An Exegetical and Theological Study of Romans 1:18–3:20* (Tübingen: Mohr Siebeck, 1998).

Belleville, Linda L., '"Under Law": Structural Analysis and the Pauline Concept of Law in Galatians 3:21–4:11', *JSNT* 26 (1986), pp. 53–78.

Benko, Stephen, 'The Edict of Claudius of A.D. 49 and the Instigator Chrestus', *TZ* 25 (1969), pp. 406–18.

Bentwich, Norman, *Josephus* (Philadelphia: The Jewish Publication Society of America, 1945), pp. 52–57.

Berger, Klaus, 'Abraham in den paulinischen Hauptbriefen', *MTZ* 17 (1966), pp. 47–89.

—'Abraham II: Im Frühjudentum und Neuen Testament' in *Theologische Realenzyklopädie* (Berlin, NY: W. de Gruyter, 1977), vol. I, pp. 372–82.

—*Das Buch der Jubiläen* (JSHRZ; Gütersloh: Gerd Mohn, 1981).

Best, E., *One Body in Christ* (London: SPCK, 1955).

Betz, H.D., *Galatians: A Commentary on Paul's Letter to the Churches in Galatia* (Hermeneia; Philadelphia: Fortress Press, 1979).

Bickerman, Elias, *The God of the Maccabees: Studies on the Meaning and Origin of the Maccabean Revolt* (SJLA, 32; Leiden: E.J. Brill, 1979).

Bilde, Per, *Flavius Josephus between Jerusalem and Rome: His Life, his Works, and their Importance* (Sheffield: JSOT Press, 1988).

Billerbeck, P., 'Abrahams Leben und Bedeutung für das Reich Gottes nach Auffassung der älterer Haggada', *Nathanael* 15 (1899), pp. 43–57, 118–128, 137–57, 161–79; 16 (1900), pp. 33–57, 65–80.

Birnbaum, Ellen. 'The Place of Judaism in Philo's Thought: Israel, Jews and Proselytes', *SBL Seminar Papers, 1992* (SBLSP, 32; Atlanta, Scholars Press, 1993), pp. 54–69.

—'What Does Philo Mean by "Seeing God"? Some Methodological Considerations', *SBL Seminar Papers, 1994* (SBLSP, 34; Atlanta, GA: Scholars Press, 1995), pp. 535–52.

—*The Place of Judaism in Philo's Thought: Israel, Jews, and Proselytes* (Studia Philonica Monographs, 2; BJS, 290; Atlanta, GA: Scholars Press, 1996).

Boccaccini, Gabriele, *Middle Judaism: Jewish Thought 300 B.C.E. to 200 C.E* (Minneapolis: Fortress Press, 1991).

Boers, H., *Theology Out of the Ghetto: A New Testament Exegetical Study Concerning Religious Exclusiveness* (Leiden: E.J. Brill, 1971).

Bogaert, P.M., 'La Figure d'Abraham dans les Antiquités Bibliques du Pseudo Philo', in *Abraham dans la Bible et dans la Tradition Juive* (Publications de 'Institutum Judaicum Bruxelles;Bruxelles: Institutum Iudaicum, Colloque de Louvain, 1977), vol. 2, pp. 40–61.

Bohrmann, Monette, *Flavius Josephus, The Zealots and Yavne: Toward a Rereading of The War of the Jews* (trans. Janet Lloyd; Bern: Peter Lang, 1989).

Borgen, Peder, *Bread from Heaven: An Exegetical Study of the Concept of Manna In the Gospel of John and the Writings of Philo* (NovTSup, 10; Leiden: E.J. Brill, 1965).

—'Philo of Alexandria', in Michael E. Stone (ed.), *Jewish Writings of the Second Temple Period* (CRINT, 2.2; Assen: Van Gorcum, 1984), pp. 233–82.

—'Philo: Survey of Research since World War II', *ANRW* 2.21.1 (Berlin: W. de Gruyter, 1984), pp. 98–154.

—*Philo, John, and Paul: New Perspectives on Judaism and Early Christianity* (Atlanta, GA: Scholars Press, 1987).

—*Philo of Alexandria, An Exegete for His Time* (NovTSup, 86; Leiden: E.J. Brill, 1997).

Bornkamm, G., 'The Letter to the Romans as Paul's Last Will and Testament', in Karl P. Donfried (ed.), *The Romans Debate* (Minneapolis, MN: Augsburg, rev. ed., 1991), pp. 16–28.

Box, G.H., and J.I. Landsman, *The Apocalypse of Abraham* (London: SPCK, 1918).

Boyarin, Daniel, 'Was Paul an "Anti-Semite"? A Reading of Galatians 3–4', *USQR* 47 (1993), pp. 47–80.

—*A Radical Jew: Paul and the Politics of Identity* (Berkeley: University of California Press, 1994).

Bréhier, E., *Les idées philosophiques et religieuses de Philon d'Alexandrie* (Paris: Librairie Alphonse Picard & Fils, 1908).

Brinsmead, B.H., *Galatians: Dialogical Response to Opponents* (SBLDS, 65; Chico, CA: Scholars Press, 1982).

Brown, R.E., and J.P. Meier, *Antioch and Rome* (London: Chapman, 1983).

Bruce, F.F., ' "Abraham Had Two Sons", A Study in Pauline Hermeneutics', in H. Drumwright (ed.), *New Testament Studies* (Waco, TX: Markham, 1975), pp. 71–84.

—'Abraham Our Father', in *The Time is Fulfilled* (Grand Rapids: Eerdmans, 1978), pp. 55–74.

—*Commentary on Galatians* (NIGTC; Grand Rapids, MI: Eerdmans, 1982).

—'The Romans Debate – Continued', *BJRL* 64 (1982), pp. 334–59.

—*The Letter of Paul to the Romans* (TNTC, 6; repr., Leicester: InterVarsity Press; rev. edn, 1987).

Burton, E. DeWitt, *A Critical and Exegetical Commentary on the Epistle to the Galatians* (ICC, 33; Edinburgh: T. & T. Clark, 1921).

Byrne, Brendan, *Son of God – 'Seed of Abraham': A Study of the Idea of the Sonship of God of All Christians in Paul against the Jewish Background* (AnBib 83; Rome: Biblical Institute Press, 1979).

—*Reckoning with Romans: A Contemporary Reading of Paul's Gospel* (Good News Studies, 18; Wilmington, DE: Michael Glazier, 1986).

Caird, G. B., *Principalities and Powers* (Oxford: Oxford University Press, 1956).

Callan, Terrance, 'Pauline Midrash: The Exegetical Background of Gal. 3:19b', *JBL* 99 (1980), pp. 549–67.

Calvert, N.L., 'Abraham and Idolatry: Paul's Comparison of Obedience to the Law to Idolatry in Galatians 4:1–10', in J. Sanders and C. Evans (eds.), *Paul and the Scriptures of Israel* (JSNTSup, 83; SSEJC, 1; Sheffield: Sheffield Academic Press, 1993), pp. 222–37.

—'Abraham Traditions in Middle Jewish Literature: Implications for the Interpretation of Galatians and Romans' (Unpublished PhD dissertation, University of Sheffield, 1993).

—'Philo's Use of Jewish Traditions about Abraham', *SBL Seminar Papers, 1993* (SBLSP 33; Atlanta: GA, Scholars Press, 1994), pp. 463–76.

Calvert-Koyzis, N., 'Josephus Among His Contemporaries: Abraham the Philosopher and Josephus' Purposes in Writing the *Antiquities of the Jews*', in John Kessler and Jeff Greenman (eds.), *Teach Us Your Paths: Studies in Old Testament Literature and Theology* (Toronto: Clements Publishing, 2001), pp. 89–110.

Carr, W., *Angels and Principalities: The Background, Meaning and Development of the Pauline Phrase 'hai archai kai hai exousiai'* (SNTSMS, 42; Cambridge: Cambridge University Press, 1981).

Charles, R.H., *The Apocrypha and Pseudepigrapha of the Old Testament in English* (2 vols.; London: Oxford University Press, 1913).

—*The Book of Jubilees* (London: SPCK, 2nd edn, 1917).

Charlesworth, James H. (ed.), *The Old Testament Pseudepigrapha* (2 vols.; Garden City, NY: Doubleday, 1983).

—'Jewish Interest in Astrology', *ANRW* 2.20.2 (ed. Wolfgang Haase and Hildegard Temporini; Berlin, N.Y.: W. de Gruyter, 1987), pp. 926–55.

Chilton, B.D., and P.R. Davies, 'The Aqedah: A Revised Tradition History', *CBQ* 40 (1978), pp. 514–46.

Christiansen, Ellen Juhl, *The Covenant in Judaism and Paul: A Study of Ritual Boundaries as Identity Markers* (Leiden: E.J. Brill, 1995).

Cicero, *Pro Flacco* (trans. C. MacDonald; LCL; London: Heinemann, 1977).

Cohen, Shaye J.D., *Josephus in Galilee and Rome: His Vita and Development as a Historian* (Leiden: E.J. Brill, 1979).

—'Crossing the Boundary and Becoming a Jew', *HTR* 82 (1989), pp. 13–33.

Cohn, L., 'An Apocryphal Work Ascribed to Philo of Alexandria', *JQR* 10 (1898), pp. 277–332.

Collins, John J., 'The Court-Tales in Daniel and the Development of Apocalyptic', *JBL* 94 (1975), pp. 218–234.

—'Jewish Apocalyptic against its Hellenistic Near Eastern Environment', *BASOR* 220 (1975), pp. 27–36.

—'The Jewish Apocalypses', *Semeia* 14 (1979), pp. 21–59.

—'Introduction: Towards the Morphology of a Genre', *Semeia* 14 (1979), pp. 1–19.

—'Sibylline Oracles: A New Translation and Introduction', in James H. Charlesworth (ed.), *The Old Testament Pseudepigrapha* (2 vols.; Garden City, NY: Doubleday, 1983), vol. I, pp. 373–472.

—'A Symbol of Otherness', in J. Neusner and E.S. Frereichs, *To See Ourselves as Others See Us: Christians, Jews, and Others in Late Antiquity* (Scholars Press Studies in the Humanities; Chico, CA: Scholars Press, 1985), pp. 163–86.

—'The Genre Apocalypse in Hellenistic Judaism', in David Hellholm (ed.), *Apocalypticism in the Mediterranean World and the Near East: Proceedings of the International Colloquium on Apocalypticism* (Tübingen: J.C.B. Mohr [Paul Siebeck], 2nd edn, 1989), pp. 531–47.

—*The Apocalyptic Imagination: An Introduction to Jewish Apocalyptic Literature* (Grand Rapids, MI; Eerdmans, 2nd edn, 1998).

Colson, F.H., 'Philo on Education', *JTS* 18 (1916–1917), pp. 151–62.

Cousar, C.B., *Galatians* (Interpretation; Atlanta, GA: John Knox Press, 1982).

Cranfield, C.E.B., *A Critical and Exegetical Commentary on the Epistle to the Romans* (ICC; 2 vols.; repr.; Edinburgh: T. & T. Clark, 1985).

Cranford, Michael, 'Abraham in Romans 4: The Father of All Who Believe', *New Testament Studies* 41 (1995), pp. 71–88.

Crispin, Derek, 'Galatians 4:1–9: the Use and Abuse of Parallels', *EvQ* 60 (1989), pp. 203–223.

Cross, Frank Moore, 'The History of the Biblical Text in the Light of the Discoveries in the Judean Desert', *HTR* 57 (1964), pp. 281–99.

Crownfield, F.R., 'The Singular Problem of the Dual Galatians', *JBL* 64 (1945), pp. 491–500.

Dahl, Nils A. 'Abrahamkindschaft'. *Das Volk Gottes: eine Untersuchung zum Kirchenbewusstsein des Urchristentums* (Darmstadt: Wissenschaftliche Buchgesellschaft, 1963), pp. 212–17.

—'The One God of Jews and Gentiles'. *Studies in Paul: Theology for the Early Christian Mission* (Minneapolis, MN: Augsburg, 1977), pp. 178–91.

Daly, R.J., 'The Soteriological Significance of the Sacrifice of Isaac', *CBQ* 39 (1977), pp. 47–75.

Daniel, Jerry L., 'Anti-Semitism in the Hellenistic-Roman Period', *JBL* 98 (1979), pp. 45–65.

Daniélou, J., 'Abraham dans la tradition Chrétienne', *Cahiers Sioniens* 5 (1952), pp. 68–87.

Das, A. Andrew, *Paul, the Law, and the Covenant* (Peabody, MA: Hendrickson, 2001).

—'Another Look at ἐὰν μὴ in Galatians 2:16', *JBL* 119 (2000), pp. 529–39.

Daube, D., 'The Interpretation of a Generic Singular in Galatians 3.16', *JQR* 35 (1944), pp. 227–30.

Davenport, Gene L., *The Eschatology of the Book of Jubilees* (SPB, 20; Leiden: E.J. Brill, 1971.

Davies, Glenn N., *Faith and Obedience in Romans: A Study in Romans 1–4* (JSNTSup, 39; Sheffield: JSOT Press, 1990).

Davis, Stephan K., *The Antithesis of the Ages: Paul's Reconfiguration of Torah* (CBQMS, 33; Washington, DC: The Catholic Biblical Association of America, 2002).

Dellling, G., 'στοιχεῖον', *TDNT*, vol. 7, p. 684.

Démann, P., 'La signification d'Abraham dans la perspective du Nouveau Testament', *Cahiers Sioniens* 5 (1952), pp. 31–43.

De Silva, David, 'Why did God Choose Abraham?', *BR* (June, 2000), pp. 17–21, 42–44.

De Vries, Simon J., *1 and 2 Chronicles* (FOTL, 11; Grand Rapids, MI: Eerdmans, 1989).

Dietzfelbinger, Christian, *Paulus und das Alte Testament: Die Hermeneutik des Paulus, untersucht an seiner Deutung der Gestalt Abrahams* (München: Chr. Kaiser Verlag, 1961).

—'Paulus und das Alte Testament: Die Hermeneutik des Paulus, untersucht an seiner Deutung der Gestalt Abrahams'. *Theologische Existenz Heute* 95 (1961), pp. 1–41.

Dillon, J., *The Middle Platonists: 80 B.C. to A.D. 220* (Ithaca, NY: Cornell University Press), 1977.

Dio Cassius, *Dio's Roman History* (trans. Earnest Cary; LCL; London: Heinemann, 1924).

Diogenes Laertius, *Lives of Eminent Philosophers* (trans. D. Hicks; LCL; London: Heinemann, 1931).

Dionysius of Halicarnassus, *Roman Antiquities* (trans. E. Cary; LCL; London: Heinemann, 1950).

Donaldson, Terence L., *Paul and the Gentiles: Remapping the Apostle's Convictional World* (Minneapolis: Fortress Press, 1997).

—'The "Curse of the Law" and the Inclusion of the Gentiles: Galatians 3:14–24', *NTS* 32 (1986), pp. 94–112.

Donfried, K.P., 'A Short Note on Romans 16', in Donfried (ed.), *The Romans Debate* (Minneapolis, MN: Augsburg, rev. edn, 1991), pp. 44–52.

Donfried, K.P. (ed.), *The Romans Debate* (Minneapolis, MN: Augsburg, rev. edn, 1991).

Donfried, K.P., and Peter Richardson, *Judaism and Christianity in First-Century Rome* (Grand Rapids, MI: Eerdmans, 1998).

Doran, Robert, 'The Jewish Historians Before Josephus', *ANRW* 2.20.1 (Berlin: W. de Gruyter, 1987), pp. 246–97.

Duling, D.C., 'Testament of Solomon', *OTP*, vol. I, pp. 935–87.

Dumbrell, William J., 'Abraham and the Abrahamic Covenant in Galatians 3:1–14', in Peter Bolt and Mark Thompson (eds.), *The Gospel to the Nations: Perspectives on Paul's Mission* (Downers Grove, IL: InterVarsity Press/Apollos, 2000), pp. 19–31.

Dunn, James D.G., 'The New Perspective on Paul', *BJRL* 65.2 (1983), pp. 95–122.

—*Romans* (WBC 38A/38B; Dallas, TX: Word Books, 1988).

—*Jesus, Paul and the Law: Studies in Mark and Galatians* (Louisville, KY: Westminster/John Knox Press, 1990).

—'Works of the Law and the Curse of the Law: (Gal. 3.10–14)', in *Jesus, Paul and the Law: Studies in Mark and Galatians* (Louisville, KY: Westminster/John Knox Press, 1990).

—*The Epistle to the Galatians* (BNTC, 9; Peabody, MA: Hendrickson, 1993).

—*The Theology of Paul's Letter to the Galatians* (New Testament Theology; Cambridge: Cambridge University Press, 1993).

—'Intra-Jewish Polemic in Galatians', *JBL* 112 (1993), pp. 459–75.

—'4QMMT and Galatians', *NTS* 43 (1997), pp. 147–53.

—'Who did Paul Think he was? A Study of Jewish-Christian Identity', *NTS* 45 (1999), pp. 174–93.

—'Noch Einmal "Works of the Law": The Dialogue Continues', in Ismo Dunderberg, Christopher Tuckett and Kari Syreeni (eds.), *Fair Play: Diversity and Conflicts in Early Christianity* (Festschrift Heikki Räisänen; NovTSup, 103; Leiden/Boston/Cologne: E.J. Brill, 2002), pp. 273–90.

Elliott, Neil, *The Rhetoric of Romans: Argumentative Constraint and Strategy and Paul's Dialogue with Judaism* (JSNTSup, 45; Sheffield: Sheffield Academic Press, 1990).

Ellis, E.E., *Paul's Use of the Old Testament* (Edinburgh: Oliver and Boyd, 1957).

—*Prophecy and Hermeneutic in Early Christianity* (WUNT, 18; Tübingen: J.C.B. Mohr [Paul Siebeck], 1978).

—*The Old Testament in Early Christianity: Canon and Interpretation in the Light of Modern Research* (Tübingen: J.C.B. Mohr, 1991).

Endres, John C., *Biblical Interpretation in the Book of Jubilee* (CBQMS, 18; Washington, DC: The Catholic Biblical Association of America, 1987).

Esler, Philip F., *Galatians* (New Testament Readings; London/New York: Routledge, 1998).

Eusebius, *Evangelicae Praeparationis* (trans. H. Gifford; Oxford: Clarendon Press, 1903).

Feldman, Louis H., 'Jewish "Sympathizers" in Classical Literature and Inscriptions', *TAPA* 81 (1950), pp. 200–208.

—*Studies in Judaica: Scholarship on Philo and Josephus (1937–1962)* (New York: Yeshiva University, 1963).

—'Abraham the Greek Philosopher in Josephus', *TAPA* 99 (1968), pp. 143–56.

—'Josephus' Version of the Binding of Isaac', *SBL Seminar Papers, 1981* (SBLSP, 21; Chico, CA: Scholars Press, 1982), pp. 113–28.

—*Josephus and Modern Scholarship (1937–1980)* (Berlin: W. de Gruyter, 1984).

—'Abraham the General in Josephus', in F.E. Greenspahn, E. Hilgert and B.L. Mack (eds.), *Nourished with Peace: Studies in Hellenistic Judaism in Memory of Samuel Sandmel* (Chico, CA: Scholars Press, 1984), pp. 43–49.

—'Flavius Josephus Revisited: the Man, His Writings, and His Significance', *ANRW* 2.21.2 (Berlin: W. de Gruyter, 1984), pp. 763–862.

—'Hellenizations in Josephus' *Jewish Antiquities:* The Portrait of Abraham', in L. Feldman and G. Hata (eds.), *Josephus, Judaism, and Christianity* (Leiden: E.J. Brill, 1987), pp. 133–53.

—'Josephus' *Jewish Antiquities* and Pseudo-Philo's *Biblical Antiquities*', in Louis H. Feldman and Gohei Hata (eds.), *Josephus, the Bible and History* (Detroit, MI: Wayne State University Press, 1989), pp. 59–80.

—*Josephus' Interpretation of the Bible* (Berkeley: University of California Press, 1998).

—*Studies in Josephus' Rewritten Bible* (Leiden: E.J. Brill, 1998).

— *Judean Antiquities: Translation and Commentary* (vol. 3 of *Flavius Josephus: Translation and Commentary*; ed. Steve Mason; Leiden: E.J. Brill, 2000).

Fisk, Bruce Norman, *Do You Not Remember? Scripture, Story and Exegesis in the Rewritten Bible of Pseudo-Philo* (JSPSup, 37; Sheffield: Sheffield Academic Press, 2001).

Fitzmyer, Joseph A., *Romans: A New Translation with Introduction and Commentary* (AB, 33; New York: Doubleday, 1993).

Foerster, W., 'κτίζω', *TDNT*, vol. III, pp. 1000–1035.

Forbes, Chris, 'Paul's Principalities and Powers: Demythologizing Apocalyptic?', *JSNT* 82 (2001), pp. 61–88.

—'Pauline Demonology and/or Cosmology? Principalities, Powers and the Elements of the World in Their Hellenistic Context', *JSNT* 85 (2002), pp. 51–73.

Fornberg, Tord, 'Abraham in the Time of Christ', *Svensk Exegetisk Årsbok* 64 (1999), pp. 115–23.

Franxmann, T.W.S., *Genesis and the 'Jewish Antiquities' of Flavius Josephus* (BibOr, 35; Rome: Biblical Institute Press, 1979).

Fraser, P.M., *Ptolemaic Alexandria* (Oxford: Clarendon Press, 1972).

Freeman, Kathleen, *Ancilla to the Pre-Socratic Philosophers* (Oxford: Basil Blackwell, 1948).

Fung, Ronald Y.K., *The Epistle to the Galatians* (NICNT; Grand Rapids, MI: Eerdmans, 1988).

Gafni, Isaiah M., 'Historical Background', in *Jewish Writings of the Second Temple Period* (CRINT, 2.2; Assen: Van Gorcum, 1984), pp. 1–31.

—'The Historical Background', *The Literature of the Sages* (CRINT, 2.3.1; Assen/Maastricht: Van Gorcum, 1987), pp. 1–34.

Gager, John, *The Origins of Anti-Semitism* (New York/Oxford: Oxford University Press, 1983).

Gagnon, Robert A.J., 'Why the "Weak" at Rome Cannot Be Non-Christian Jews', *CBQ* 62 (2000), pp. 64–82.

Garlington, Don, *'The Obedience of Faith': A Pauline Phrase in Historical Context* (WUNT, 38;Tübingen: J.C.B. Mohr [Paul Siebeck], 1991).

—*Faith, Obedience and Perseverance: Aspects of Paul's Letter to the Romans* (WUNT, 79; Tübingen: J.C.B. Mohr [Paul Siebeck], 1994).

—'Role Reversal and Paul's Use of Scripture', *JSNT* 65 (1997), pp. 85–121.

Gaston, L., 'For All the Believers: the Inclusion of Gentiles as the Ultimate Goal of Torah in Romans', *Paul and the Torah* (Vancouver, B.C.: University of British Columbia Press, 1987), pp. 116–34.

Ginzberg, Louis, *The Legends of the Jews* (5 vols.; Philadelphia: The Jewish Publication Society of America, 5728–1968).

152   *Paul, Monotheism and the People of God*

Goodenough, E.R., 'Philo's Exposition of the Law and his *De vita Mosis*', *HTR* 27 (1933), pp. 109–125.

—*By Light, Light: The Mystic Gospel of Hellenistic Judaism* (New Haven: Yale University Press, 1935).

—*The Politics of Philo Judaeus: Practice and Theory* (New Haven, NJ: Yale University Press, 1938).

—*Jewish Symbols in the Greco-Roman Period* (13 vols.; New York: Pantheon Books for the Bollingen Foundation, 1958).

Goodman, M., *The Ruling Class of Judaea* (Cambridge: Cambridge University Press, 1987).

—*Jews in a Graeco-Roman World* (Oxford: Clarendon Press, 1998).

Gordon, T. David, 'The Problem at Galatia', *Int.* 41 (1987), pp. 32–43.

—'A Note on ΠΑΙΔΑΓΩΓΟΣ in Galatians 3:24–25', *NTS* 35 (1989), pp. 150–54.

Gosling, J.C.B., *Plato* (The Arguments of the Philosophers; London: Routledge & Kegan Paul, 1973).

Grant, Michael, *The Jews in the Roman World* (London: Weidenfeld and Nicolson, 1973).

Grant, Michael (ed.), *Greek and Latin Authors* (New York: The H.W. Wilson Co., 1980).

Gray, Rebecca, *Prophetic Figures in Late Second Temple Jewish Palestine: The Evidence From Josephus* (New York: Oxford University Press, 1993).

Green, Arthur. *Devotion and Commandment: The Faith of Abraham in the Hasidic Imagination* (Cincinnati: Hebrew Union College Press, 1989).

Gruenwald, Ithamar, 'Jewish Apocalyptic Literature', *ANRW* 2.19.1 (Berlin: W. de Gruyter, 1979), pp. 89–118.

Guillet, J., 'Figure d'Abraham dans l'Ancient Testament', *Cahiers Sioniens* 5 (1952), pp. 31–43.

Gundry, R.H., 'Grace, Works, and Staying Saved in Paul', *Bib* 66 (1985), pp. 1–38.

Guthrie, D., *Galatians* (NCBC; repr., London: Marshall, Morgan & Scott, 1984).

Hadas-Lebel, Mireille, *Flavius Josephus: Eyewitness to Rome's First-Century Conquest of Judea* (trans. Richard Miller; New York: Macmillan Publishing Company, 1993).

Hahn, Ferdinand, 'Die Gestalt Abrahams in der Sicht Philos', in Ferdinand Hahn, *et al.* (eds.), *Zion Ort der Begegnung* (Festschrit Laurentius Klein; BBB, 90; Bodenheim: Athenäum Hain Hanstein, 1993), pp. 203–215.

Hall, Robert G., 'The "Christian Interpolation" in the Apocalypse of Abraham', *JBL* 107 (1988), pp. 107–110.

Hamerton-Kelly, Robert G., 'Sources and Traditions in Philo Judaeus: Prolegomena to an Analysis of His Writings', *Studia Philonica* 1 (1972), pp. 3–26.

Hansen, G. Walter, *Abraham in Galatians: Epistolary and Rhetorical Contexts* (JSNTSup, 29; Sheffield: Sheffield Academic Press, 1989).

Hanson, A.T., 'Abraham the Justified Sinner', in *Studies in Paul's Technique and Theology* (London: SPCK, 1974), pp. 52–66.

—'The Origin of Paul's Use of the ΠΑΙΔΑΓΩΓΟΣ for the Law', *JSNT* 34 (1988), pp. 71–76.

Harrelson, Walter, 'The Significance of "Last Words" for Intertestamental Ethics', in James L. Crenshaw and John T. Willis (eds.), *Essays in Old Testament Ethics* (New York: KTAV, 1974), pp. 205–23.

Harrington, Daniel J., 'The Original Language of Pseudo–Philo's Liber Antiquitatum Biblicarum', *HTR* 63 (1970), pp. 503–14.

—'The Biblical Text of Pseudo-Philo's Liber Antiquitatum Biblicarum', *CBQ* 33 (1971), pp. 1–17.

—*The Hebrew Fragments of Pseudo-Philo's Liber Antiquitatum Biblicarum Preserved in the Chronicles of Jerahmeel* (SBLTT Pseudepigrapha, 3; Missoula, MT: Scholars Press, 1974).

—'Abraham Traditions in the Testament of Abraham and in the "Rewritten Bible" of the Intertestamental Period', *Studies on the Testament of Abraham* (SBLSCS, 6; Missoula, MT: Scholars Press, 1976).

—'Pseudo-Philo: A New Translation and Introduction', *OTP* (ed. James H. Charlesworth; 2 vols.; Garden City, NY: Doubleday, 1983), vol. II, pp. 297–377.

—'Pseudo-Philo: Liber Antiquitatum Biblicarum', in M. de Jonge (ed.), *Outside the Old Testament* (Cambridge Commentaries on Writings of the Jewish and Christian World 200 B.C. to A.D. 200, 4; Cambridge: Cambridge University Press, 1985), pp. 6–25.

—'Palestinian Adaptations of Biblical Narratives and Prophecies', in Robert A. Kraft and George W.E. Nickelsburg (eds.), *Early Judaism and Its Modern Interpreters* (SBLBMI, 2; Atlanta, GA: Scholars Press, 1986), pp. 239–58.

Harrisville, Roy A., III, *The Figure of Abraham in the Epistles of St. Paul: In the Footsteps of Abraham* (San Francisco: Mellen Research University Press, 1992).

Hayman, Peter, 'Monotheism – A Misused Word in Jewish Studies?', *Journal of Jewish Studies* 42 (1991), pp. 1–15.

Hays, Richard, *The Faith of Jesus Christ: An Investigation of the Narrative Substructure of Galatians 3:1–4:11* (SBLDS, 56; Chico, CA: Scholars Press, 1983).

—' "Have We Found Abraham to be Our Forefather According to the Flesh?" A Reconsideration of Rom. 4:1', *NovT* 27 (1985), pp. 76–98.

—*Echoes of Scripture in the Letters of Paul* (New Haven: Yale University Press, 1989).

Hengel, M., *Judaism and Hellenism* (trans. John Bowden; 2 vols.; Philadelphia: Fortress Press, 1974).

Hicks, R.D., *Stoic and Epicurean* (New York: Russell & Russell, 1962).

Himmelfarb, Martha, *Ascent to Heaven in Jewish and Christian Apocalypses* (New York: Oxford University Press, 1993).

Hofius, O., 'Eine altjüdische Parallele zu Röm IV. 17b', *NTS* 18 (1971–72), pp. 93–94.

Holladay, Carl R., *Theios Aner in Hellenistic Judaism: A Critique of the Use of this Category in New Testament Christology* (SBLDS, 40; Missoula, MT: Scholars Press, 1977), p. 73.

—*Fragments from Hellenistic Jewish Authors* (trans. Carl R. Holladay; SBLTT 20, 39, 40; Pseudepigrapha 10, 13, 14; Chico, CA: Scholars Press, 1983).

Hollis, Hilda, 'The Phrase "God is One" in the New Testament: A Study of Romans 3:30, Galatians 3:20, and James 2:19' (Unpublished MA thesis, McGill University Faculty of Religious Studies, 1985).

Holst, Richard, 'The Meaning of "Abraham Believed God" in Romans 4:3', *WTJ* 59 (1997), pp. 319–26.

Hooker, M.D., 'Adam in Romans 1', *NTS* 6 (1959–60), pp. 297–306.

—'A Further Note on Romans 1', *NTS* 13 (1966–67), pp. 181–83.

—'Paul and "Covenantal Nomism" ', in M.D.Hooker and S.G. Wilson (eds.), *Paul and Paulinism: Essays in honour of C.K. Barrett* (London: SPCK, 1982), pp. 57–66.

Horace, *Satires, Epistles, and Ars Poetica* (trans. Rushton Fairclough; LCL; London: Heinemann, 1936).

Horsley, Richard A., Hanson, John S. *Bandits, Prophets and Messiahs: Popular Movements at the Time of Jesus* (San Francisco: Harper & Row, 1988).

Howard, G., *Paul, Crisis in Galatia: A Study in Early Christian Theology* (SNTSMS, 35; New York: Cambridge University Press, 1979).

Hübner, Hans, *Law in Paul's Thought* (trans. James C.G. Greig; Edinburgh: T. & T. Clark, 1984).

Huffman, Carl A., 'The Pythagorean tradition' in A.A. Long (ed.), *The Cambridge Companion to Early Greek Philosophy* (Cambridge: Cambridge University Press, 1999), pp. 66–87.

Hurtado, L.W., *One God, One Lord* (London: SCM Press, 1988).

—'First-Century Jewish Monotheism', *JSNT* 71 (1998), pp. 3–26.

154   *Paul, Monotheism and the People of God*

Jacobson, Howard, *A Commentary on Pseudo-Philo's Liber Antiquitatum Biblicarum with Latin Text and English Translation* (2 vols.; AGJU, 31; Leiden: E.J. Brill, 1996).
James, M.R., *The Biblical Antiquities of Philo* (repr., New York: KTAV, 1971).
Jervell, Jacob, 'The Letter to Jerusalem', in Karl P. Donfried (ed.), *The Romans Debate* (Minneapolis, MN: Augsburg, rev. edn, 1991), pp. 53–64.
Jewett, R., 'The Agitators and the Galatian Congregation', *NTS* 17 (1971), pp. 198–212.
Josephus, *The Life of Josephus* (trans. H. St. J. Thackeray; LCL; London: Heinemann, 1926).
—*The Jewish War Books I–III* (trans. H. St. J. Thackeray; LCL; London: Heinemann, 1927).
—*Jewish Antiquities Books I–IV* (trans. H. St. J. Thackeray; Cambridge, MA: Harvard University, 1930).
—*Jewish Antiquities Books XII–XIV* (trans. Ralph Marcus; LCL; Cambridge, MA: Harvard, 1966).
—*Jewish Antiquities Books XV–XVII* (trans. Ralph Marcus; LCL; Cambridge, MA: Harvard, 1963.
— *Jewish Antiquities Books XVIII–XX* (trans. Louis H. Feldman; LCL; Cambridge, MA: Harvard, 1965).
Juvenal, *Juvenal and Persius* (trans. G.G. Ramsay; Cambridge, MA: Harvard, 1920).
Karris, R.J., 'The Occasion of Romans,' in Karl P. Donfried (ed.), *The Romans Debate* (Minneapolis, MN: Augsburg, rev. edn, 1991), pp. 65–84.
Käsemann, E., *Perspectives on Paul* (London: SCM Press, 1971).
—*Commentary on Romans* (trans. Geoffrey Bromiley; London: SCM Press, 1980).
Kasher, Aryeh, *The Jews in Hellenistic and Roman Egypt: The Struggle for Equal Rights* (Tübingen: J.C.B. Mohr [Paul Siebeck], 1985).
Kim, Seyoon, *Paul and the New Perspective* (Tübingen: Mohr Siebeck, 2002).
Kisch, Guido, *Pseudo-Philo's Liber Antiquitatum Biblicarum* (Publications in Medieval Studies; Notre Dame, IN: University of Notre Dame, 1949).
Klijn, A.F.J., '2 (Syriac Apocalypse of) Baruch: A New Translation and Introduction', *OTP* (ed. James H. Charlesworth; 2 vols.; Garden City, NY: Doubleday, 1983), I, pp. 615–52.
Knox, J., 'Romans', in George A. Buttrick (ed.), *The Interpreter's Bible* (12 vols.; New York: Abingdon Press, 1954), vol. IX, pp. 355–72.
Knox, W.L., 'Abraham and the Quest for God', *HTR* 28 (1935), pp. 55–60.
—*St. Paul and the Church of the Gentiles* (Cambridge: Cambridge University Press, 1961).
Koester, H., *History, Culture and Religion of the Hellenistic Age* (Philadelphia: Fortress Press, 1982).
Kraemer, R.S., 'On the Meaning of the Term "Jew" in Greco-Roman Inscriptions', *HTR* 82 (1989), pp. 35–53.
Kraft, Robert A., and George W.E. Nickelsburg (eds.), *Early Judaism and Its Modern Interpreters* (SBLBMI, 2; Atlanta: GA: Scholars Press, 1986).
Kugel, James L., and Rowan A Greer, *Early Biblical Interpretation* (Library of Early Christianity, 3; Philadelphia: Westminster Press, 1986).
LaHurd, Carol S., 'One God, One Father: Abraham in Judaism, Christianity, and Islam', *Dialog* 29.1 (1990), pp. 17–24.
Lambrecht, J., Abraham, ' "Notre père à tous": la figure d'abraham dans les écrits pauliniens', *Publications de l'Institutum Judaicum* 2 (1979), pp. 118–58.
—'Abraham and His Offspring: A Comparison of Galatians 5, 1 with 3,13', *Biblica* 80 (1999), pp. 525–36.
—'Paul's Logic in Romans 3:29–30', *JBL* 119 (2000), pp. 526–28.
Lampe, P., *Die stadtrömischen Christen in den ersten beiden Jahrhunderten: Untersuchungen zur Sozialgeschichte* (Tübingen: J.C.B. Mohr, 2nd edn, 1989).
—'The Roman Christians of Romans 16', in Karl P. Donfried (ed.), *The Romans Debate* (Minneapolis, MN: Augsburg, rev. edn, 1991), pp. 216–30.

Leon, H.J., *The Jews of Ancient Rome* (Philadelphia: The Jewish Publication Society of America, 1960).
—'The Jews of Rome in the First Centuries of Christianity', in E.J. Vardanam and J.L. Garrett, Jr (eds.), *The Teacher's Yoke: Studies in Memory of Henry Trantham* (Waco, TX: Baylor University Press, 1964), pp. 154–63.
Lightfoot, J.B., *St. Paul's Epistle to the Galatians* (London: Macmillan & Co., 1884).
Lincoln, A.T., *Paradise Now and Not Yet: Studies in the Role of the Heavenly Dimension in Paul's Thought with Special Reference to his Eschatology* (repr., Grand Rapids, MI: Baker Book House, 1991).
—'Abraham Goes to Rome: Paul's Treatment of Abraham in Romans 4', in Michael J. Wilkins and Terance Paige (eds.), *Worship, Theology and Ministry in the Early Church* (JSOTSup, 87; Sheffield: Sheffield Academic Press, 1992).
Lindsay, Dennis R., *Josephus and Faith: Πίστις and Πιστεύειν as Faith Terminology in the Writings of Flavius Josephus and in the New Testament* (AGJU, 19; Leiden/New York: E.J. Brill, 1993).
Long, A.A., *Hellenistic Philosophy: Stoics, Epicureans, Sceptics* (Berkeley/Los Angeles: University of California Press, 2nd edn, 1986.)
—'Soul and body in Stoicism', in A.A. Long (ed.), *Stoic Studies* (Cambridge: Cambridge University Press, 1996), pp. 224–49.
Longenecker, Bruce, *The Triumph of Abraham's God: The Transformation of Identity in Galatians* (Nashville: Abingdon Press, 1998).
Longenecker, Richard N., 'The "Faith of Abraham" Theme in Paul, James, and Hebrews: A Study in the Circumstantial Nature of New Testament Teaching', *JETS* 20 (1977), pp. 203–212.
—'The Pedagogical Nature of the Law in Galatians 3:19–4:7', *JETS* 25 (1982), pp. 53–61.
—*Galatians* (WBC 41; Dallas, TX: Word Books, 1990).
—'Graphic Illustrations of a Believer's New Life in Christ: Galatians 4:21–31', *RevExp* 91 (1994), pp. 183–99.
Luedemann, G., *Paul: Apostle to the Gentiles* (Philadelphia: Fortress Press, 1984).
Lull, David J., '"The Law was our Pedagogue"': A Study in Galatians 3:19–25', *JBL* 105 (1986), pp. 481–98.
Mack, B., *Logos und Sophia: Untersuchungen zur Weisheitstheologie im hellenistischen Judentum* (SUNT, 10; Göttingen: Vandenhoeck & Ruprecht, 1973).
—'Philo Judaeus and Exegetical Traditions in Alexandria', *ANRW* 2.21.1 (Berlin: W. de Gruyter, 1984), pp. 227–71.
Marrou, H. I., *A History of Education in Antiquity* (New York: Sheed and Ward, 1956).
Martin, Troy, 'Apostasy to Paganism: The Rhetorical Stasis of the Galatian Controversy', *JBL* 114 (1995), pp. 437–61.
Martin-Achard, R., *Actualité d'Abraham* (Bibliothèque théologique; Neuchâtel: Delachaux et Niestlé, 1969).
Martinez, Florintino Garcia, 'The Heavenly Tablets in the Book of *Jubilees*', in Matthias Albani, *et al.* (eds.), *Studies in the Book of Jubilees* (Texte und Studienzum Antiken Judentum, 65; Tübingen: Mohr Siebeck, 1997).
Martyn, J.L., 'A Law-Observant Mission to Gentiles: The Background of Galatians', *SJT* 38 (1985), pp. 307–24.
—*Galatians: A New Translation with Introduction and Commentary* (AB, 33A; New York: Doubleday, 1997).
Mason, Steve, *Josephus and the New Testament* (Peabody, MA: Hendrickson, 1992).
—'"Should Any Wish to Enquire Further" (*Ant.* 1.25): The Aim and Audience of Josephus' *Jewish Antiquities/Life*', in Steve Mason (ed.), *Understanding Josephus: Seven Perspectives* (JSPSup, 32; Sheffield Academic Press, 1998), pp. 64–103.

Mason, Steve (ed.), *Understanding Josephus: Seven Perspectives* (JSPSup, 32; Sheffield: Shef–field Academic Press, 1998).

Matera, Frank, 'The Culmination of Paul's Argument to the Galatians: Gal 5,1–6,17', *JSNT* 32 (1988), pp. 79–91.

McEleney, N.J., 'Conversion, Circumcision, and the Law', *NTS* 20 (1974), pp. 319–41.

Meeks, Wayne A., *The First Urban Christians: The Social World of the Apostle Paul* (New Haven: Yale University Press, 1983).

—*The Moral World of the First Christians* (London: SPCK, 1987).

Mendelson, Alan, *Secular Education in Philo of Alexandria* (Cincinnati: Hebrew Union College Press, 1982).

—*Philo's Jewish Identity* (Brown Judaic Studies 161; Atlanta: Scholar's Press, 1988).

Metzger, Bruce M., *A Textual Commentary on the Greek New Testament* (Stuttgart: Deutsche Bibelgesellschaft, 1994).

Minar, Edwin L., *Early Pythagorean Politics in Practice and Theory* (Baltimore, MD: Waverly Press, Inc., 1942).

Minear, P.S., *The Obedience of Faith: The Purposes of Paul in the Epistle to the Romans* (SBT, 2.19; Naperville, IL: Alec R. Allenson, Inc., 1974).

Momigliano, A., *Claudius: The Emperor and his Achievement* (repr., New York: Barnes & Noble, Inc., 1961).

Moo, Douglas J., 'Paul and the Law in the Last Ten Years', *SJT* 40 (1987), pp. 287–307.

—*The Epistle to the Romans* (NICNT; Grand Rapids, MI: Eerdmans, 1996).

Morland, Kjell Arne, *The Rhetoric of Curse in Galatians: Paul Confronts Another Gospel* (Emory Studies in Early Christianity, 5; Atlanta: Scholars Press, 1995).

Moxnes, Halvor, *Theology in Conflict: Studies in Paul's Understanding of God in Romans* (Leiden: E.J. Brill, 1980).

Mueller, James R., 'The Apocalypse of Abraham and the Destruction of the Second Jewish Temple', *SBL Seminar Papers, 1981* (*SBLSP* 21; Chico, CA: Scholars Press, 1982), pp. 341–49.

Müller, Mogens, 'Die Abraham-Gestalt im Jubiläenbuch: Versuch einer Interpretation', *SJOT* 19 (1996), pp. 238–57.

Munck, Johannes, *Paul and the Salvation of Mankind* (trans. F. Clark; London: SCM Press, 1959).

Murphy, F.J., 'Retelling the Bible: Idolatry in Pseudo-Philo', *JBL* 107 (1988), pp. 275–87.

—*Pseudo-Philo: Rewriting the Bible* (New York: Oxford University Press, 1993).

Murphy O'Connor, J., 'Prisca and Aquila: Traveling Tentmakers and Church Builders', *BR* 8.6 (1992), pp. 40–62.

—'The Irrevocable Will (Gal 3:15)', *RB* 106 (1999), pp. 224–35.

Nanos, Mark D., *The Mystery of Romans: The Jewish Context of Paul's Letter* (Minneapolis, MN: Fortress Press, 1996).

—'Some Problems with Reading Romans through the Lens of the Edict of Claudius', *The Mystery of Romans*, pp. 372–87.

—'The Jewish Context of the Gentile Audience Addressed in Paul's Letter to the Romans', *CBQ* 61 (1999), pp. 283–304.

Neusner, J., 'The Use of the Later Rabbinic Evidence for the Study of Paul', *Approaches to Ancient Judaism 2* (BJS, 9; Chico, CA: Scholars Press, 1980), pp. 43–63.

—'Scripture and Tradition in Judaism', *Approaches to Ancient Judaism 2* (BJS 9; Chico, CA: Scholars Press, 1980), pp. 173–91.

Nickelsburg, George W.E., 'Good and Bad Leaders in Pseudo-Philo's Liber Antiquitatum Biblicarum', in G.W.E. Nickelsburg and J.J. Collins (eds.), *Ideal Figures in Ancient Judaism* (SCS, 12; Chico, CA: Scholars Press, 1980), pp. 49–65.

—*Jewish Literature Between the Bible and the Mishnah* (Philadelphia: Fortress Press, 1981).

—'The Bible Rewritten and Expanded', in Michael E. Stone (ed.), *Jewish Writings of the Second Temple Period* (CRINT, 2.2; Assen: Van Gorcum, 1984), pp. 89–156.

—'Stories of Biblical and Early Post-Biblical Times', in Michael E. Stone (ed.), *Jewish Writings of the Second Temple Period* (CRINT, 2.2. Assen: Van Gorcum, 1984), pp. 33–87.

—'Palestinian Adaptations of Biblical Narratives and Prophecies', R.A. Kraft and G.W.E. Nickelsburg (eds.), *Early Judaism and Its Modern Interpreters* (Atlanta, GA: Scholars Press, 1986), pp. 239–47.

Niditch, Susan, *The Symbolic Vision in Biblical Tradition* (HSM, 30; Chico, CA: Scholars Press, 1983).

Niehoff, Maren, 'Two Examples of Josephus' Narrative Technique in his "Rewritten Bible" ', *JSJ* 27.1 (1996), pp. 31–45.

—*Philo on Jewish Identity and Culture* (Texts and Studies in Ancient Judiasm, 86; Tübingen: Mohr Siebeck, 2001).

Nikiprowetzky, V., *La Troisième Sibylle* (Études Juives, IX; Paris: Mouton, 1970).

— *Le commentaire de l'écriture chez Philon d'Alexandrie* (ALGHJ, 11; Leiden: E.J. Brill, 1977).

Nolland, John, 'Uncircumcised Proselytes?' *JSJ* 12 (1981), pp. 173–94.

Oates, Whitney J. (ed.), *The Stoic and Epicurean Philosophers: the Complete Extant Writings of Epicurus, Epictetus, Lucretius, Marcus Aurelius* (trans. P.E. Matheson; New York: Random House, 1940).

Obolensky, Dmitri, *The Bogomils: A Study in Balkan Neo-Manichaeism* (Cambridge: Cambridge University Press, 1948).

Oepke, A., 'μεσίτης', *TDNT*, vol. 4, pp. 598–624.

Oppenheim, A. Leo, *Ancient Mesopotamia: Portrait of a Dead Civilization* (Chicago: University of Chicago Press, 1964).

Park, Ik Soo, 'Paul and the Abraham Tradition: A Challenge for the Church Today' (Unpublished PhD dissertation, Drew University, 1985).

Perrot, Charles, Pierre-Maurice Bogaert, *Pseudo-Philon Les Antiquités* (Paris: Les Éditions du Cerf, 1976).

Philo, *Philo in Ten Volumes* (and Two Supplementary Volumes) (trans. F.H. Colson, G.H. Whitaker and Ralph Marcus; LCL; London: Heinemann, 1968).

Philonenko-Sayar, Belkis, and Marc Philonenko, *Die Apocalypse Abrahams* (JSHRZ, 5; Gütersloh: Gütersloher Verlagshaus Gerd Mohn, 1982).

Plato, *Euthyphro, Apology, Crito, Phaedo, Phaedrus* (vol. I of *Plato in Ten Volumes*; trans. H.N. Fowler; Cambridge, MA: Harvard University Press, 1982).

Porter, Calvin L., 'Romans 1.18–32: Its Role in the Developing Argument', *NTS* 40 (1994), pp. 210–28.

Porton, Gary G., 'Diversity in Postbiblical Judaism', in R.A. Kraft and G.W.E. Nickelsburg (eds.), *Early Judaism and Its Modern Interpreters* (SBLBMI 2; Philadelphia: Fortress Press, 1986), pp. 57–80.

Räisänen, Heiki. *Paul and the Law* (Tübingen: J.C.B. Mohr [Paul Siebeck], 2nd edn, 1987).

Rajak, Tessa, 'Josephus and the "Archaeology" of the Jews', *JJS* 33 (1982), pp. 465–77.

—*Josephus: The Historian and His Society* (Philadelphia: Fortress Press, 1984).

Rapa, Robert Keith, *The Meaning of "Works of the Law" in Galatians and Romans* (Studies in Biblical Literature, 31; New York: Peter Lang, 2001).

Rappaport, Salomo, *Agada und Exegese bei Flavius Josephus* (Wien: Verlag der Alexander Kohut Memorial Foundation, 1930).

Reicke, B., 'The Law and this World According to Paul: Some Thoughts Concerning Gal 4:1–11', *JBL* 70 (1951), pp. 259–74.

Rengstorf, Karl Heinrich (ed.), *A Complete Concordance to Flavius Josephus* (4 vols., Leiden: E.J. Brill, 1979).

Rhoads, David M., *Israel in Revolution: 6–74 C.E* (Philadelphia: Fortress Press, 1976).
Rhyne, C.T., *Faith Establishes the Law* (SBLDS, 55; Chico, CA: Scholars Press, 1981).
Roberts, Alexander, and James Donaldson, *The Anti-Nicene Father* (repr., Buffalo: The Christian Literature Publishing Co., 1887).
Roetzel, C.J., *The Letters of Paul: Conversations in Context* (London: SCM Press, 1983).
Ropes, J.H., *The Singular Problem of the Epistle to the Galatians* (Cambridge, MA: Harvard University Press, 1929).
Rowland, Christopher, *The Open Heaven: A Study of Apocalyptic in Judaism and Early Christianity* (London: SPCK, 1982).
Rubinkiewicz, R., 'La vision de l'histoire dans l'Apocalypse d'Abraham', *ANRW* 2.19.1 (Berlin: W. de Gruyter, 1979), pp. 137–51.
—'The Apocalypse of Abraham: A New Translation and Introduction', *OTP* (ed. James H. Charlesworth; 2 vols.; Garden City, NY: Doubleday, 1983), vol. I, pp. 681–719.
—*L'Apocalypse d'Abraham, en vieux slave: Introduction, texte critique, traduction et commentaire* (Lublin: Société des Lettres et des Sciences de l'Université Catholique de Lublin, 1987), pp. 137–51.
Rubinstein, A., 'A Problematic Passage in the Apocalypse of Abraham', *JJS* 8 (1957), pp. 45–50.
Runia, David, *Philo of Alexandria and the Timaeus of Plato* (Leiden: E.J. Brill, 1986).
—*Philo in Early Christian Literature: A Survey* (Assen: Van Gorcum, 1993).
Rusam, Dietrich, 'Neue Belege zu den stoicheia tou kosmou', *ZNW* 83 (1992), pp. 119–25.
Russell, D.S., *The Method and Message of Jewish Apocalyptic* (London: SCM Press, 1964).
—*Apocalyptic, Ancient and Modern* (London: SCM Press, 1978).
—*The Old Testament Pseudepigrapha: Patriarchs and Prophets in Early Judaism* (London: SCM Press, 1987).
Rutgers, Leonard Victor, 'Roman Policy towards the Jews: Expulsions from the City of Rome during the First Century C.E.', *Classical Antiquity* 13 (1994), pp. 56–74.
Safrai, S., 'Relations Between the Diaspora and the Land of Israel', *Jewish People in the First Century* (CRINT, 1.1; Assen: Van Gorcum, 1974), pp. 184–215.
Sandbach, F.H., *The Stoics* (New York: W.W. Norton, 1975).
Sanday, W., and A.C. Headlam, *The Epistle to the Romans* (ICC; New York: Charles Scribner's Sons, 1911).
Sanders, E.P., 'Patterns of Religion in Paul and Rabbinic Judaism: A Holistic Method of Comparison', *HTR* 66 (1973), pp. 455–78.
—'The Covenant as a Soteriological Category and the Nature of Salvation in Palestinian and Hellenistic Judaism', *Jews, Greeks and Christians: Religious Cultures in Late Antiquity* (Festschrift W.D. Davies; Leiden: E.J. Brill, 1976), pp. 11–44.
—*Paul and Palestinian Judaism* (repr., Philadelphia: Fortress Press, 1983).
—*Paul, the Law, and the Jewish People* (Philadelphia: Fortress Press, 1983).
—'The Genre of Palestinian Jewish Apocalypses', in David Hellholm (ed.), *Apocalypticism in the Mediterranean World and the Near East: Proceedings of the International Colloquium on Apocalypticism* (Tübingen: J.C.B. Mohr [Paul Siebeck], 2nd edn, 1989), pp. 447–59.
—*Paul* (Past Masters; Oxford: Oxford University Press, 1991).
—'Defending the Indefensible', *JBL* 110 (1991), pp. 463–77.
Sandmel, Samuel, 'Abraham in Normative and Hellenistic Jewish Traditions' (Unpublished PhD dissertation; Yale University Press, 1949).
—'Abraham's Knowledge of the Existence of God', *HTR* 44 (1951), pp. 137–39.
—'Philo's Place in Judaism: A Study of Conceptions of Abraham in Jewish Literature', *HUCA* 25 (1954), pp. 137–48.

—'Philo's Place in Judaism: A Study of Conceptions of Abraham in Jewish Literature, II', *HUCA* 26 (1955), pp. 151–332.

—'Parallelomania'. *JBL* 81 (1962), pp. 1–13.

—*Philo's Place in Judaism: A Study of Conceptions of Abraham in Jewish Literature* (New York: KTAV, 1971).

—*Philo of Alexandria: An Introduction* (New York, Oxford: Oxford University Press, 1979).

—'Philo: The Man, His Writings, His Significance', *ANRW* 2.21.1 (Berlin: W. de Gruyter, 1984), pp. 3–46.

—'Palestinian and Hellenistic Judaism and Christianity: The Question of the Comfortable Theory', *HUCA* 50 (1979), pp. 137–48.

Schalit, A., 'Josephus Flavius', in Cecil Roth and Geoffrey Widoger (eds.), *Encyclopaedia Judaica* (16 vols.; Jerusalem: MacMillan, 1971), vol. X, pp. 251–66.

Schmithals, W., 'Die Häretiker in Galatien', *ZNW* 47 (1956), pp. 25–66.

Schmitz, Otto, 'Abraham im Spätjudentum und im Urchristentum', *Aus Schrift und Geschichte* (Stuttgart: Calwer Vereinsbuchhandlung, 1922), pp. 99–123.

Schoeps, H. J., 'The Sacrifice of Isaac in Paul's Theology', *JBL* 65 (1946), pp. 385–92.

—*The Theology of the Apostle in Light of Jewish Religious History* (Philadelphia: Westminster Press, 1961).

Scott, James M., *Adoption as Sons of God: An Exegetical Investigation into the Background of ΥΙΟΘΕΣΙΑ in the Pauline Corpus* (WUNT 48;Tübingen: J.C.B. Mohr [Paul Siebeck], 1992).

Schreckenberg, Heinz, 'Preliminaries to the Early Christian Reception of Josephus', in Heinz Schreckenberg and Kurt Schubert (eds.), *Jewish Historiography and Iconography in Early and Medieval Christianity* (CRINT, III.2; Assen/Maastricht: Van Gorcum, 1992), pp. 17–50.

Schreiner, Thomas R., *The Law and Its Fulfilment: A Pauline Theology of Law* (Grand Rapids: Baker Book House, 1993).

Schürer, E., *The History of the Jewish People in the Age of Jesus Christ* (4 vols.; repr., Edinburgh: T & T Clark, rev. edn, 1987).

Schwartz, Seth, *Josephus and Judaean Politics* (Columbia Studies in the Classical Tradition, 18; Leiden: E.J. Brill, 1990).

Schwarz, Eberhard. *Identität durch Abgrenzung: Abgrenzungprozesse in Israel im 2. vorchristlichen Jahrhundert und ihre traditiongeschichtlichen Voraussetzungen. Zugleich ein Beirag zur Erforschung des Jubiläenbuches* (Europäische Hochschulschriften, 23.162; Frankfurt/Bern: Peter Lang, 1982).

Scroggs, R. 'Paul as Rhetorician: Two Homilies in Romans 1–11', in R. Hamerton-Kelly, *et al.* (eds.), *Jews, Greeks, and Christian* (Festschrift for W.D. Davies; Leiden: E.J. Brill, 1976), pp. 270–98.

Segal, Alan F., *Paul the Convert* (New Haven: Yale University Press, 1990).

Segal, J.B., 'Intercalation and the Hebrew Calendar', *VT* 7 (1957), pp. 250–307.

Seifrid, Mark, *Justification by Faith: The Origin and Development of a Central Pauline Theme* (Leiden: E.J. Brill, 1992).

—*Christ our Righteousness: Paul's Theology of Justification* (Downers Grove, IL: InterVarsity, 2000).

Seneca, *Ad Lucilium, Epistulae Morales* (trans. Richard M. Gummere; LCL; Cambridge, MA: Harvard University Press, 1934).

Sextus Empiricus, *Against the Physicists, Against the Ethicists* (trans. R.G. Bury; LCL; Cambridge, MA: Harvard University Press, 1936).

Sherwin-White, A.N., *Racial Prejudice in Imperial Rome* (Cambridge: Cambridge University Press, 1970).

Siker, Jeffrey, 'Disinheriting the Jews: The Use of Abraham in Early Christian Controversy with Judaism from Paul through Justin Martyr' (Unpublished PhD dissertation, Princeton Theological Seminary, 1989).

—'From Gentile Inclusion to Jewish Exclusion: Abraham in Early Christian Controversy with Jews', *BTB* 19.1 (1989), pp. 30–36.

—*Disinheriting the Jews: Abraham in Early Christian Controversy* (Louisville, KY: Westminster/John Knox Press, 1991).

Slingerland, Dixon, 'Chrestus: Christus?', in Alan J. Avery-Peck *et al.* (eds.), *The Literature of Early Rabbinic Judaism: Issues in Talmudic Redaction and Interpretation* (Vol. 4 of *New Perspectives on Ancient Judaism*; Studies in Judaism; Lanham: University Press of America, 1989).

—'Suetonius *Claudius* 25.4 and the Account in Cassius Dio', *JQR* 79 (1989), pp. 305–322.

Smallwood, E.M., 'Some Notes on the Jews under Tiberius', *Latomus* 15 (1956), pp. 314–29.

—*The Jews Under Roman Rule* (SJLA, 20; Leiden: E.J. Brill, 1976).

Smiles, Vincent, *The Gospel and the Law in Galatia: Paul's Response to Jewish Christian Separatism and the Threat of Galatian Apostasy* (Collegeville, MN: Michael Glazier/Liturgical Press, 1998).

Smith, J.Z., 'Wisdom and Apocalyptic', in B.A. Pearson (ed.), *Religious Syncretism in Antiquity: Essays in Conversation with Geo Widengren* (Santa Barbara, CA: Scholars Press for the AAR and Institute of Religious Studies, 1975), pp. 131–56.

Smith, Robert W., *The Art of Rhetoric in Alexandria* (The Hague: Martinus Nijhoff, 1974).

Snyder, Graydon F., 'The Interaction of Jews with Non-Jews in Rome', in Karl P. Donfried and Peter Richardson (eds.), *Judaism and Christianity in First Century Rome* (Grand Rapids, MI: Eerdmans, 1998).

Speiser, E.A., *Genesis* (AB, 1; Garden City, NY: Doubleday, 1964).

Spilsbury, Paul, *The Image of the Jew in Flavius Josephus' Paraphrase of the Bible* (Texte und Studien zum Antiken Judentum, 69; Tübingen: Mohr Siebeck, 1998).

—'God and Israel in Josephus: A Patron-Client Relationship', in Steve Mason (ed.), *Understanding Josephus: Seven Perspectives* (JSPSSup, 32; Sheffield: Sheffield Academic Press, 1998), pp. 172–91.

Stambaugh, John E., and David L. Balch, *The New Testament in Its Social Environment* (Library of Early Christianity, 2; Philadelphia: Westminster Press, 1986).

Stendahl, Krister, 'The Apostle Paul and the Introspective Conscience of the West', *Paul Among Jews and Gentiles and Other Essays* (Philadelphia: Fortress Press, 1976), pp. 78–96.

—*Final Account: Paul's Letter to the Romans* (Minneapolis: Fortress Press, 1995).

Sterling, Gregory E., *Historiography and Self-Definition: Josephos, Luke–Acts and Apologetic Historiography* (NovTSup, 64; Leiden: E.J. Brill, 1992).

Stern, Menahem, *Greek and Latin Authors on Jews and Judaism* (2 vols.; Jerusalem: The Israel Academy of Sciences and Humanities, 1974).

—'The Jewish Diaspora', in S. Safari *et al.* (eds.), *Jewish People in the First Century* (CRINT 1.1; Assen: Van Gorcum, 1974), pp. 117–83.

—'The Jews in Greek and Latin Literature,' *The Jewish People in the First Century* (CRINT, 1.2; Assen: Van Gorcum, 1974), pp. 1101–159.

—'Aspects of Jewish Society: The Priesthood and other Classes', *The Jewish People in the First Century* (CRINT, 1.2. Assen: Van Gorcum, 1974), pp. 561–630.

Stockhausen, Carol. K., '2 Corinthians 3 and the Principles of Pauline Exegesis', in *Paul and the Scriptures of Israel* (ed. Craig A. Evans and James A. Sanders; JSNTSup, 83; SSEJC, 1; Sheffield: JSOT Press, 1993).

Stone, Michael E., 'Apocalyptic Literature', *Jewish Writings of the Second Temple Period* (CRINT, 2.2; Minneapolis: Fortress Press, 1986), pp. 383–441.

Stowers, S.K., *The Diatribe and Paul's Letter to the Romans* (SBLDS, 57; Chico, CA: Scholar's Press, 1981).

—*A Rereading of Romans: Justice, Jews and Gentiles* (New Haven/London: Yale University Press, 1994).

Strabo, *Geography* (trans. Horace L. Jones; LCL; London: Heinemann, 1930).

Stuhlmacher, Peter, *Paul's Letter to the Romans: A Commentary* (Louisville, KY: Westminster/ John Knox Press, 1994).

—*Revisting Paul's Doctrine of Justification: A Challenge to the New Perspective, with an Essay by Donald A. Hagner* (Downers Grove, IL: InterVarsity Press, 2001).

Suetonius, *Suetonius in Two Volumes* (trans. J.C. Rolfe; LCL ; London: William Heinemann, 1920).

Sumney, Jerry L. *'Servants of Satan', 'False Brothers' and Other Opponents of Paul* (JSNTSup, 188; Sheffield: Sheffield Academic Press, 1999).

Tacitus. *Tacitus* (trans. John Jackson; LCL; London: Heinemann, 1969).

Tcherikover, Victor, and Alexander Fuks (eds.), *Corpus Papyrorum Judaicarum* (2 vols.; Cambridge, MA: Harvard University Press for The Magnes Press, The Hebrew University, 1957.

—*Hellenistic Civilization and the Jews* (Philadelphia: Magnes Press, The Hebrew University for the Jewish Publication Society of America, 1966).

Testuz, Michel, *Les Idées Religieuses du Livre des Jubilés* (Geneva: Droz, 1960).

Thackeray, H. St. John, *Josephus: The Man and the Historian* (New York: KTAV, 1967).

Thielman, Frank. *From Plight to Solution: A Jewish Framework for Understanding Paul's View of the Law in Galatians and Romans* (NovTSup, 61; Leiden: E.J. Brill, 1989).

—*Paul and the Law: A Contextual Approach* (Downers Grove, IL: Inter Varsity Press, 1994).

Thompson, Richard W., 'The Inclusion of Gentiles in Rom 3,27–30', *Bib* 69 (1988), pp. 543–46.

—'Paul's Double Critique of Jewish Boasting: A Study of Rom 3,27 in Its Context', *Bib* 67 (1986), pp. 520–31.

Tobin, Thomas H., 'What Shall We Say that Abraham Found? The Controversy behind Romans 4', *HTR* 88 (1995), pp. 437–52.

Tyson, Joseph B., 'Paul's Opponents in Galatia.', *NovT* 10 (1968), pp. 241–54.

VanderKam, James C., *Textual and Historical Studies in the Book of Jubilees* (HSM, 14; Missoula, MT: Scholars Press for Harvard Semitic Museum, 1977).

—The Putative Author of the Book of Jubilees', *JSS* 26 (1981), pp. 209–17.

—*Enoch and the Growth of an Apocalyptic Tradition* (CBQMS, 15; Washington, DC: Catholic Biblical Association of America, 1984).

—'The *Book of Jubilees*', in M. De Jonge (ed.), *Outside the Old Testament* (Cambridge Commentaries on Writings of the Jewish and Christian World, 200 B.C. to A.D. 200, 4; Cambridge: Cambridge University Press, 1985), pp. 111–44.

—*The Book of Jubilees* (CSCO, 510–511; Scriptores Aethiopici, 87–88; Leuven: Peeters, 1989).

—'The Origins and Purposes of the Book of Jubilees', in Matthias Albani, Jorg Frey and Armin Lange (eds.), *Studies in the Book of Jubilees* (Tübingen: Mohr Siebeck, 1997).

—'Genesis 1 in *Jubilees* 2', in *From Revelation to Canon: Studies in the Hebrew Bible and Second Temple Literature* (Leiden: E.J. Brill, 2000), pp. 500–521.

—Biblical Interpretation in *1 Enoch* and *Jubilees*', in *From Revelation to Canon: Studies in the Hebrew Bible and Second Temple Literature* (Leiden: E.J. Brill, 2000), pp. 276–304.

—*An Introduction to Early Judaism* (Grand Rapids, MI: Eerdmans, 2001).

—*The Book of Jubilees* (Guides to Apocrypha and Pseudepigrapha; Sheffield: Sheffield Academic Press, 2001).

Vermes, Geza, *Scripture and Tradition in Judaism: Haggadic Studies* (Studia post biblica, 4; Leiden: E.J. Brill, 1961).

Villalba I Varneda, Peri. *The Historical Method of Flavius Josephus* (ALGHJ, 29; Leiden: E.J. Brill, 1986).

Wacholder, B.Z., 'Pseudo-Eupolemus' Two Greek Fragments on the Life of Abraham', *HUCA* 34 (1963), pp. 83–113.

—'How Long did Abram Stay in Egypt?', *HUCA* 35 (1964), pp. 43–56.

Wadsworth, M., 'A New Pseudo-Philo', *JJS* 29 (1978), pp. 185–91.

Walker, William O., Jr, 'Romans 1.18–2.29: A non-Pauline Interpolation?', *NTS* 45 (1999), pp. 533–52.

Walters, James C. *Ethnic Issues in Paul's Letter to the Romans: Changing Self-Definitions in Earliest Roman Christianity* (Valley Forge, PA: Trinity Press, 1993).

Wan, Sze-kar, 'Abraham and the Promise of the Spirit: Galatians and the Hellenistic-Jewish Mysticism of Philo', *SBL Seminar Papers, 1994* (*SBLSP*, 34; Atlanta: Scholars Press, 1995), pp. 6–22.

Ward, Roy Bowen, 'The Works of Abraham: James 2:14–26', *HTR* 61 (1968), pp. 283–90.

—'Abraham Traditions in Early Christianity', in G.W.E. Nickelsburg, Jr (ed.), *Studies on the Testament of Abraham* (SCS, 6; Missoula, MT: Scholars Press, 1976), pp. 173–84.

Watson, F., *Paul, Judaism, and the Gentiles: A Sociological Approach* (SNTSMS, 56; Cambridge: Cambridge University Press, 1986).

—*Text, Church and World: Biblical Interpretation in Theological Perspective* (Grand Rapids: Eerdmans, 1994).

—'The Triune Divine Identity: Reflections on Pauline God-Language, in Disagreement with J.D.G. Dunn', *JSNT* 80 (2000), pp. 99–124.

Wedderburn, A.J.M., 'Adam in Paul's Letter to the Romans', in E.A. Livingstone (ed.), *Papers on Paul and Other New Testament Authors* (Studia Biblica 3; JSNTSup, 3; Sheffield: Sheffield Academic Press, 1980), pp. 413–30.

—*The Reasons for Romans* (Minneapolis, MN: Fortress Press, 1991).

—'The Purpose and Occasion of Romans Again', in Karl P. Donfried (ed.), *The Romans Debate* (Minneapolis, MN: Augsburg, rev. edn, 1991), pp. 195–202.

Weitzman, Steven, 'The Song of Abraham', *HUCA* 65 (1994), pp. 21–33.

Westerholm, S., *Israel's Law and the Church's Faith: Paul and his Recent Interpreters* (Grand Rapids, MI: Eerdmans, 1988).

—'The "New Perspective" at Twenty-five', in D.A. Carson, Peter T. O'Brien and Mark A. Seifried (eds.), *Justification and Variegated Nomism* (Grand Rapids: Baker Academic Books, forthcoming).

Whittaker, M., *Jews and Christians: Greco-Roman Views* (Cambridge Commentries on Writings of the Jewish & Christian World 200 BC to AD 200, 6; Cambridge: Cambridge University Press, 1984).

Wiefel, W., 'The Jewish Community in Ancient Rome and the Origins of Roman Christianity', in Karl P. Donfried (ed.), *The Romans Debate* (Minneapolis, MN: Augsburg, rev. edn, 1991), pp. 85–101.

Wieser, Friedrich E., *Die Abrahamvorstellungen im Neuen Testament* (Europäische Hochschulschriften 23/317; Bern: Peter Lang, 1987).

Wilckens, U., 'Die Rechtfertigung Abrahams nach Römer 4', in R. Rendtorff and K. Koch (eds.), *Studien zur Theologie der alttestamentlichen Überlieferungen* (Festschrift G. von Rad; Neukirchen–Vluyn: Neukirchener Verlag, 1961), pp. 33–49.

—*Der Brief an die Römer* (3 vols.; EKKNT; Köln: Benziger Verlag, 1978).

Wilken, Robert L., 'The Christianization of Abraham: Jewish Roots of the Christian Faith', *Concordia Theological Monthly* 43 (1972), pp. 723–26.

Williamson, Ronald, *Jews in the Hellenistic World: Philo* (Cambridge Commentaries on Writings of the Jewish and Christian World, 200 BC to AD 200, 1.2; Cambridge: Cambridge University Press, 1989).

Winston, David, 'Philo's Ethical Theory', *ANRW* 2.21.1 (Berlin: W. de Gruyter, 1984), pp. 372–416.

Wintermute, O.S., 'Jubilees: A New Translation and Introduction', *OTP* (ed. J.H. Charlesworth; London: Darton, Longman, and Todd, 1985), vol. 2, pp. 35–142.

Wolfson, Harry A., *Philo: Foundations of Religious Philosophy in Judaism, Christianity, and Islam* (2 vols.; repr., Cambridge, MA: Harvard University Press, rev. edn, 1948).

Wright, N.T., *The Climax of the Covenant: Christ and the Law in Pauline Theology* (repr., Minneapolis: Fortress Press, 1992).

—*The New Testament and the People of God* (vol. I of *Christian Origins and the Question of God*; Minneapolis: Fortress Press, 1992).

—*What Saint Paul Really Said: Was Paul of Tarsus the Real Founder of Christianity?* (Grand Rapids, MI: Eerdmans, 1997).

—'The Letter to the Romans', in Leander Keck *et al.* (eds.), *The New Interpreter's Bible: A Commentary in Twelve Volumes* (Nashville: Abingdon Press, 2002), pp. 393–770.

Young, Norman H., 'PAIDAGOGOS: The Social Setting of a Pauline Metaphor', *NovT* 29 (1987), pp. 150–76.

—'The Figure of the Paidagōgos in Art and Literature', *BA* June (1990), pp. 80–86.

Young, Richard Alan, 'The Knowledge of God in Romans 1:18–23: Exegetical and Theological Reflections', *JETS* 43 (2000), pp. 695–707.

Zeitlin, Solomon, *The Book of Jubilees: Its Character and Significance* (Philadelphia, 1939).

—'The Book of Jubilees and the Pentateuch', *JQR* 48 (1957), pp. 218–35.

Ziesler, J., *Paul's Letter to the Romans* (London: SCM Press, 1989).

INDEXES

INDEX OF REFERENCES

OLD TESTAMENT

NEW TESTAMENT

73	127
74–75	27
75	127
77–80	25
78	31
79	128
80	128
81–84	27, 107
84	28
84–88	128
85–87	24
88	28, 128
107–114	119
185–186	33
262	28
275–276	36–7

De cherubim

	22
4	28
7	28

De congressu eruditionis gratia

35	20
74–78	19

De ebrietate

	22
106–110	28

Contra Flaccum

8	21
25–35	8
53–54	21
55	20
55–72	21
68	22
73–85	22
95–96	22

De fuga et inventione

	22

De gigantibus

62	28
64	28

Quis rerum divinarum heres sit

	22

18	24
69–70	29
78	32
93	30
94	30
95	30
96–99	31
105	19
279	31, 32

Quod Deus sit immutabilis

144	31

Legum allegoriae

	22
3.228	31

Legatio ad Gaium

120–131	21
130	22
132–139	21
350–372	22

De migratione Abrahami

	22
7	29
13	39
44	31
54	31
92	23, 38
129–130	37, 95, 119
176–179	33
177–179	29
178–179	58
183	127
184–185	29
185–186	29
194	29, 33
195	29

De mutatione nominum

66–67	28
253–63	20
258	31

De opificio mundi

172	34–5

De posteritate Caini

7	24
18–20	31

De praemiis et poenis

	22
27	28

Quaestiones et solutiones in Exodum

	22

Quaestiones et solutiones in Genesin

	22
3.3	27
3.45–50	38
3.46	37
3.46–52	37, 38
3.49	32, 37, 103–4
3.51	37
3.52	38
4.4	31

De somniis

1.52–60	29, 33
1.66–67	31

De specialibus legibus

	37
1.9	38
1.52	121

De virtutibus

	22
212–213	25, 107, 127
214	121
216	28, 94
219	28

Josephus

	4, 141–2

Antiquitates judaicae

	51–69
1.4	53
1.5	53, 55
1.14	65, 66
1.14–15	56, 64
1.17	55
1.23–24	56
1.24	56

INDEX OF AUTHORS